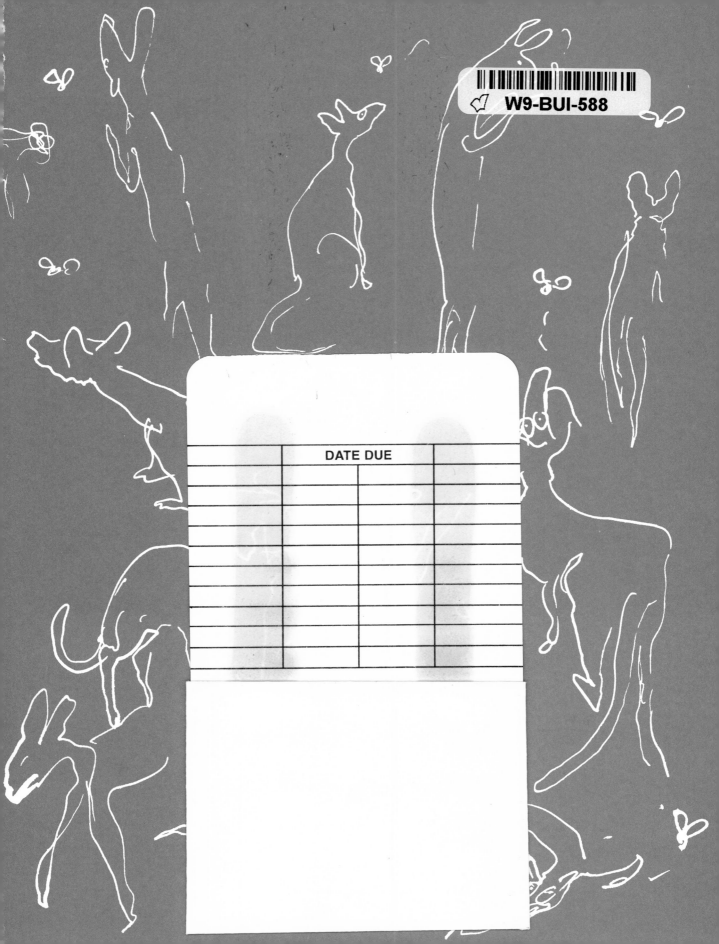

W9-BUI-588

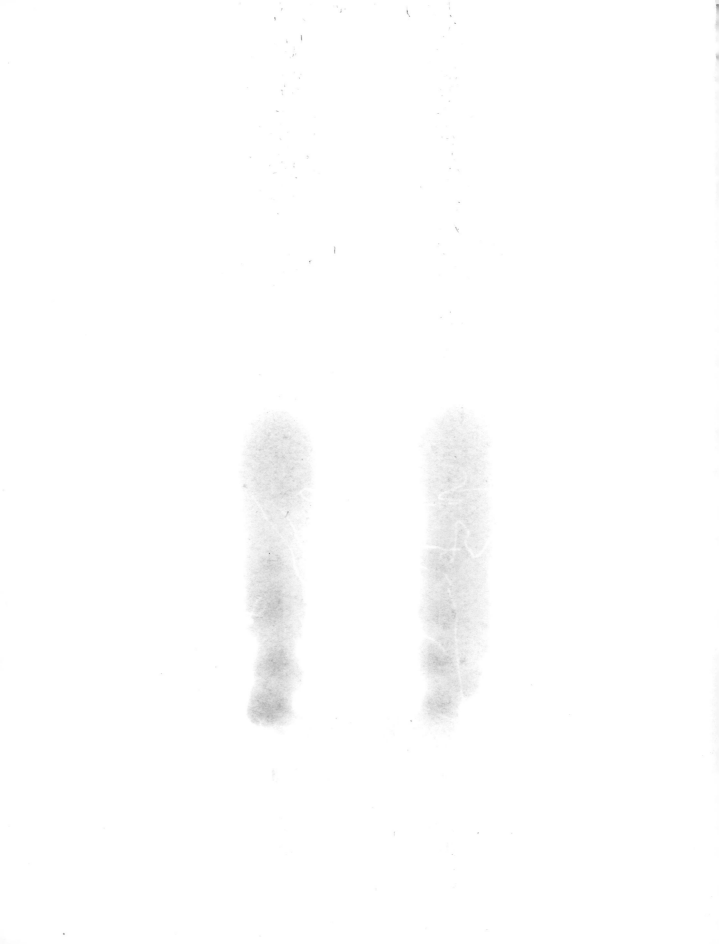

Also by Joann Sfar

The Rabbi's Cat

The Rabbi's Cat
2

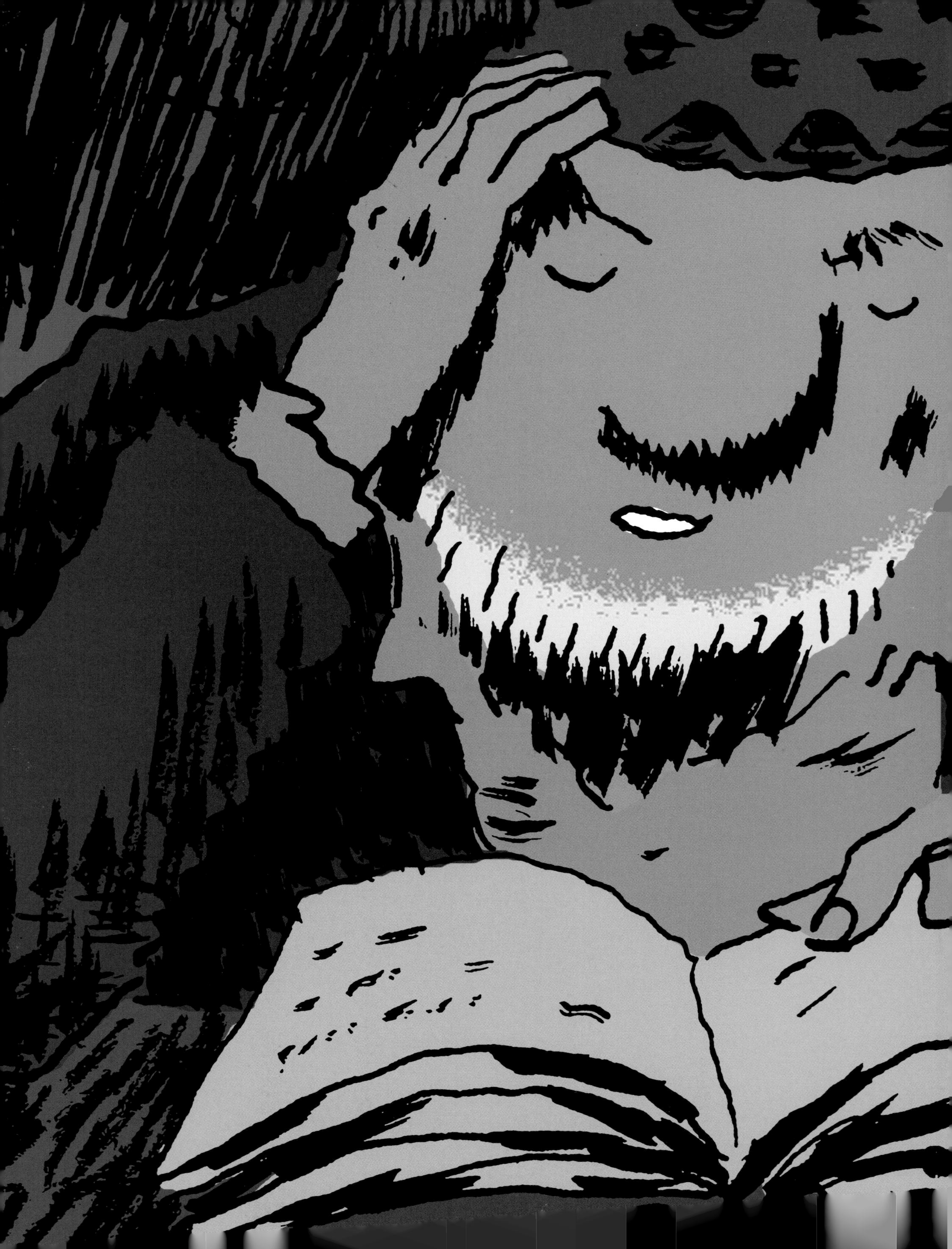

The Rabbi's Cat 2

JOANN SFAR

Color by Brigitte Findakly

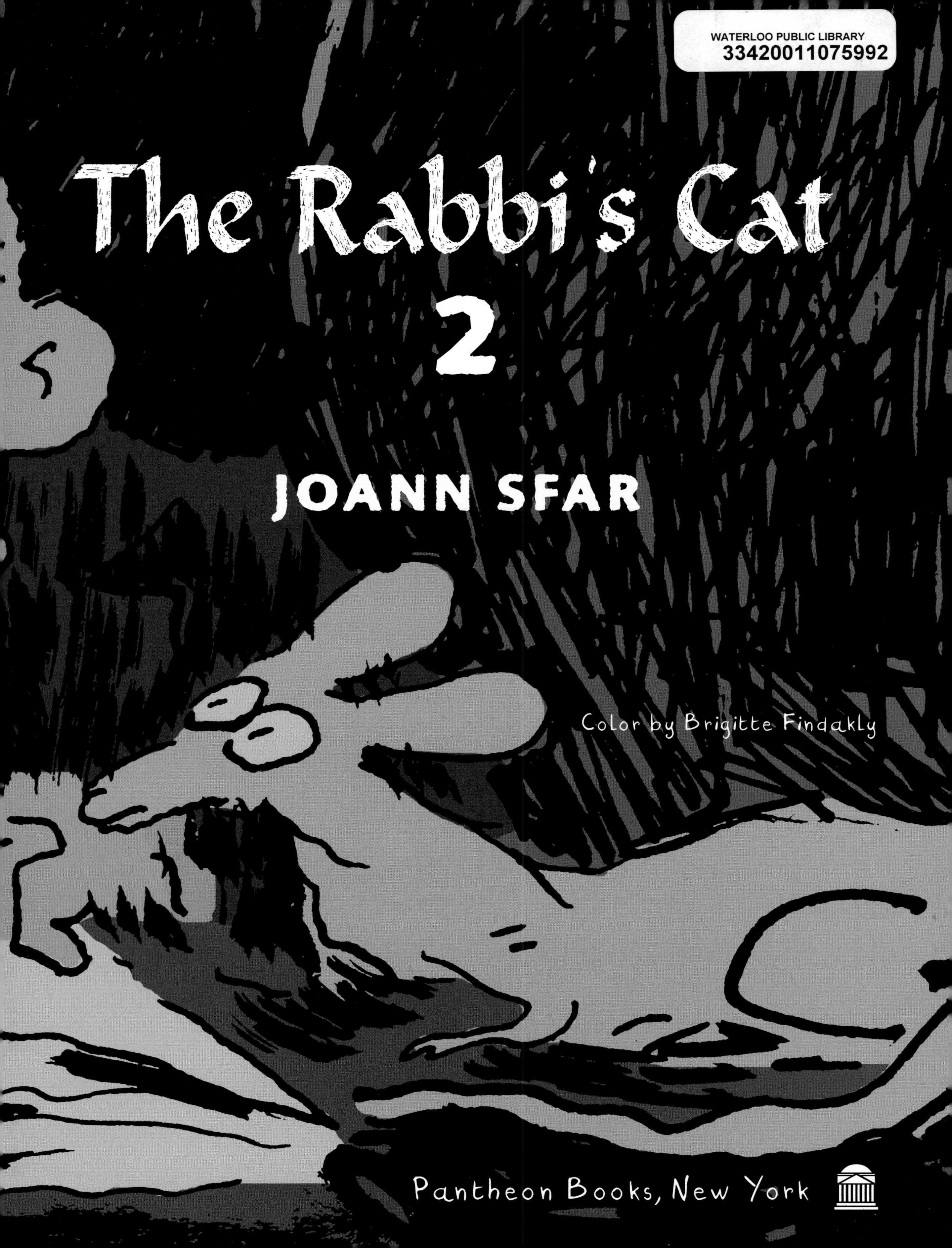

Pantheon Books, New York

Originally published in France by Dargaud, Paris, in two volumes: *Le Chat du Rabbin: 4. Le Paradis terrestre* in 2005, and *Le Chat du Rabbin: 5. Jérusalem d'Afrique* in 2006.

www.dargaud.com

Pantheon Books and colophon are registered trademarks of Random House, Inc.

Library of Congress Cataloging-in-Publication Data
Sfar, Joann.
[Chat du rabbin. English]
The rabbi's cat / Joann Sfar.
p. cm.
ISBN 978-0-375-42507-3
I. Title.
PN6747.S48C4813 2005 741.5′944—dc22 2004061406

www.pantheonbooks.com
Printed in Singapore
First American Edition
2 4 6 8 9 7 5 3 1

I

HEAVEN ON EARTH

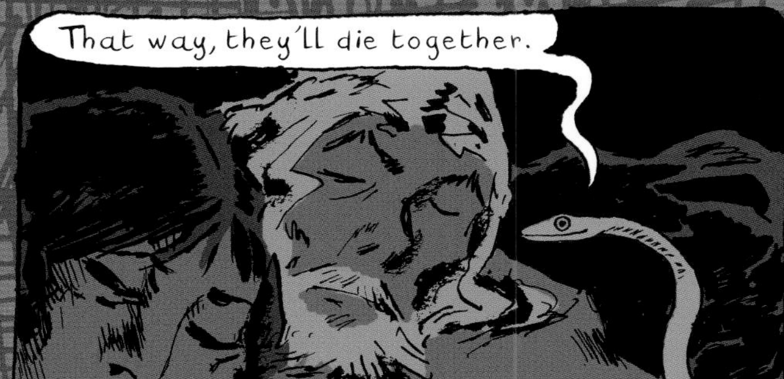
That way, they'll die together.

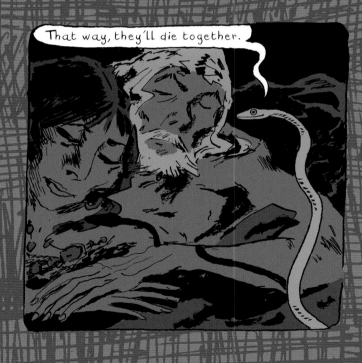

For Romain Gary, Hugo Pratt, Joseph Kessel,
and for my daddy who is a hero.

The anecdotes mentioned in this book are strictly accurate
and never exaggerated, 'cause my granny told them to me.

Thank you to my uncle Fernand Taïeb
for his precious memories.

—JOANN SFAR

I'm the rabbi's cat. Tons of things happen to me. For instance, I once went to Paris and it rained. So I came back to my hometown, in Algeria.

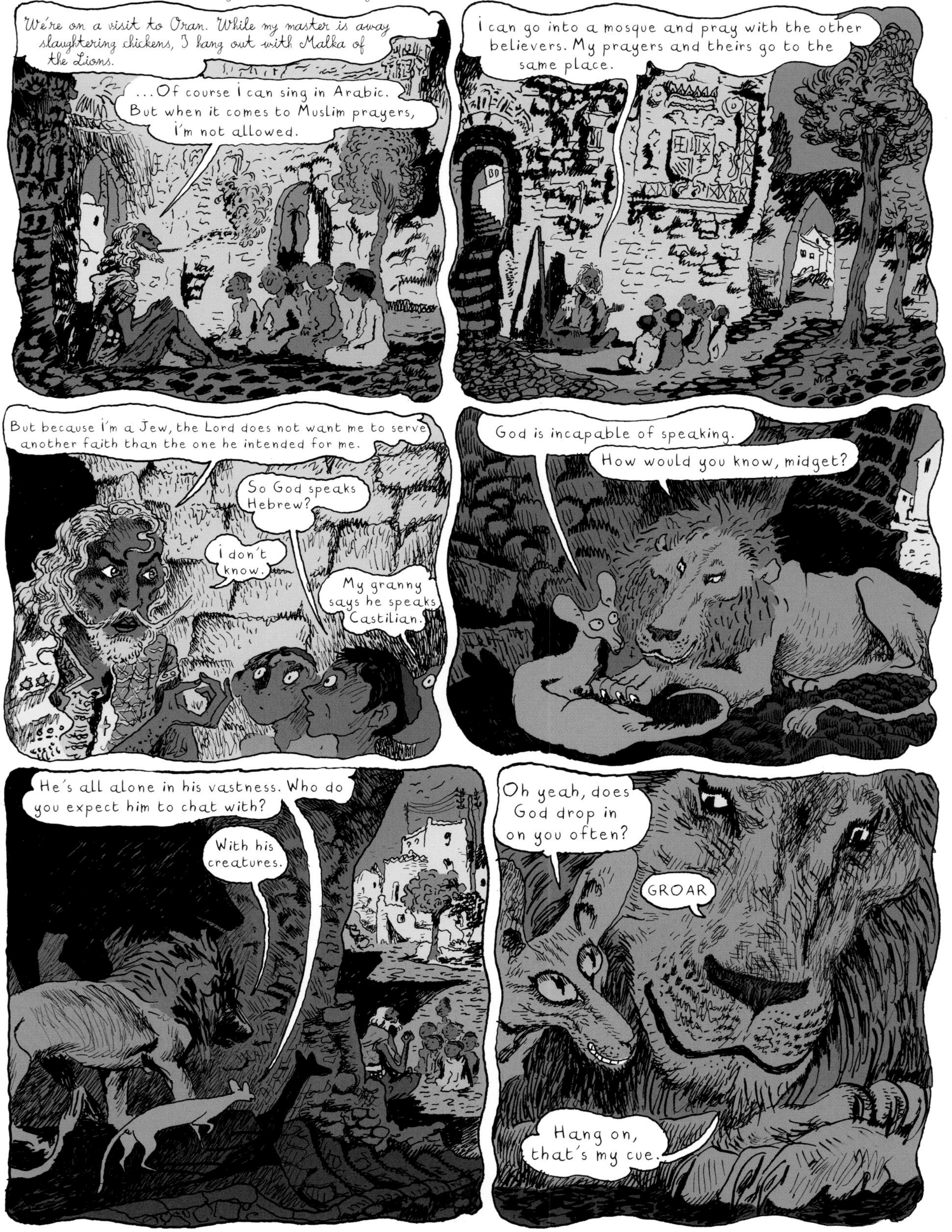
We're on a visit to Oran. While my master is away slaughtering chickens, I hang out with Malka of the Lions.
...Of course I can sing in Arabic. But when it comes to Muslim prayers, I'm not allowed.
I can go into a mosque and pray with the other believers. My prayers and theirs go to the same place.
But because I'm a Jew, the Lord does not want me to serve another faith than the one he intended for me.
So God speaks Hebrew?
I don't know.
My granny says he speaks Castilian.
God is incapable of speaking.
How would you know, midget?
He's all alone in his vastness. Who do you expect him to chat with?
With his creatures.
Oh yeah, does God drop in on you often?
GROAR
Hang on, that's my cue.

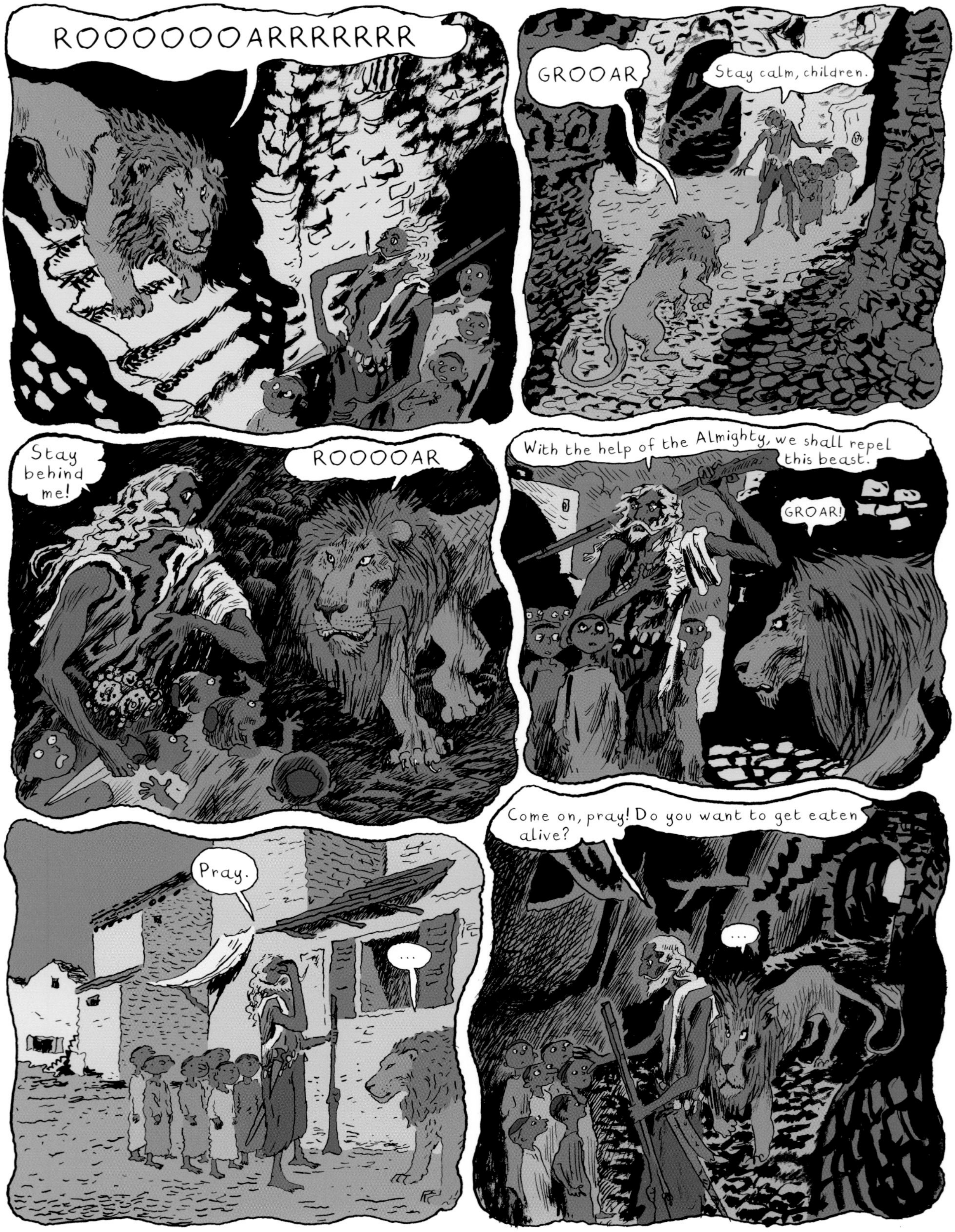
ROOOOOOARRRRRRR
GROOAR
Stay calm, children.
Stay behind me!
ROOOOAR
With the help of the Almighty, we shall repel this beast.
GROAR!
Pray.
...
Come on, pray! Do you want to get eaten alive?
...

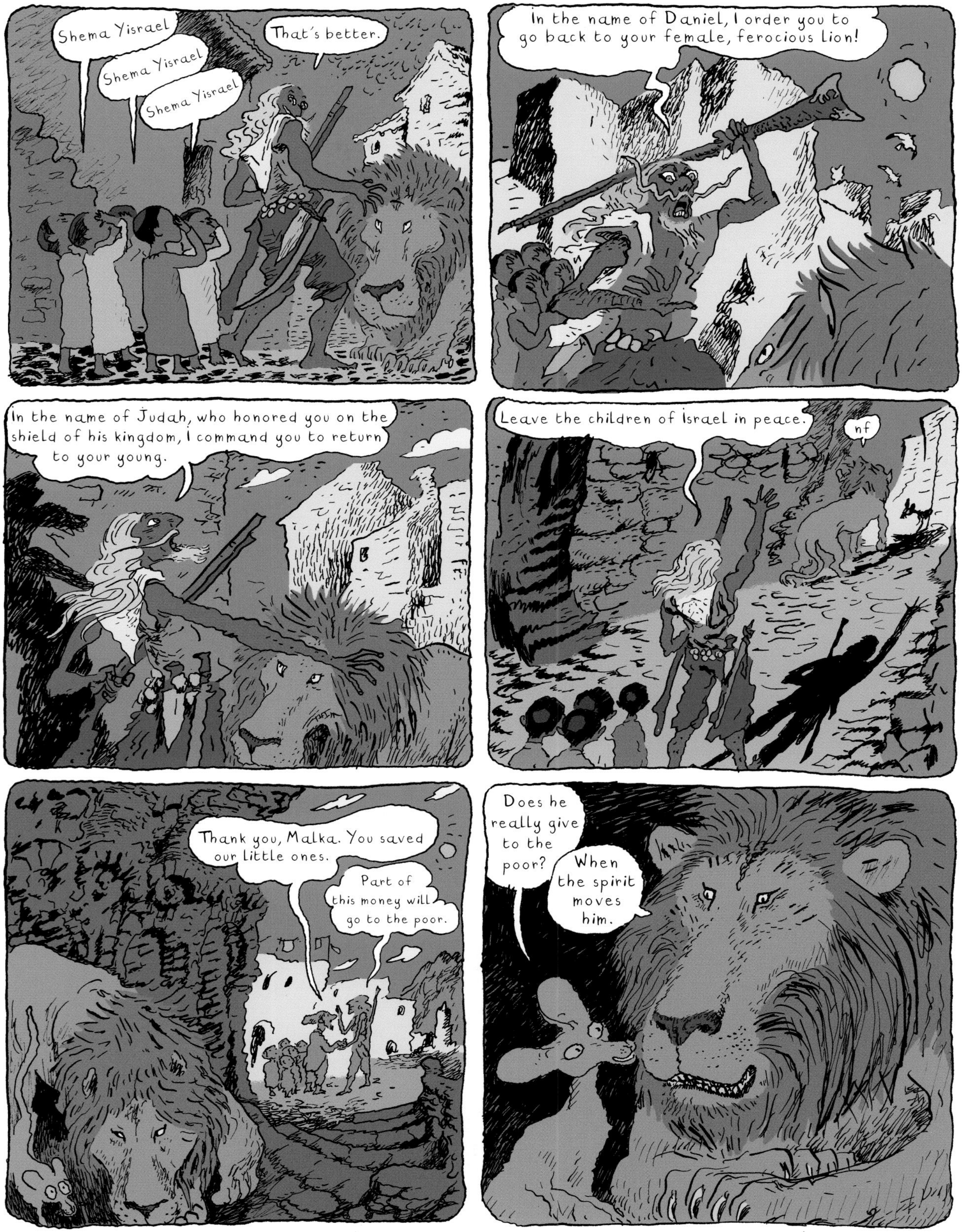
Shema Yisrael
Shema Yisrael
Shema Yisrael
That's better.
In the name of Daniel, I order you to go back to your female, ferocious Lion!
In the name of Judah, who honored you on the shield of his kingdom, I command you to return to your young.
Leave the children of Israel in peace.
nf
Thank you, Malka. You saved our little ones.
Part of this money will go to the poor.
Does he really give to the poor?
When the spirit moves him.

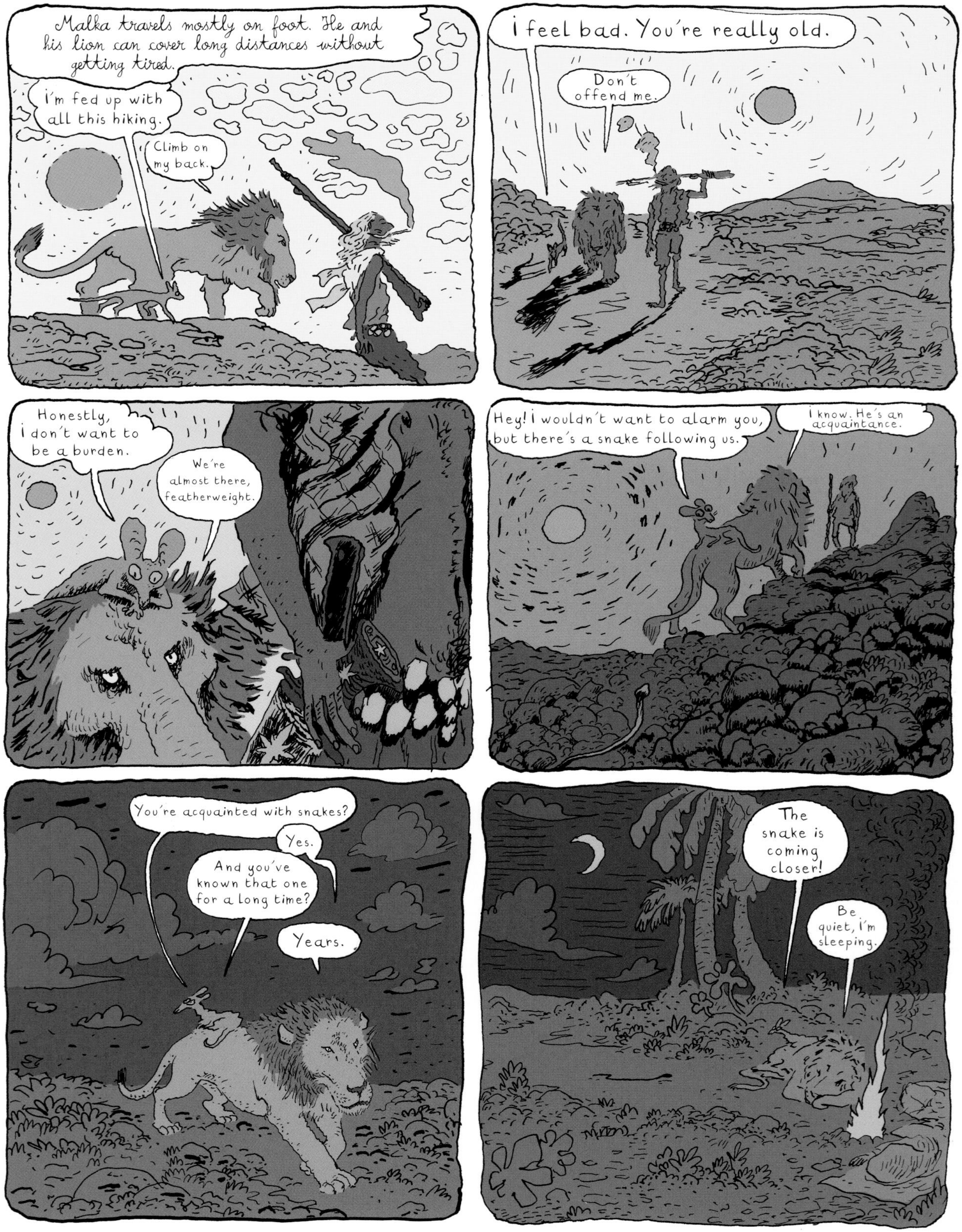
Malka travels mostly on foot. He and his lion can cover long distances without getting tired.
I'm fed up with all this hiking.
Climb on my back.
I feel bad. You're really old.
Don't offend me.
Honestly, I don't want to be a burden.
We're almost there, featherweight.
Hey! I wouldn't want to alarm you, but there's a snake following us.
I know. He's an acquaintance.
You're acquainted with snakes?
Yes.
And you've known that one for a long time?
Years.
The snake is coming closer!
Be quiet, I'm sleeping.

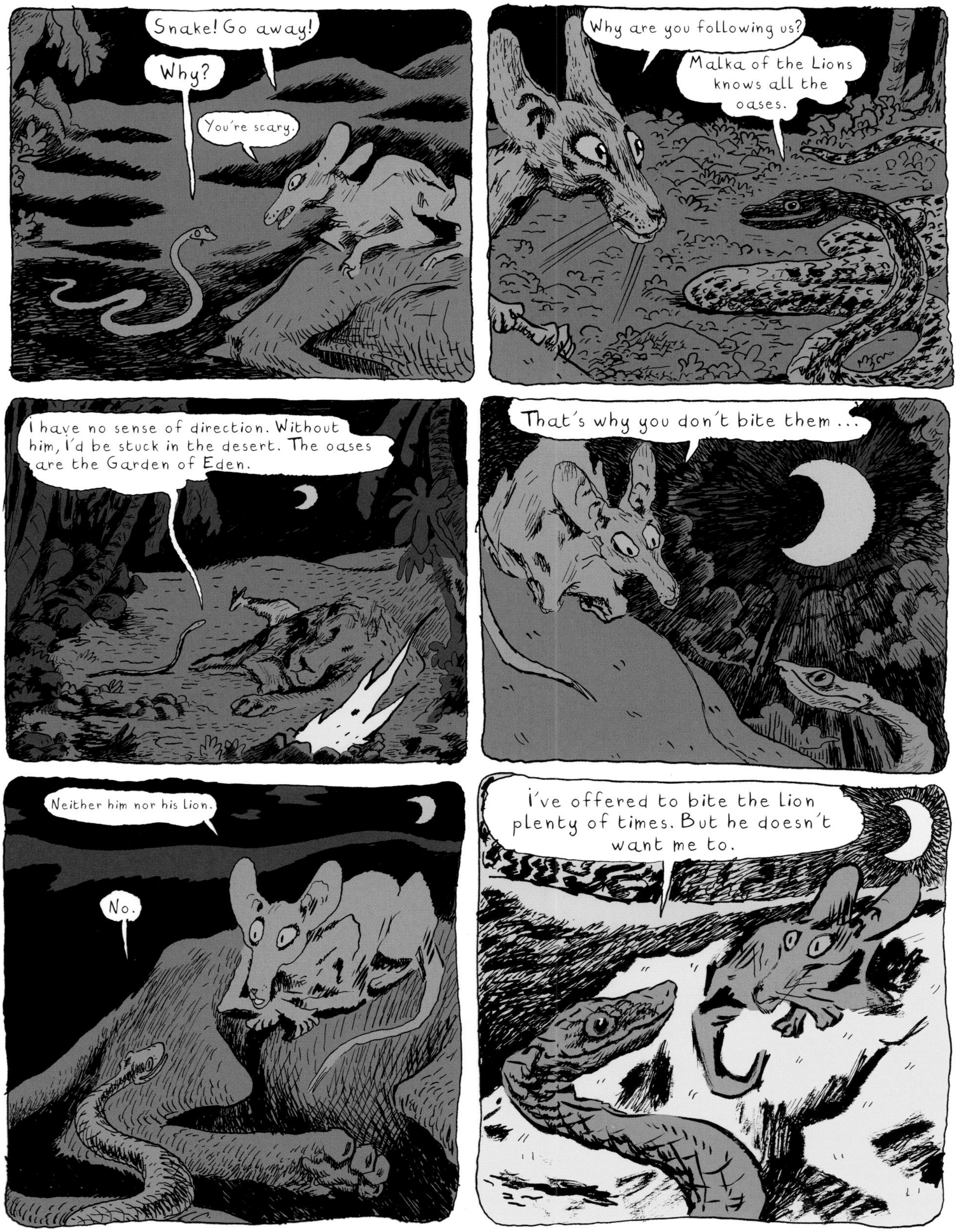
Snake! Go away!
Why?
You're scary.
Why are you following us?
Malka of the Lions knows all the oases.
I have no sense of direction. Without him, I'd be stuck in the desert. The oases are the Garden of Eden.
That's why you don't bite them...
Neither him nor his Lion.
No.
I've offered to bite the Lion plenty of times. But he doesn't want me to.

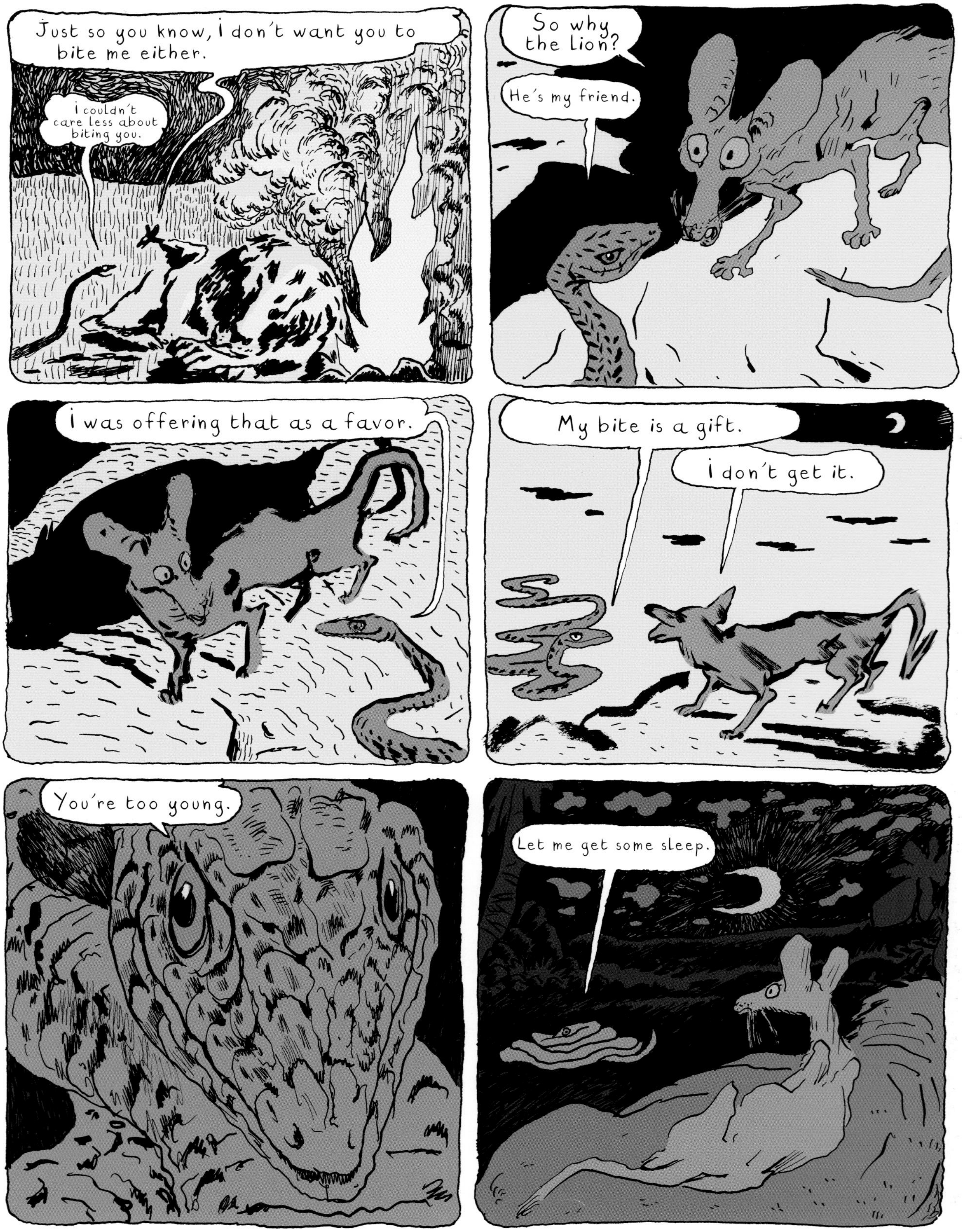
Just so you know, I don't want you to bite me either.
I couldn't care less about biting you.
So why the Lion?
He's my friend.
I was offering that as a favor.
My bite is a gift.
I don't get it.
You're too young.
Let me get some sleep.

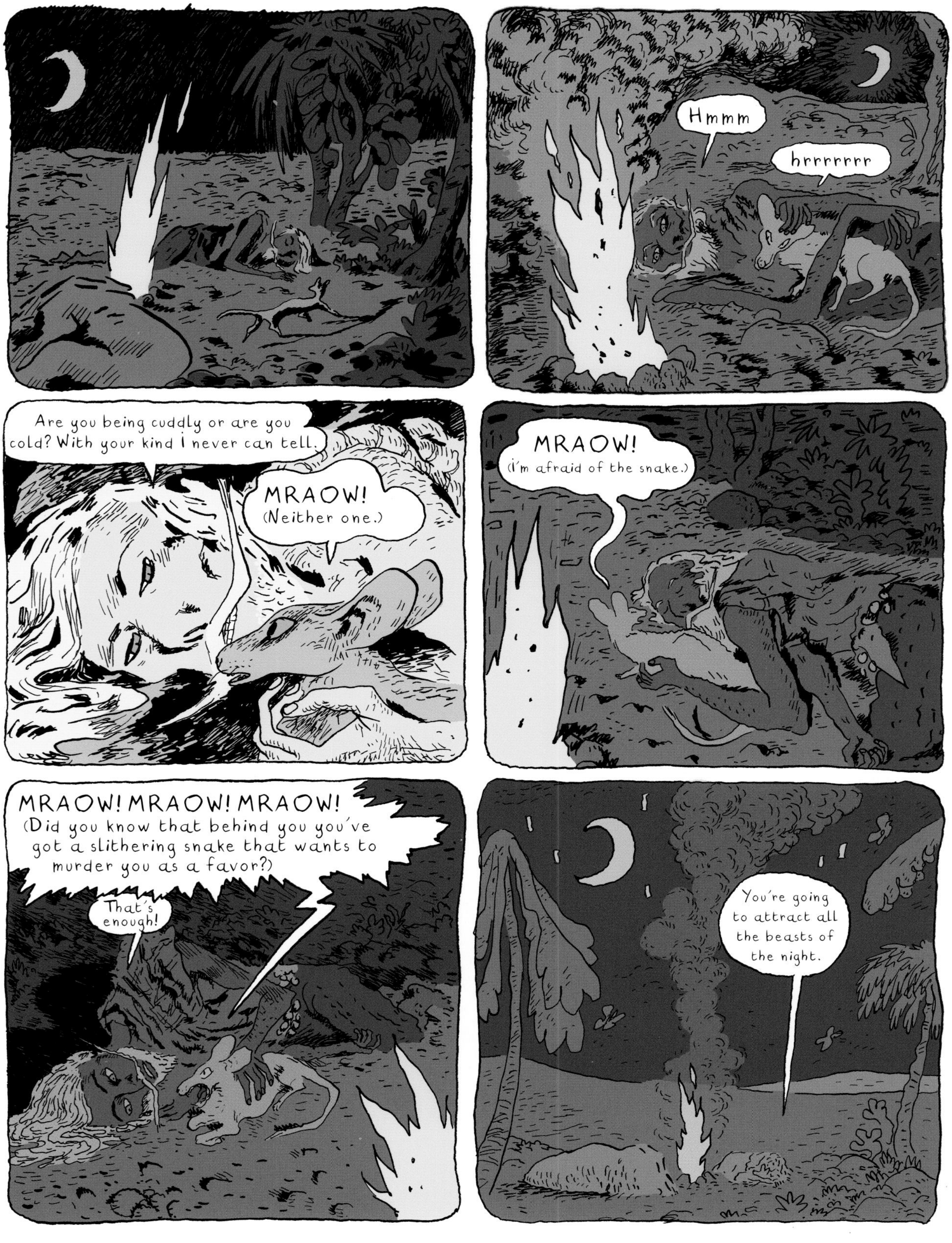
Hmmm
hrrrrrrr
Are you being cuddly or are you cold? With your kind I never can tell.
MRAOW! (Neither one.)
MRAOW! (I'm afraid of the snake.)
MRAOW! MRAOW! MRAOW! (Did you know that behind you you've got a slithering snake that wants to murder you as a favor?)
That's enough!
You're going to attract all the beasts of the night.

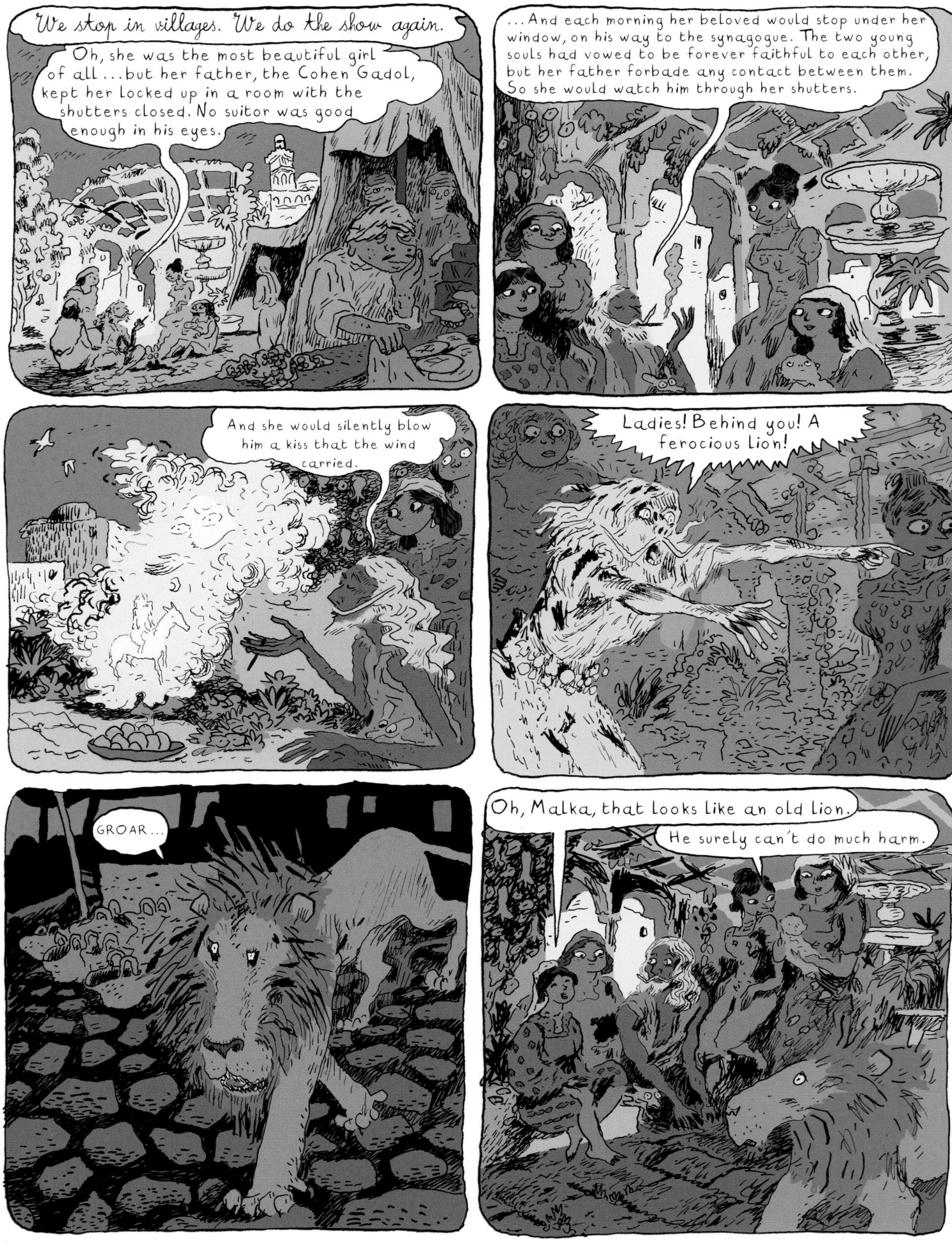
We stop in villages. We do the show again.
Oh, she was the most beautiful girl of all... but her father, the Cohen Gadol, kept her locked up in a room with the shutters closed. No suitor was good enough in his eyes.
...And each morning her beloved would stop under her window, on his way to the synagogue. The two young souls had vowed to be forever faithful to each other, but her father forbade any contact between them. So she would watch him through her shutters.
And she would silently blow him a kiss that the wind carried.
Ladies! Behind you! A ferocious lion!
GROAR...
Oh, Malka, that looks like an old lion.
He surely can't do much harm.

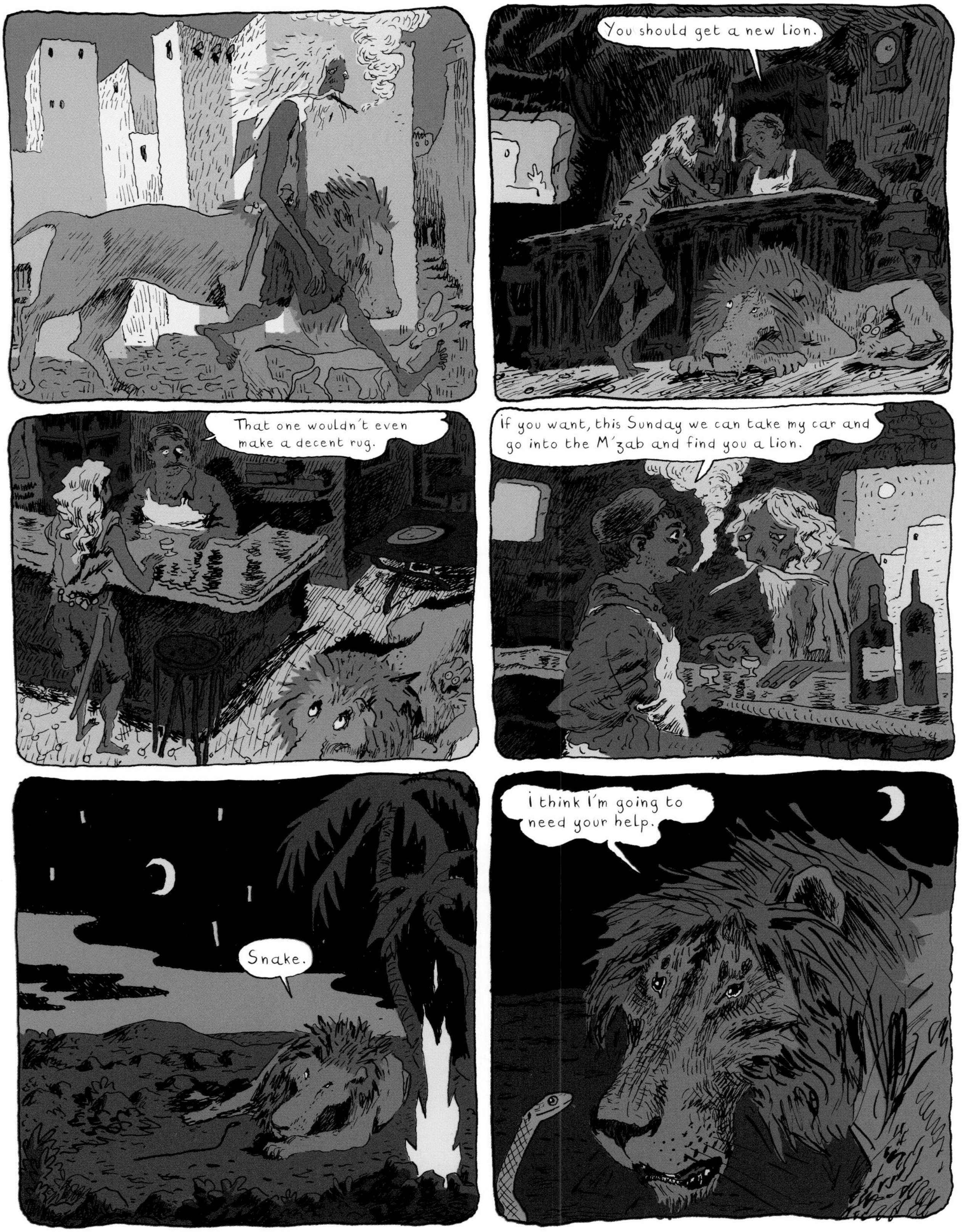
You should get a new lion.
That one wouldn't even make a decent rug.
If you want, this Sunday we can take my car and go into the M'zab and find you a lion.
Snake.
I think I'm going to need your help.

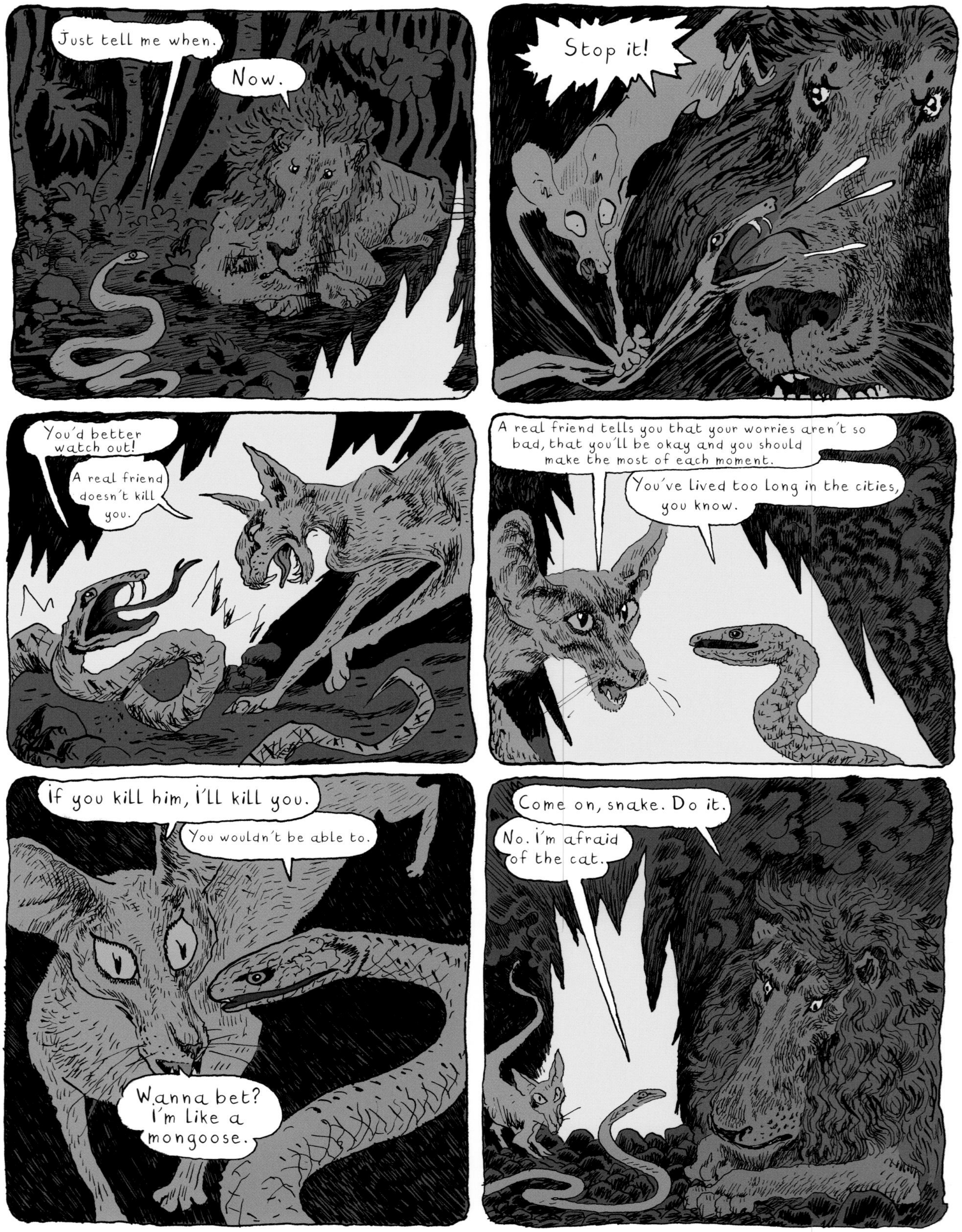
Just tell me when.
Now.
Stop it!
You'd better watch out!
A real friend doesn't kill you.
A real friend tells you that your worries aren't so bad, that you'll be okay and you should make the most of each moment.
You've lived too long in the cities, you know.
If you kill him, I'll kill you.
You wouldn't be able to.
Wanna bet? I'm like a mongoose.
Come on, snake. Do it.
No. I'm afraid of the cat.

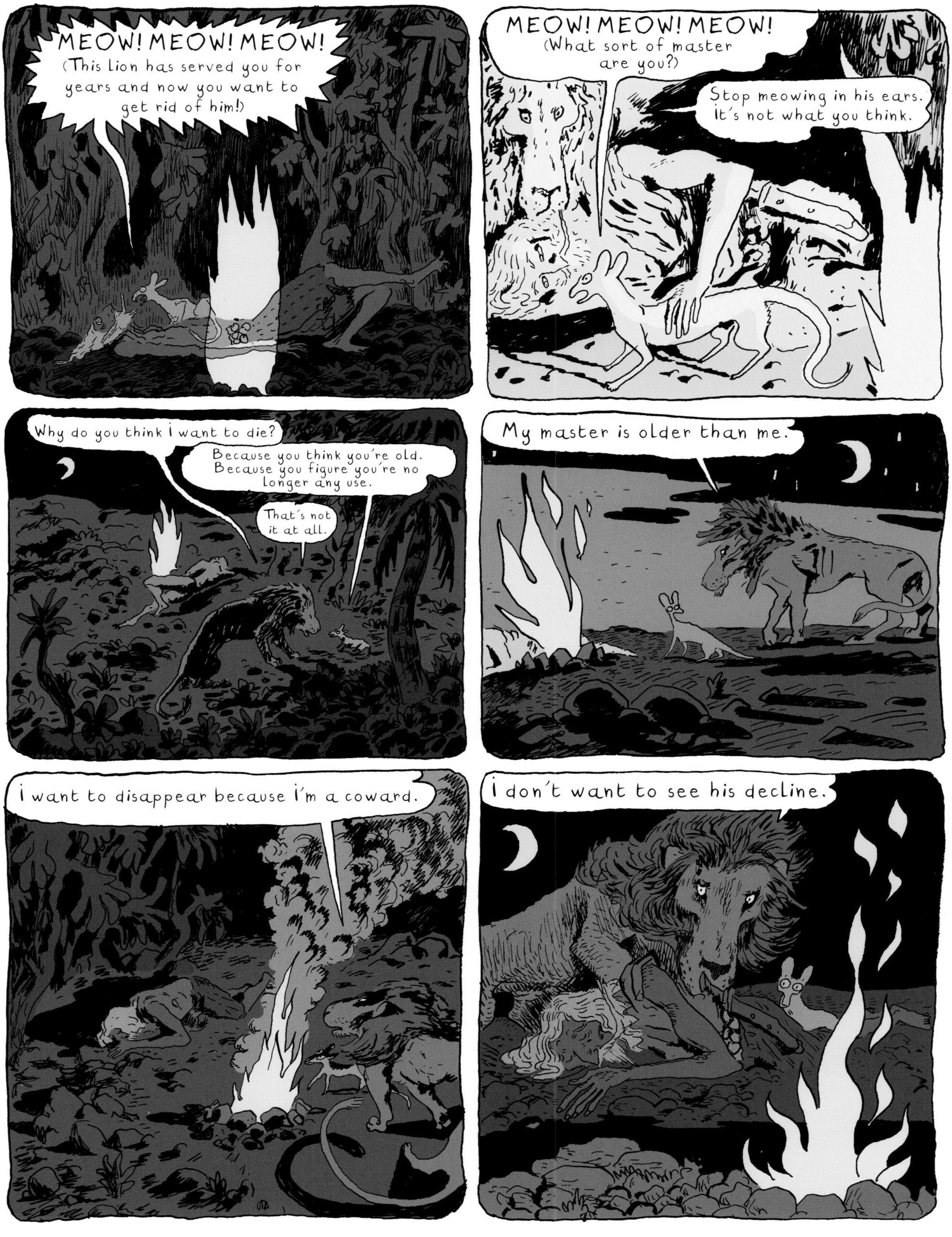
MEOW! MEOW! MEOW!
(This Lion has served you for years and now you want to get rid of him!)
MEOW! MEOW! MEOW!
(What sort of master are you?)
Stop meowing in his ears. It's not what you think.
Why do you think I want to die?
Because you think you're old. Because you figure you're no longer any use.
That's not it at all.
My master is older than me.
I want to disappear because I'm a coward.
I don't want to see his decline.

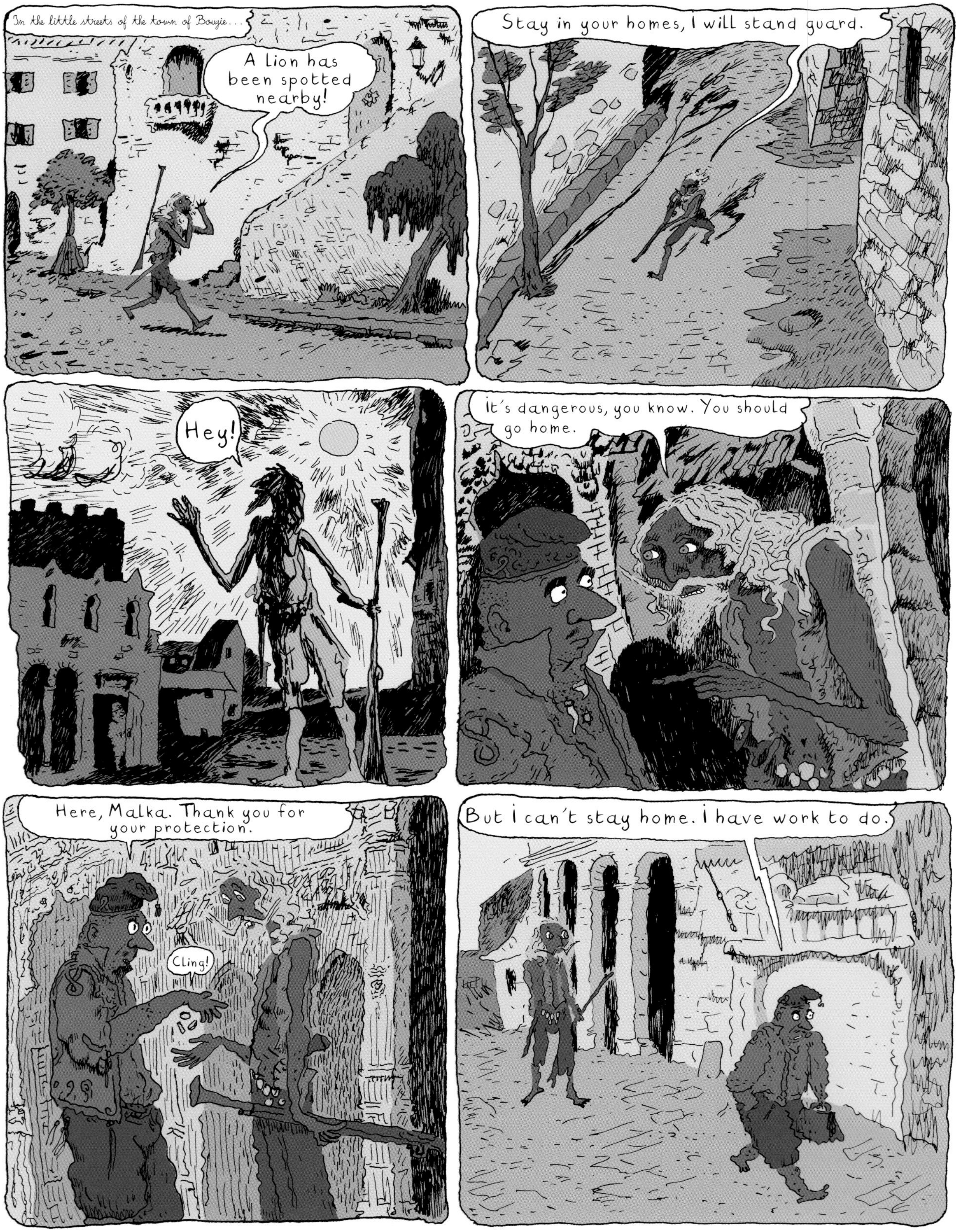
In the little streets of the town of Bougie...
A Lion has been spotted nearby!
Stay in your homes, I will stand guard.
Hey!
It's dangerous, you know. You should go home.
Here, Malka. Thank you for your protection.
Cling!
But I can't stay home. I have work to do.

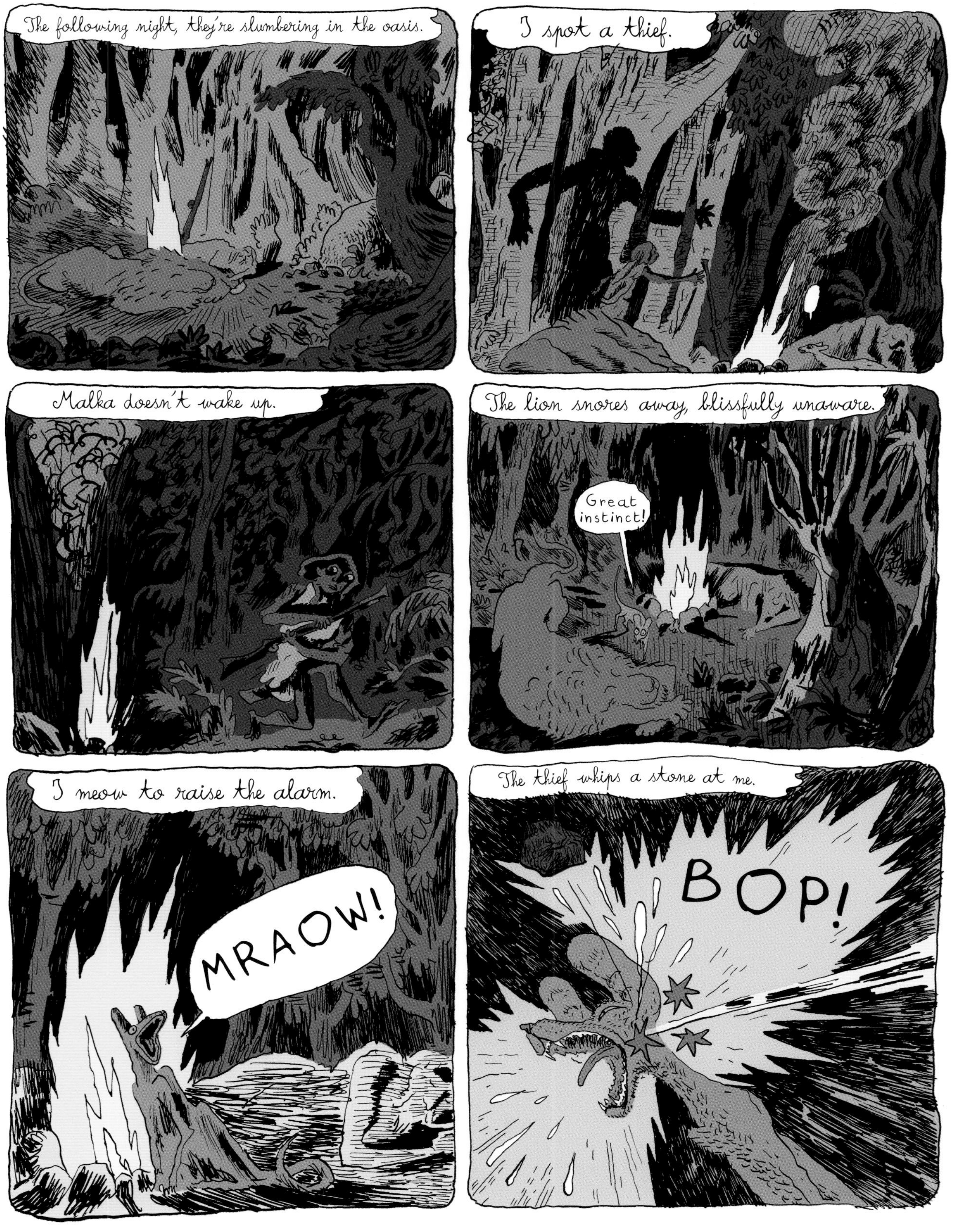
The following night, they're slumbering in the oasis.
I spot a thief.
Malka doesn't wake up.
The lion snores away, blissfully unaware.
Great instinct!
I meow to raise the alarm.
MRAOW!
The thief whips a stone at me.
BOP!

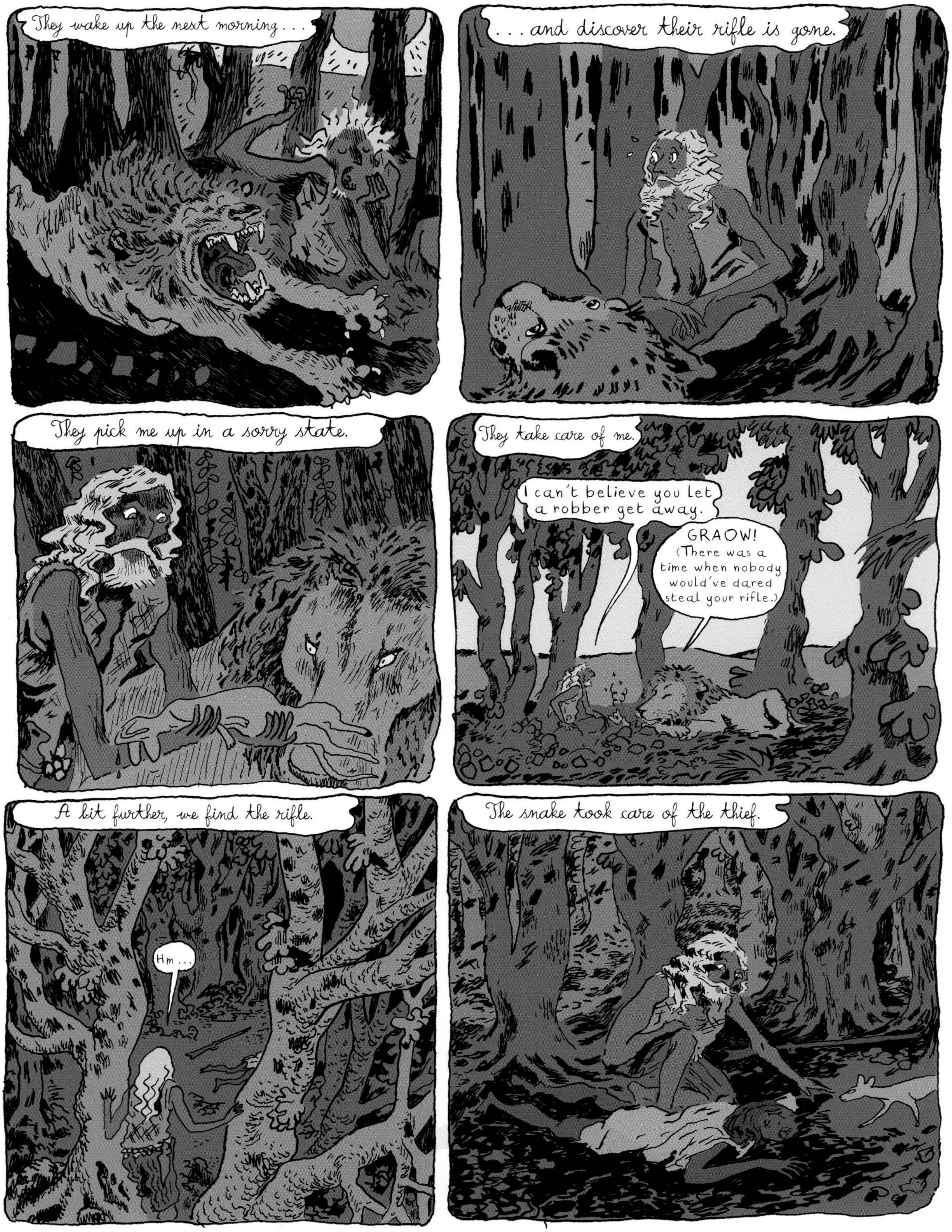
They wake up the next morning . . .
. . . and discover their rifle is gone.
They pick me up in a sorry state.
They take care of me.
I can't believe you let a robber get away.
GRAOW! (There was a time when nobody would've dared steal your rifle.)
A bit further, we find the rifle.
Hm . . .
The snake took care of the thief.

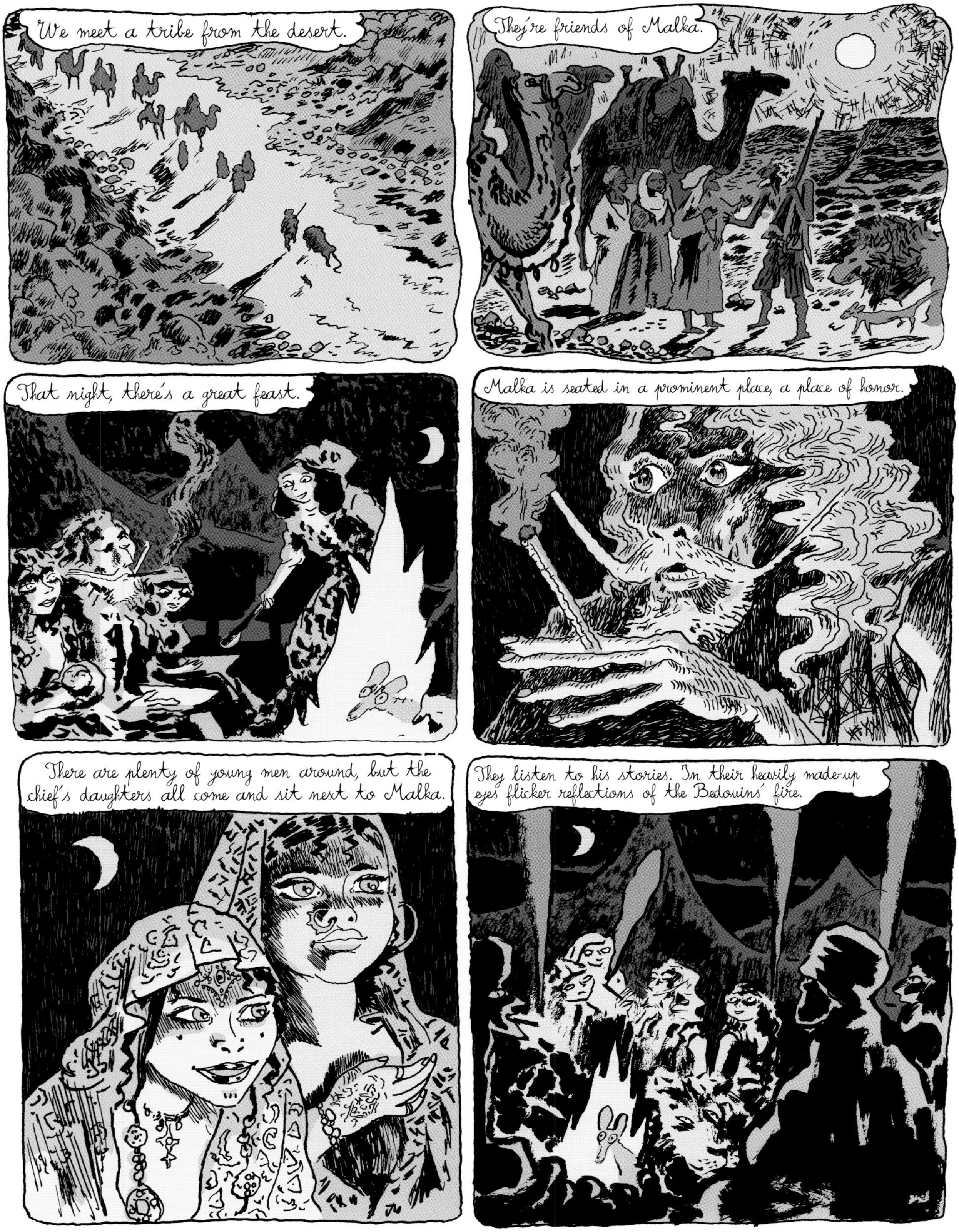
We meet a tribe from the desert.
They're friends of Malka.
That night, there's a great feast.
Malka is seated in a prominent place, a place of honor.
There are plenty of young men around, but the chief's daughters all come and sit next to Malka.
They listen to his stories. In their heavily made-up eyes flicker reflections of the Bedouins' fire.

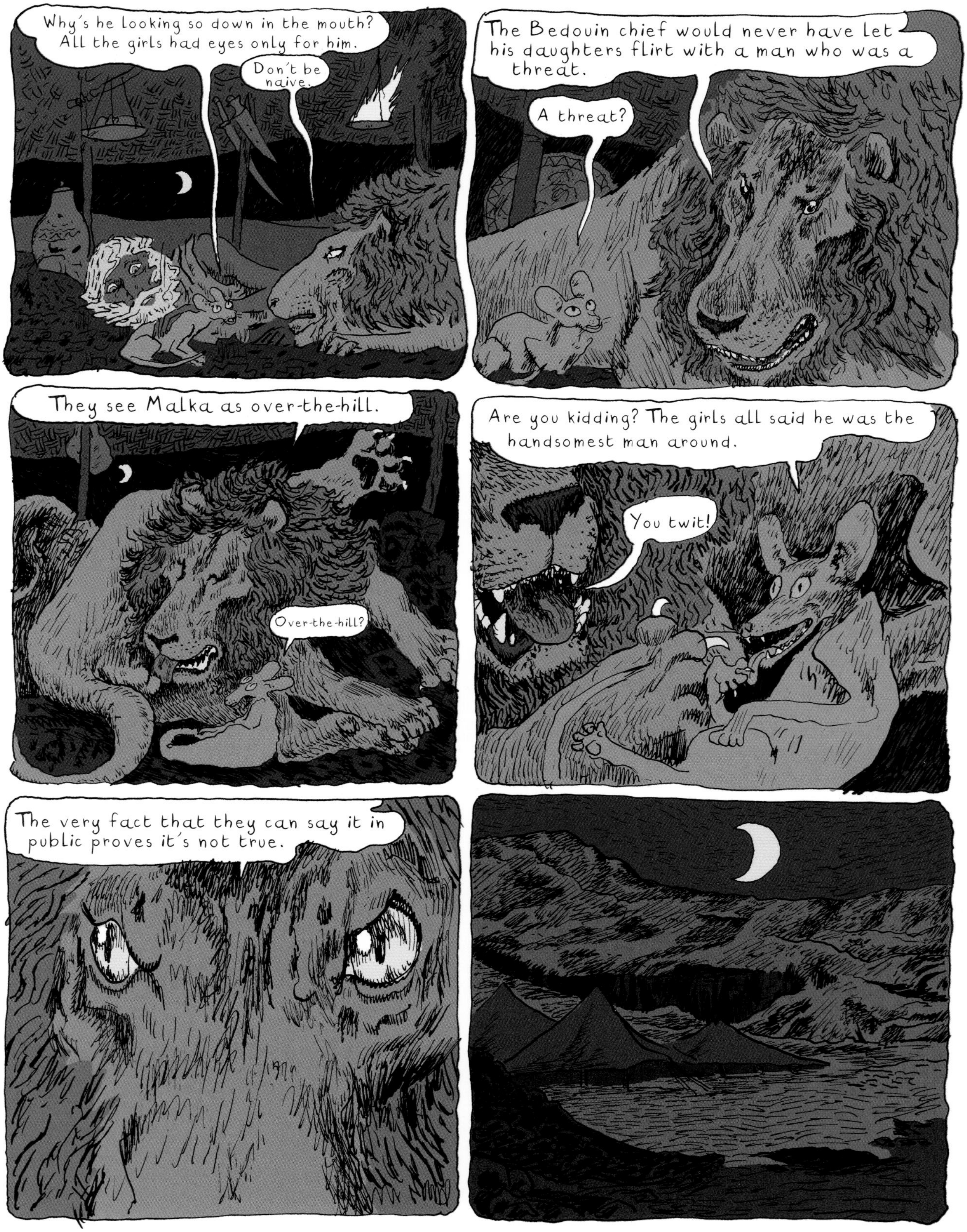
Why's he looking so down in the mouth? All the girls had eyes only for him.
Don't be naive.
The Bedouin chief would never have let his daughters flirt with a man who was a threat.
A threat?
They see Malka as over-the-hill.
Over-the-hill?
Are you kidding? The girls all said he was the handsomest man around.
You twit!
The very fact that they can say it in public proves it's not true.

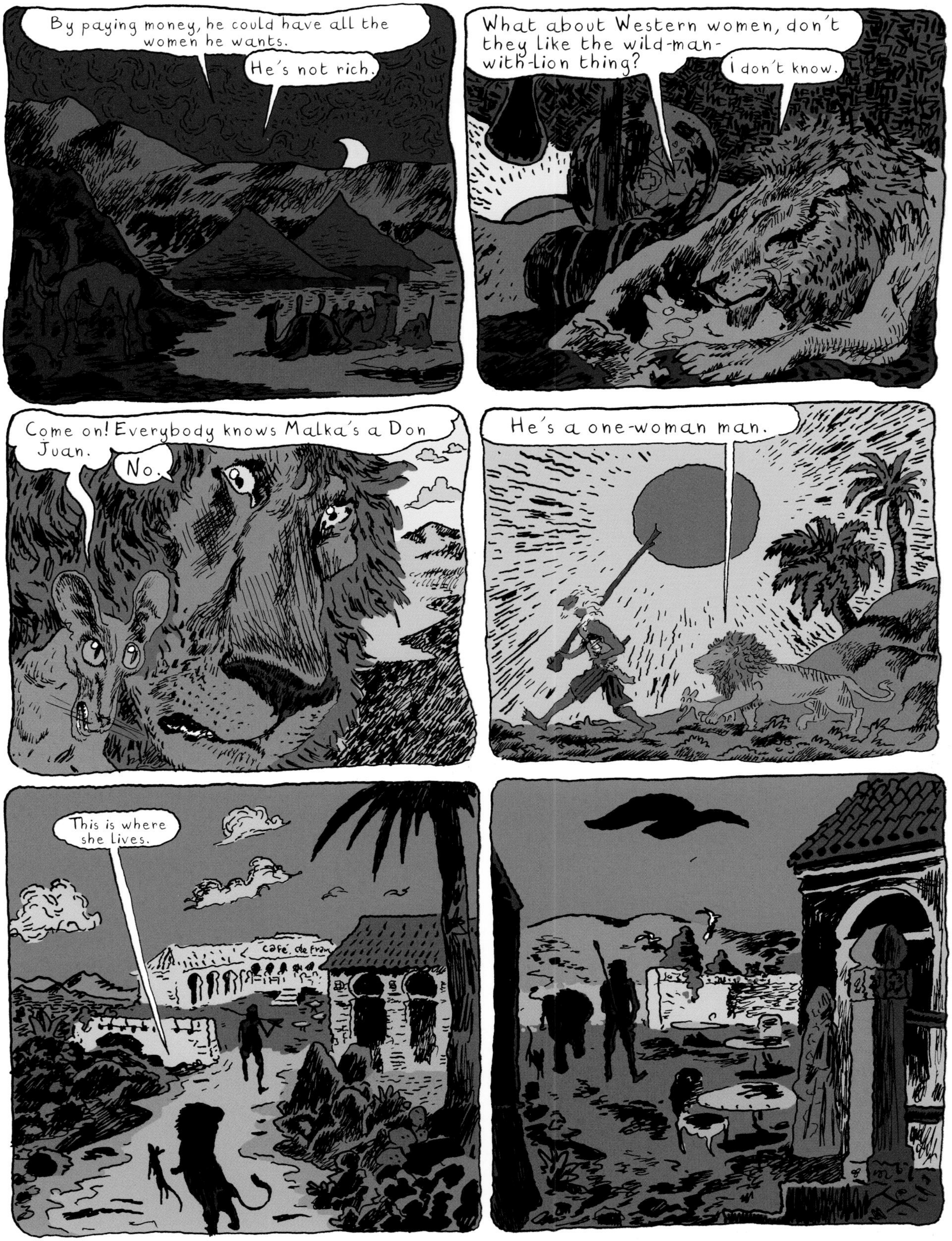
By paying money, he could have all the women he wants.
He's not rich.
What about Western women, don't they like the wild-man-with-lion thing?
I don't know.
Come on! Everybody knows Malka's a Don Juan.
No.
He's a one-woman man.
This is where she lives.
café de fran

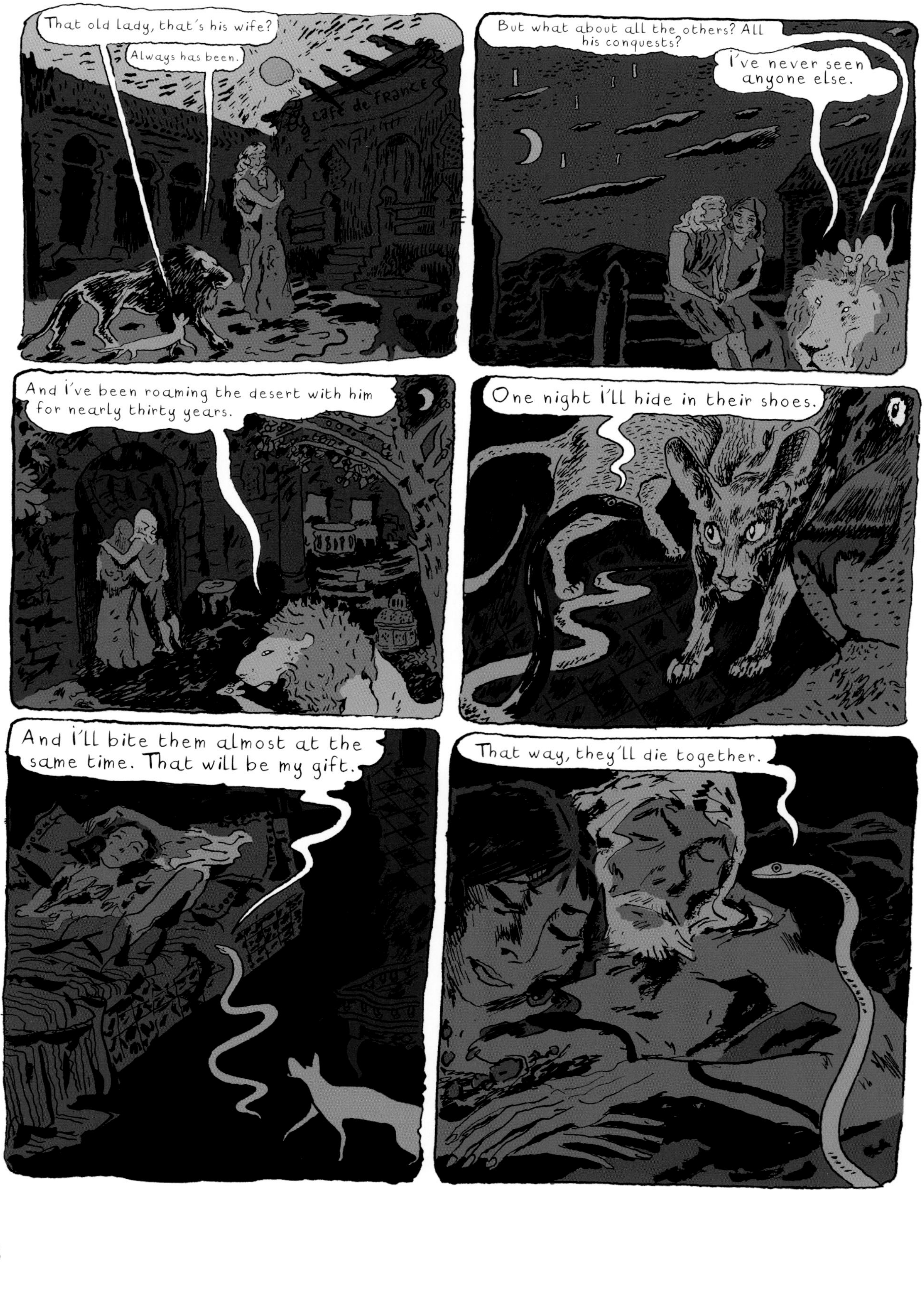
That old lady, that's his wife?
Always has been.
Café de France
But what about all the others? All his conquests?
I've never seen anyone else.
And I've been roaming the desert with him for nearly thirty years.
One night I'll hide in their shoes.
And I'll bite them almost at the same time. That will be my gift.
That way, they'll die together.

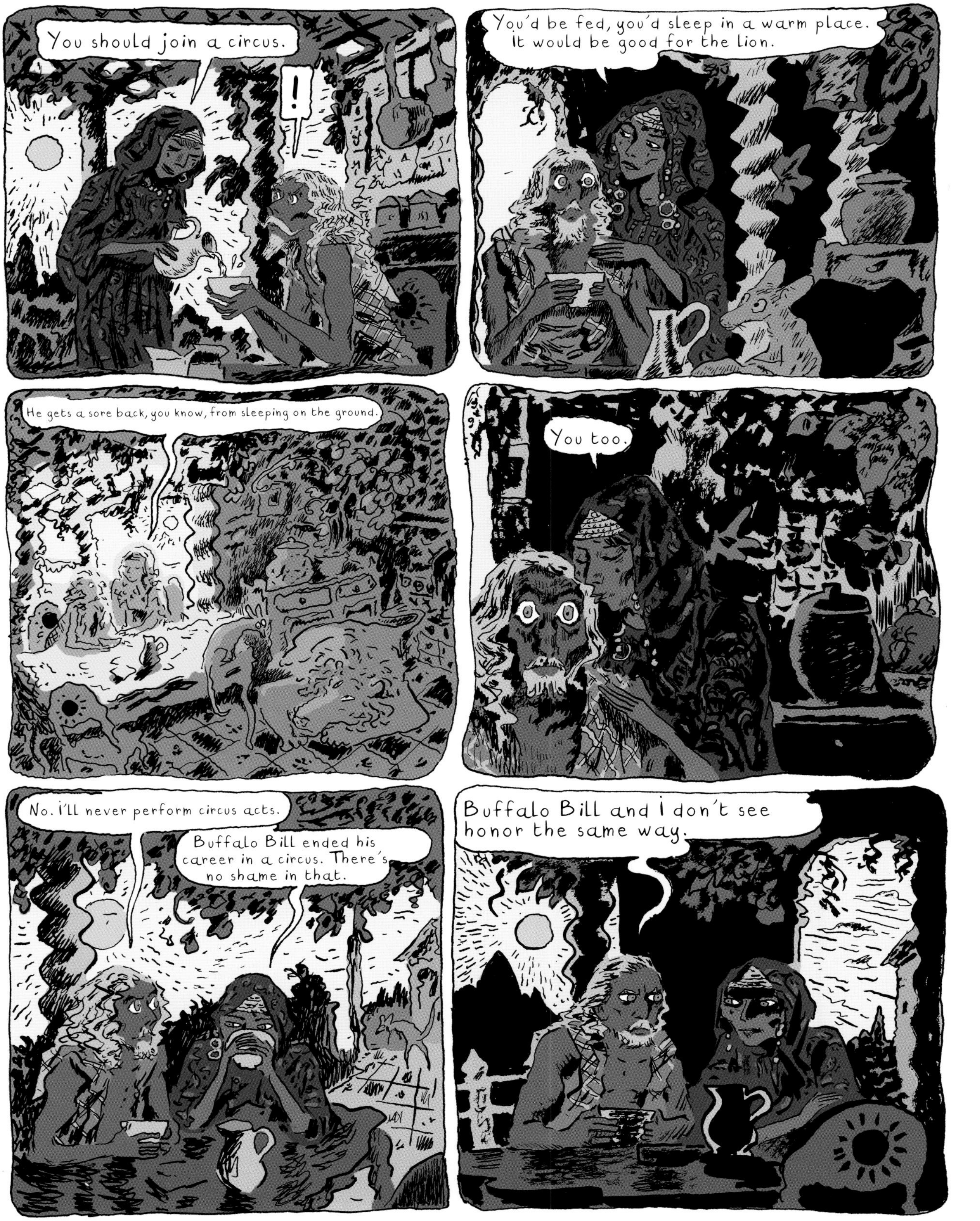
You should join a circus.
!
You'd be fed, you'd sleep in a warm place. It would be good for the Lion.
He gets a sore back, you know, from sleeping on the ground.
You too.
No. I'll never perform circus acts.
Buffalo Bill ended his career in a circus. There's no shame in that.
Buffalo Bill and I don't see honor the same way.

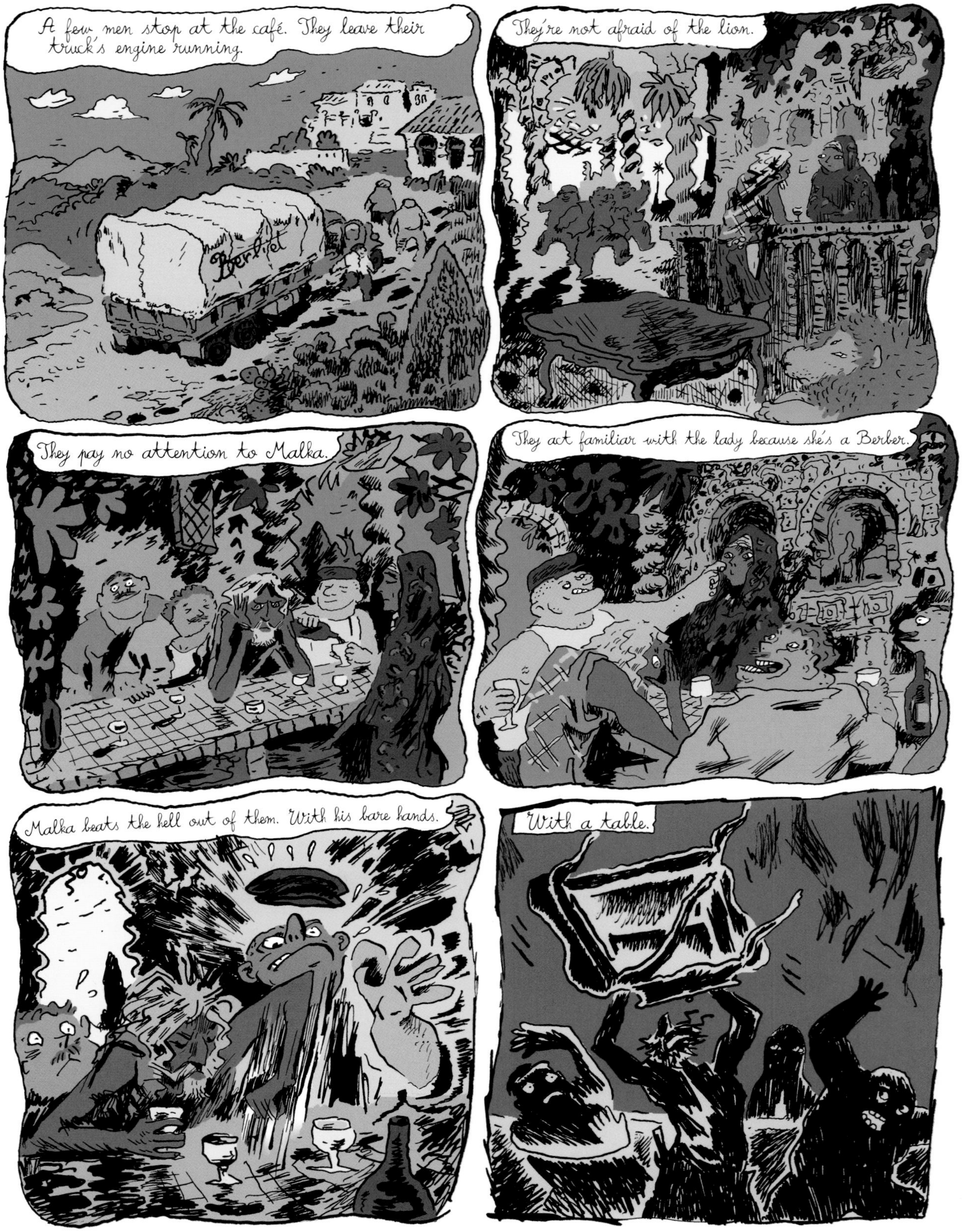
A few men stop at the café. They leave their truck's engine running.
Berliet
They're not afraid of the lion.
They pay no attention to Malka.
They act familiar with the lady because she's a Berber.
Malka beats the hell out of them. With his bare hands.
With a table.

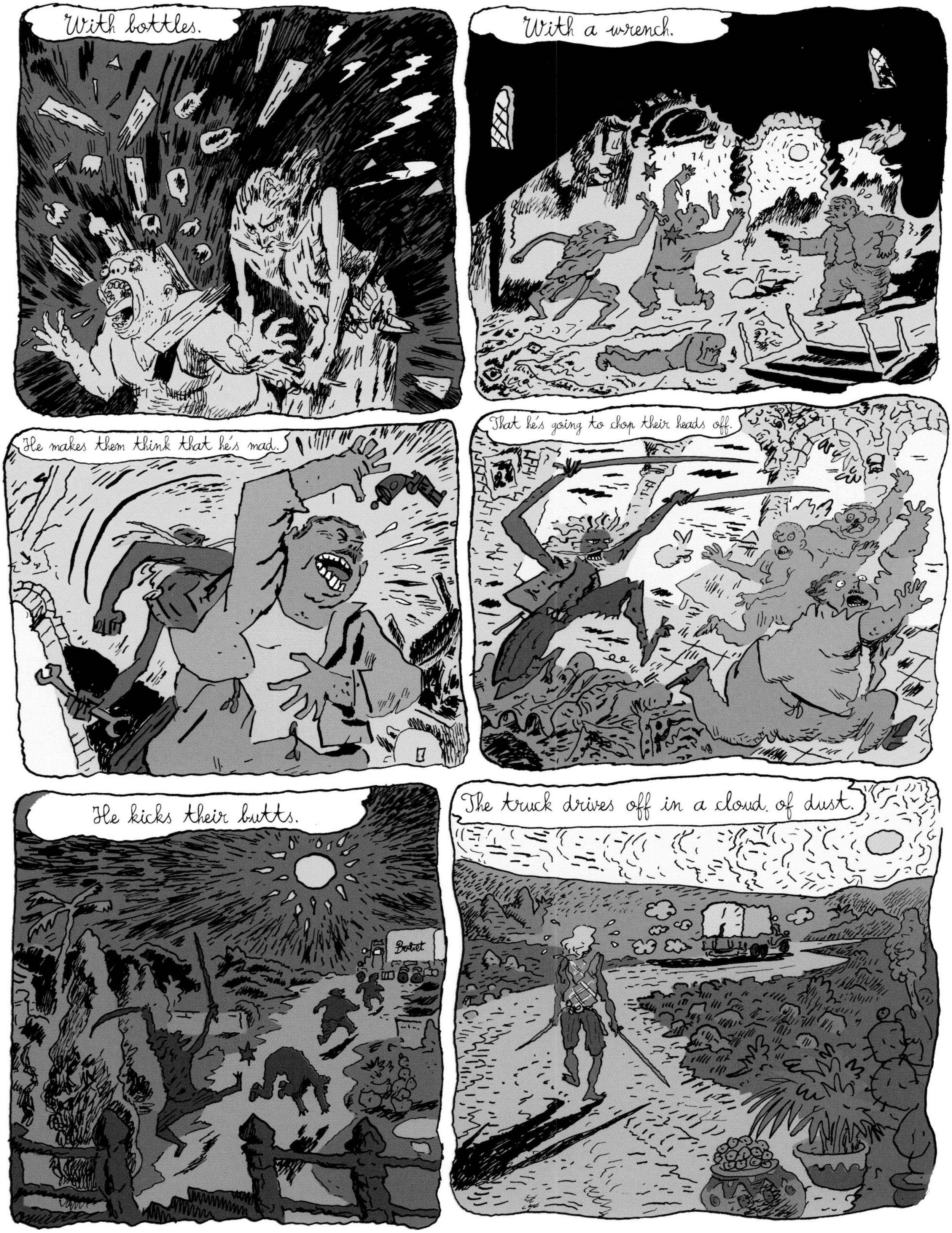
With bottles.
With a wrench.
He makes them think that he's mad.
That he's going to chop their heads off.
He kicks their butts.
The truck drives off in a cloud of dust.

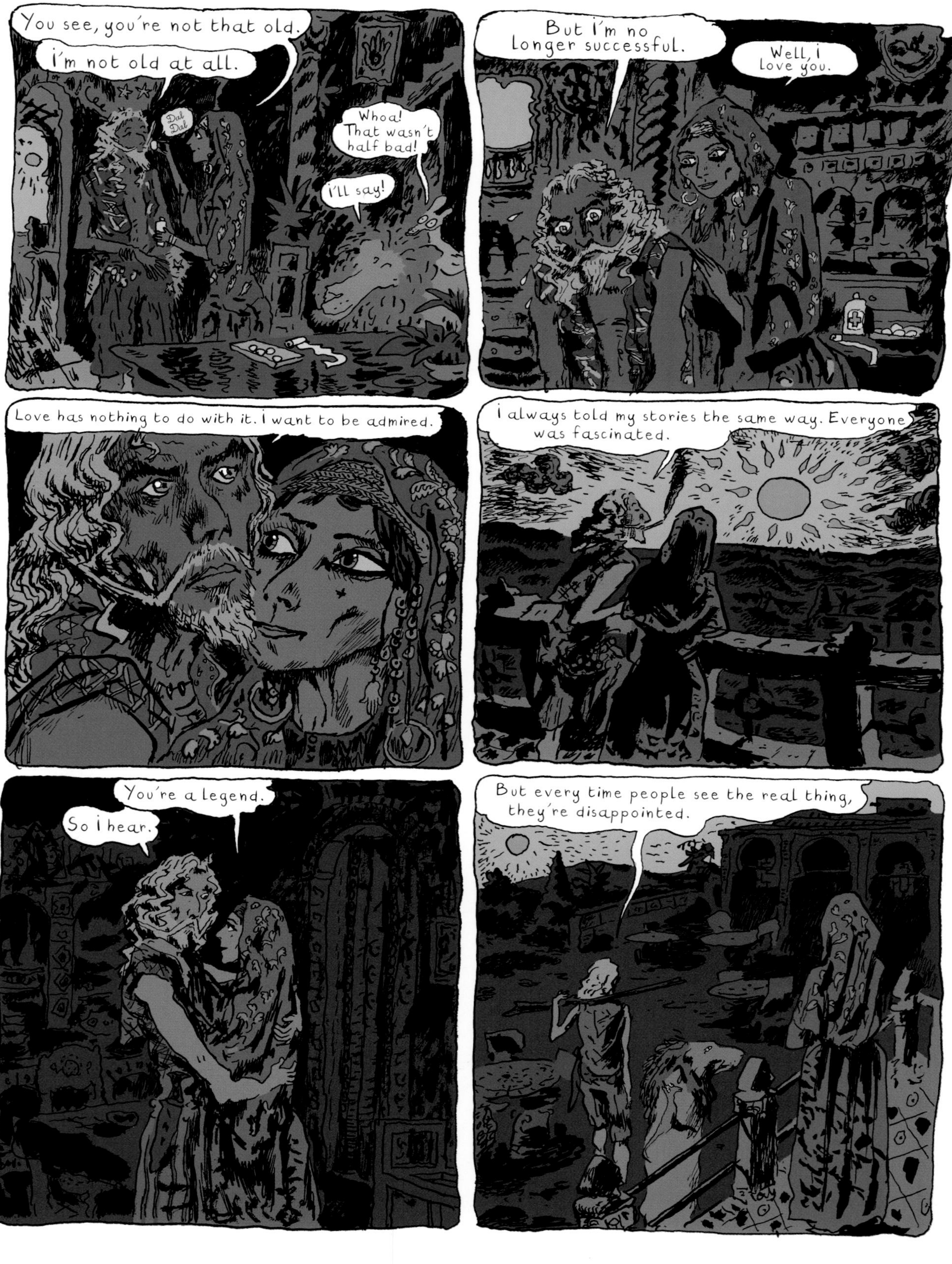
You see, you're not that old.
I'm not old at all.
Dal Dal
Whoa! That wasn't half bad!
I'll say!
But I'm no longer successful.
Well, I love you.
Love has nothing to do with it. I want to be admired.
I always told my stories the same way. Everyone was fascinated.
You're a legend.
So I hear.
But every time people see the real thing, they're disappointed.

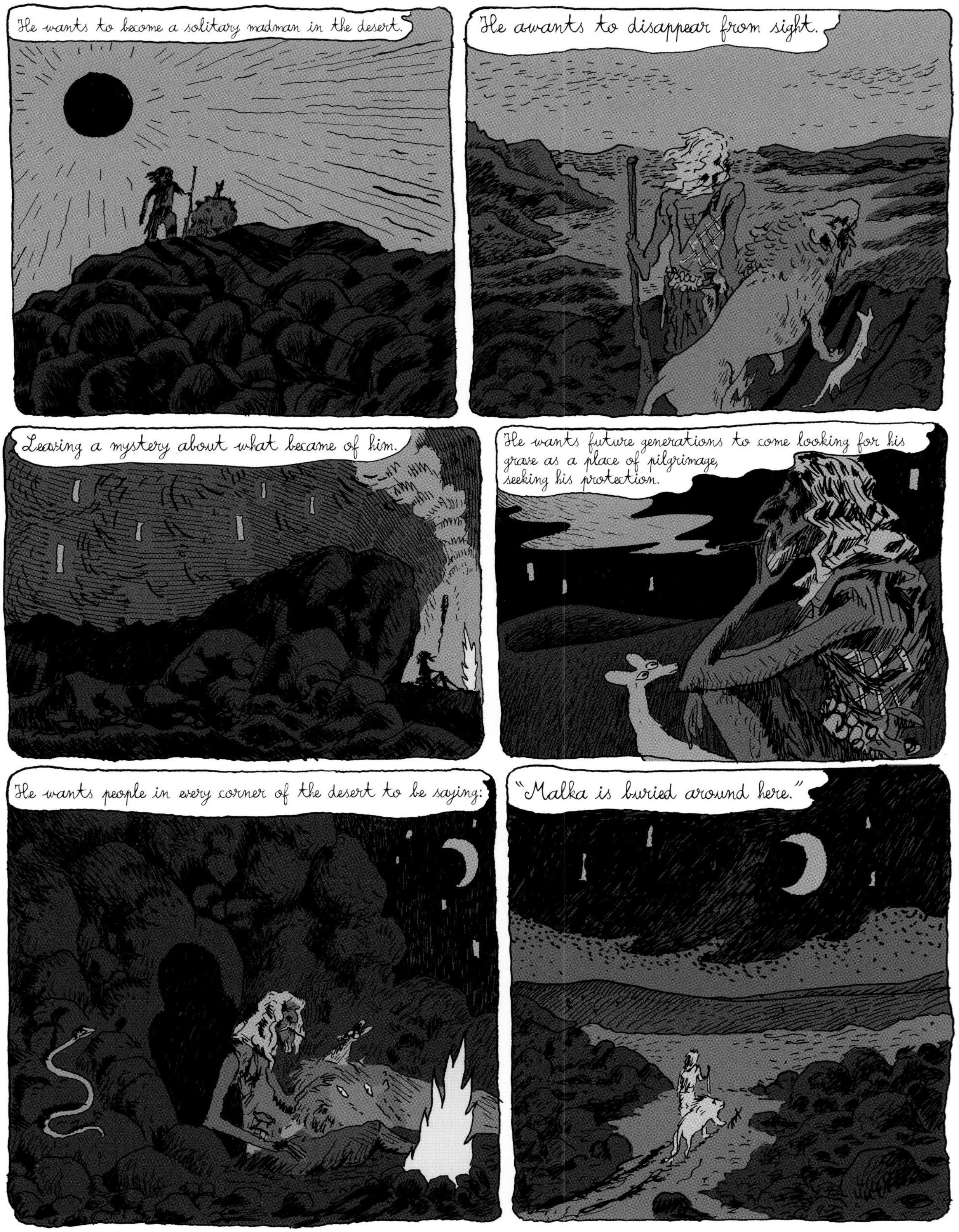
He wants to become a solitary madman in the desert.
He awants to disappear from sight.
Leaving a mystery about what became of him.
He wants future generations to come looking for his grave as a place of pilgrimage, seeking his protection.
He wants people in every corner of the desert to be saying:
"Malka is buried around here."

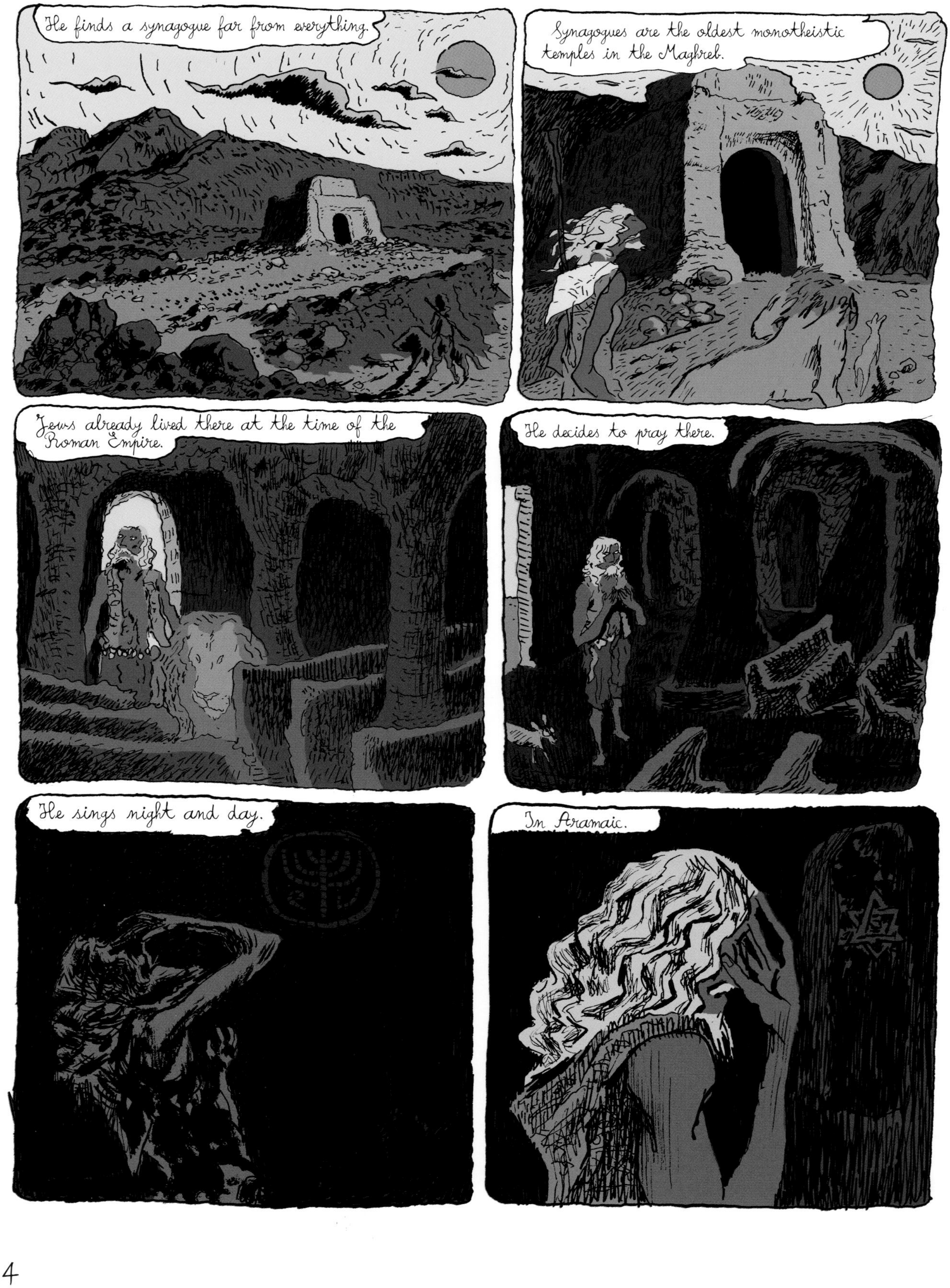
He finds a synagogue far from everything.
Synagogues are the oldest monotheistic temples in the Maghreb.
Jews already lived there at the time of the Roman Empire.
He decides to pray there.
He sings night and day.
In Aramaic.

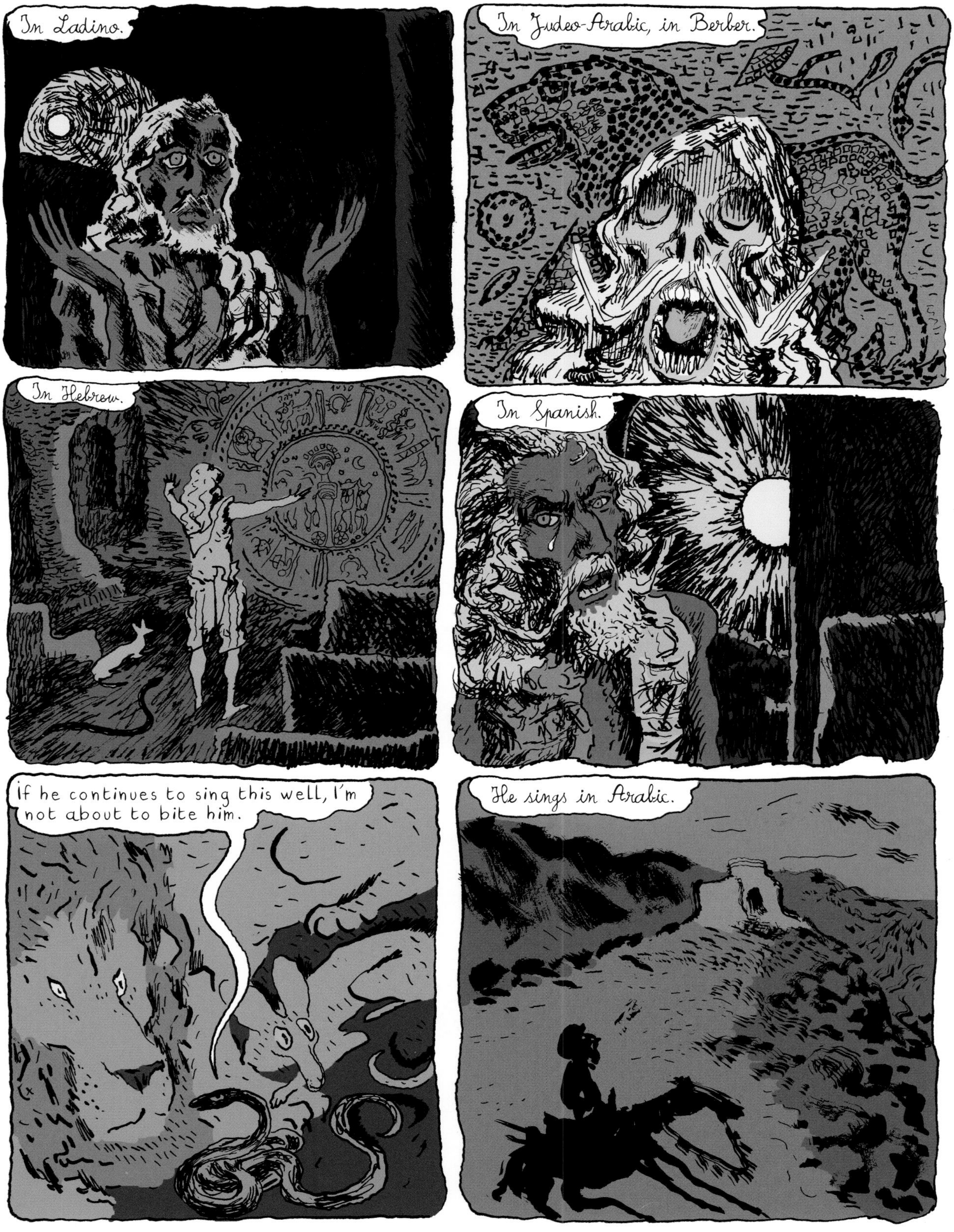
In Ladino.
In Judeo-Arabic, in Berber.
In Hebrew.
In Spanish.
If he continues to sing this well, I'm not about to bite him.
He sings in Arabic.

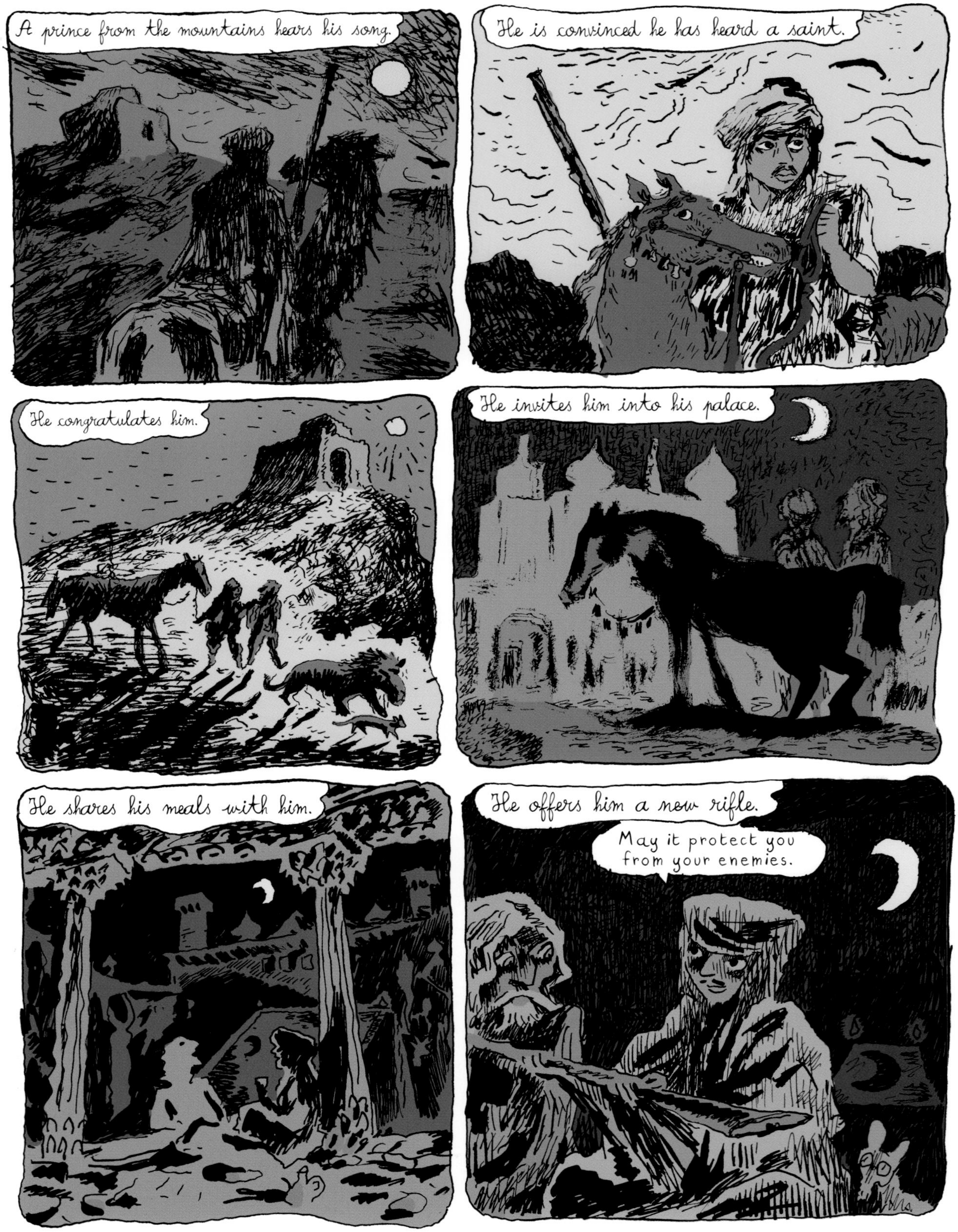
A prince from the mountains hears his song.
He is convinced he has heard a saint.
He congratulates him.
He invites him into his palace.
He shares his meals with him.
He offers him a new rifle.
May it protect you from your enemies.

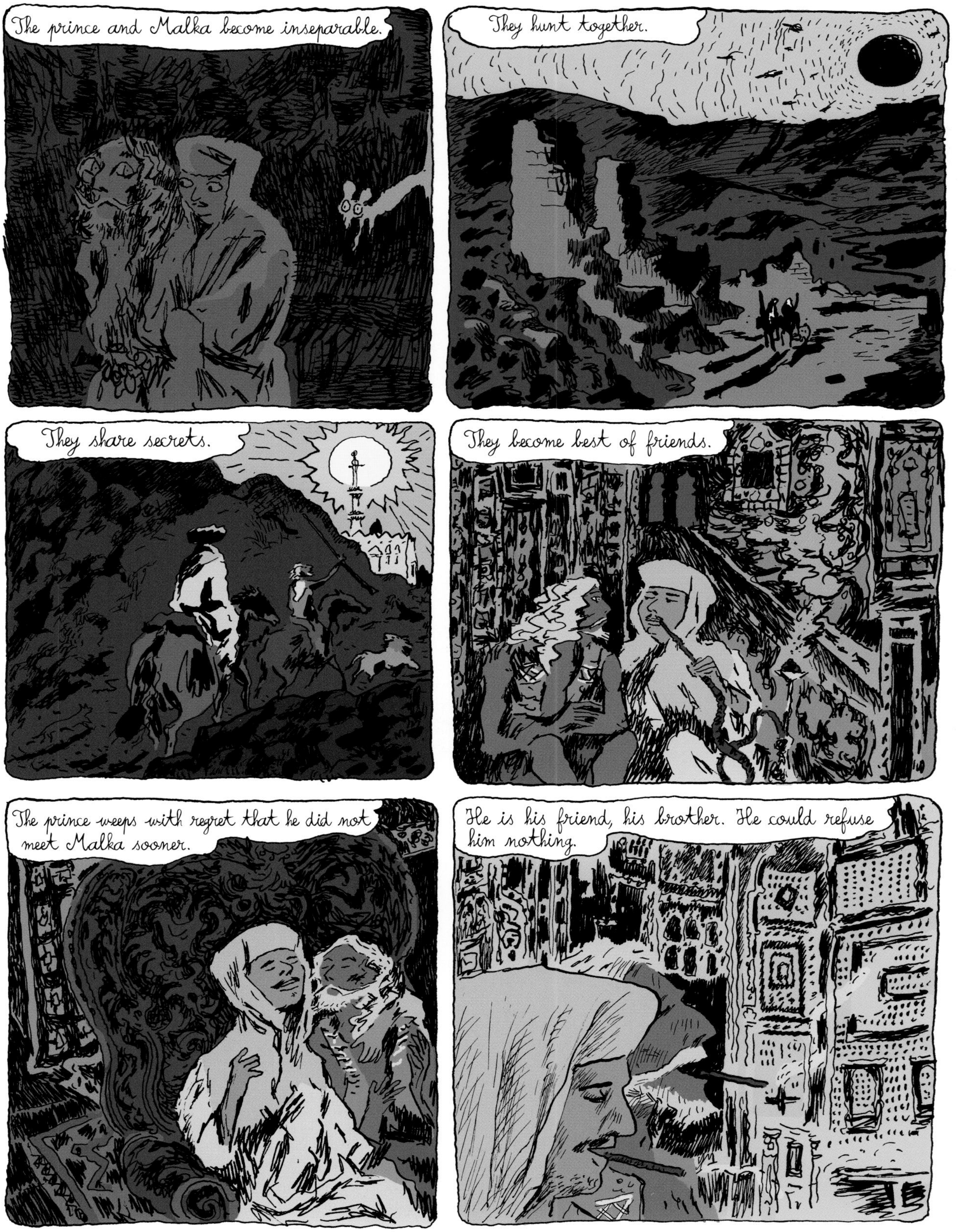
The prince and Malka become inseparable.
They hunt together.
They share secrets.
They become best of friends.
The prince weeps with regret that he did not meet Malka sooner.
He is his friend, his brother. He could refuse him nothing.

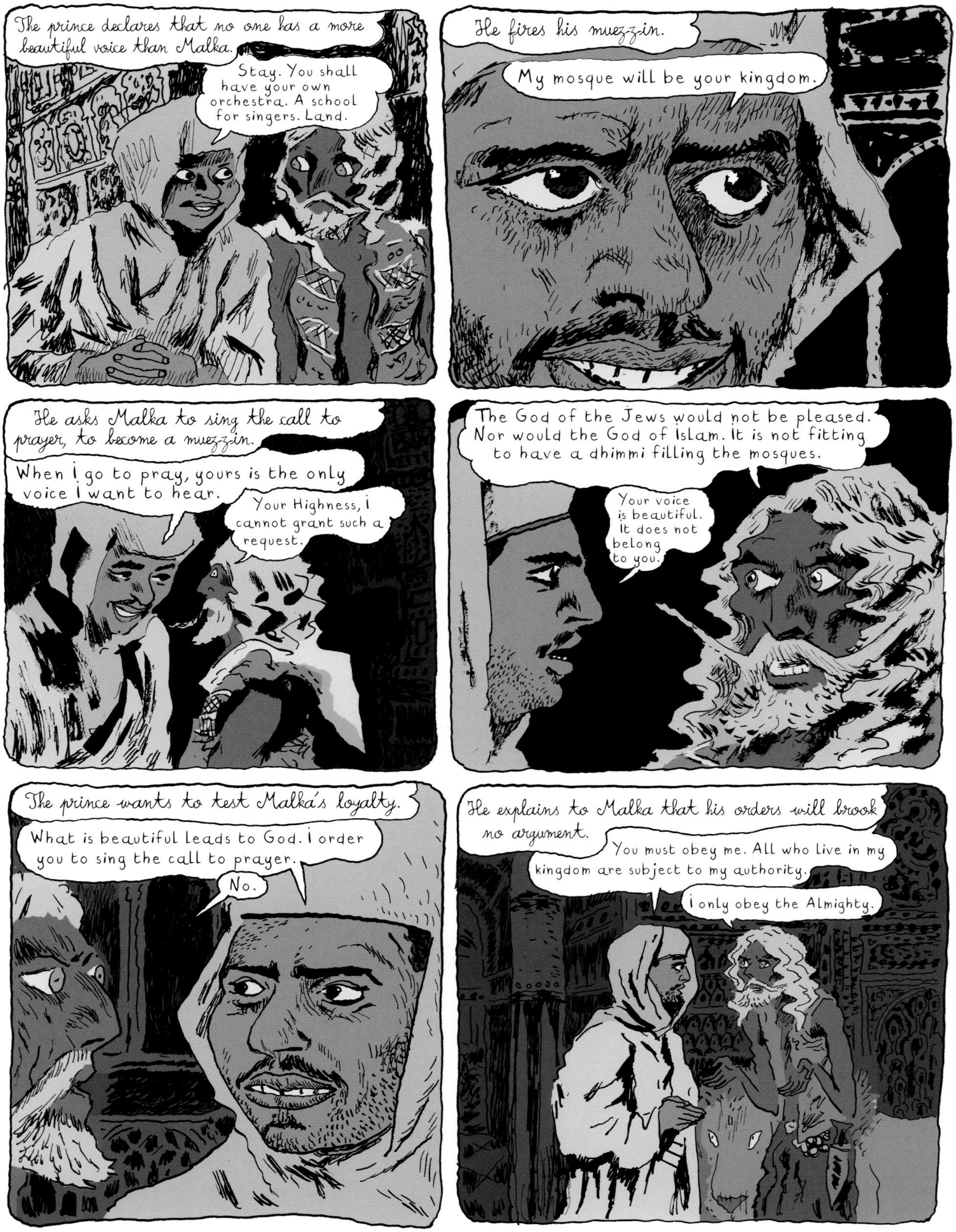
The prince declares that no one has a more beautiful voice than Malka.
Stay. You shall have your own orchestra. A school for singers. Land.
He fires his muezzin.
My mosque will be your kingdom.
He asks Malka to sing the call to prayer, to become a muezzin.
When I go to pray, yours is the only voice I want to hear.
Your Highness, I cannot grant such a request.
The God of the Jews would not be pleased. Nor would the God of Islam. It is not fitting to have a dhimmi filling the mosques.
Your voice is beautiful. It does not belong to you.
The prince wants to test Malka's loyalty.
What is beautiful leads to God. I order you to sing the call to prayer.
No.
He explains to Malka that his orders will brook no argument.
You must obey me. All who live in my kingdom are subject to my authority.
I only obey the Almighty.

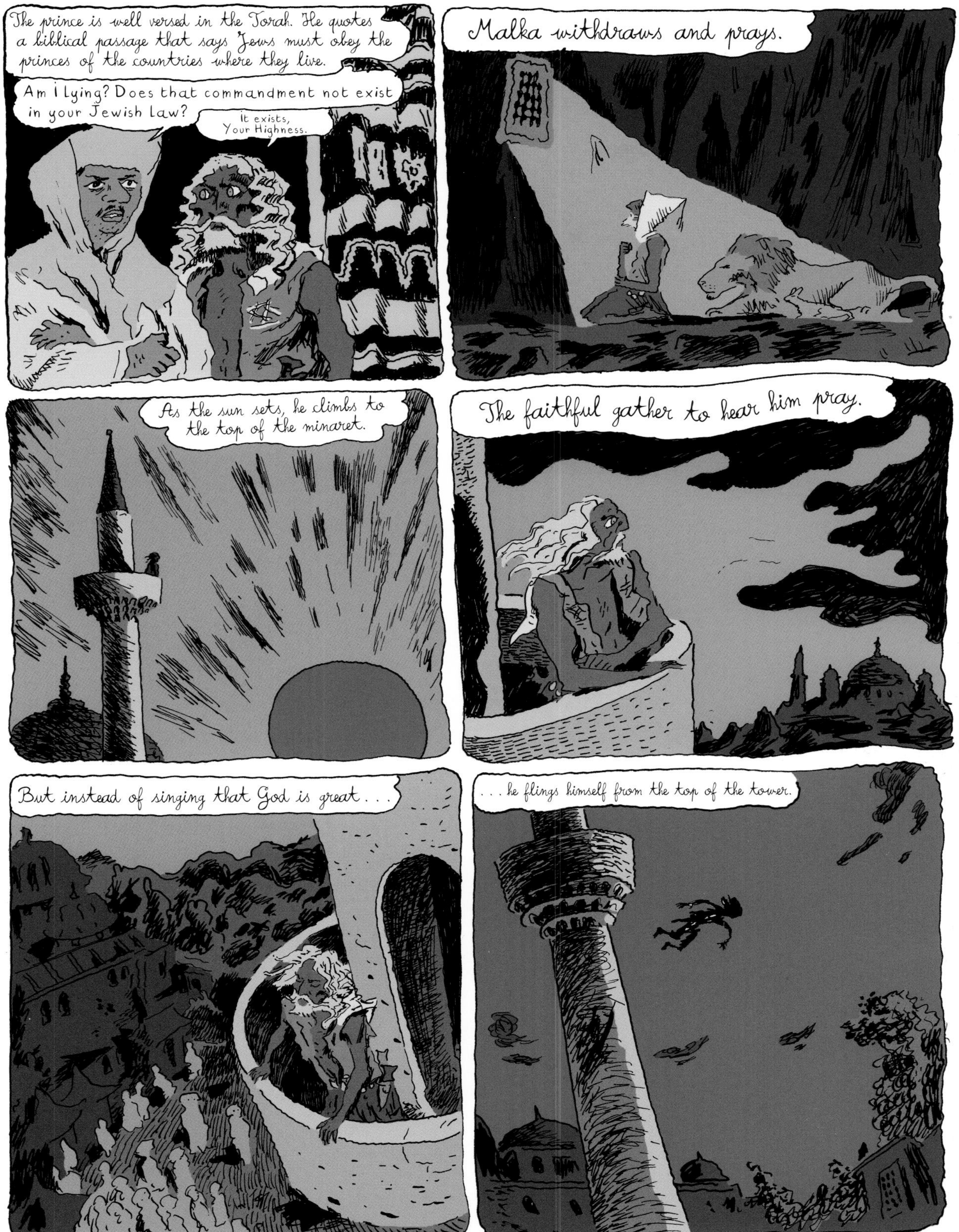
The prince is well versed in the Torah. He quotes a biblical passage that says Jews must obey the princes of the countries where they live.
Am I Lying? Does that commandment not exist in your Jewish Law?
It exists, Your Highness.
Malka withdraws and prays.
As the sun sets, he climbs to the top of the minaret.
The faithful gather to hear him pray.
But instead of singing that God is great . . .
. . . he flings himself from the top of the tower.

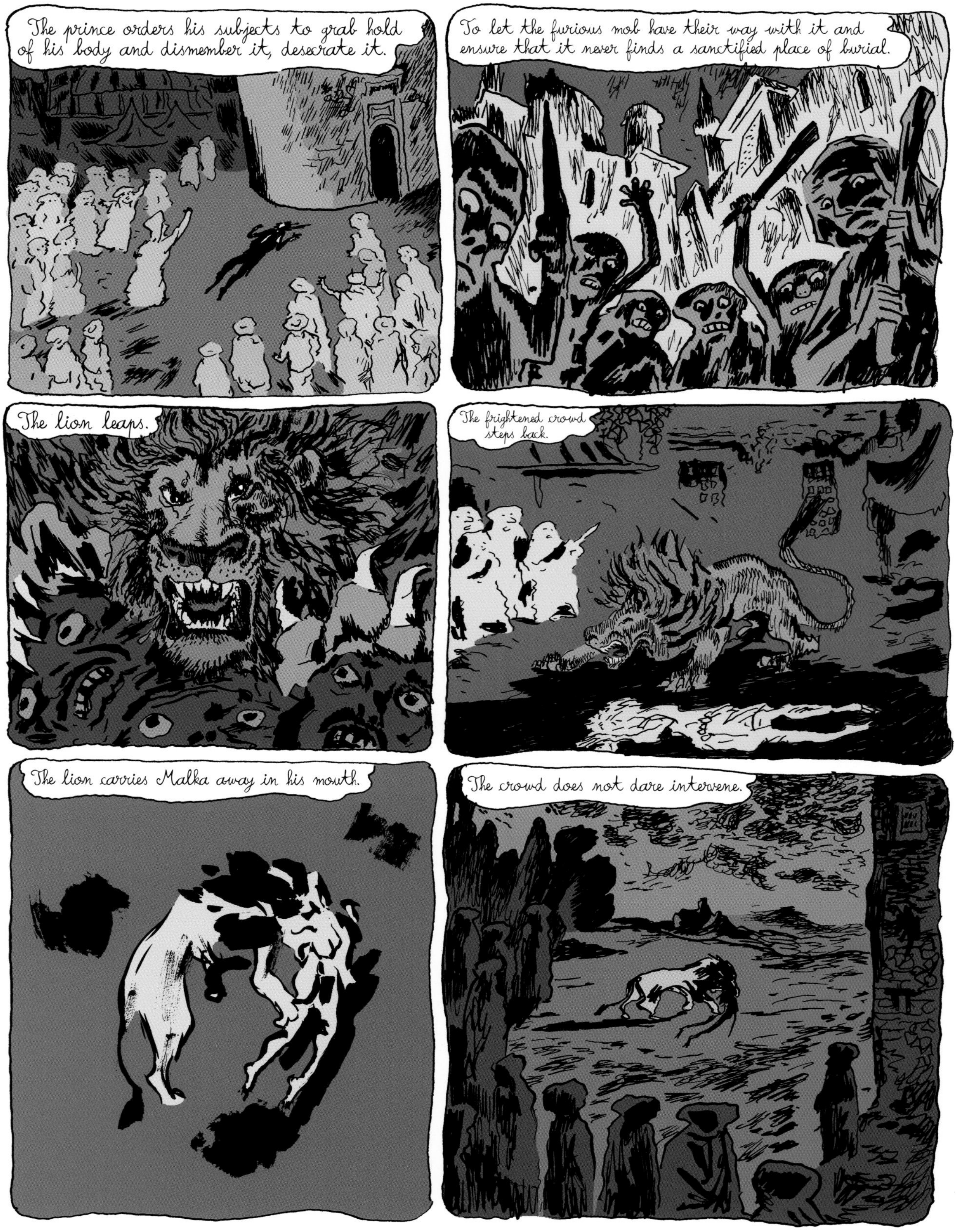
The prince orders his subjects to grab hold of his body and dismember it, desecrate it.
To let the furious mob have their way with it and ensure that it never finds a sanctified place of burial.
The lion leaps.
The frightened crowd steps back.
The lion carries Malka away in his mouth.
The crowd does not dare intervene.

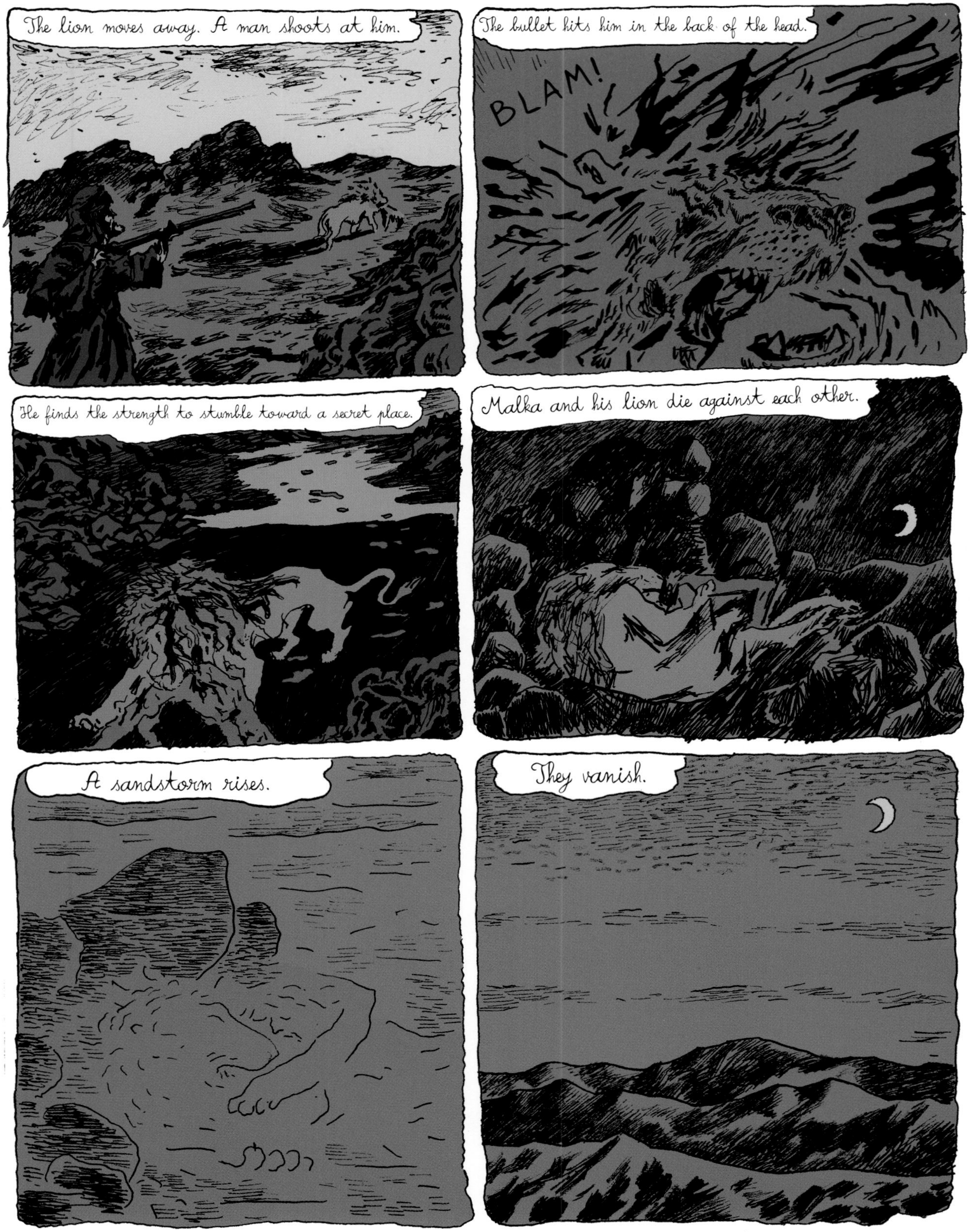

The lion moves away. A man shoots at him.
The bullet hits him in the back of the head.
BLAM!
He finds the strength to stumble toward a secret place.
Malka and his lion die against each other.
A sandstorm rises.
They vanish.

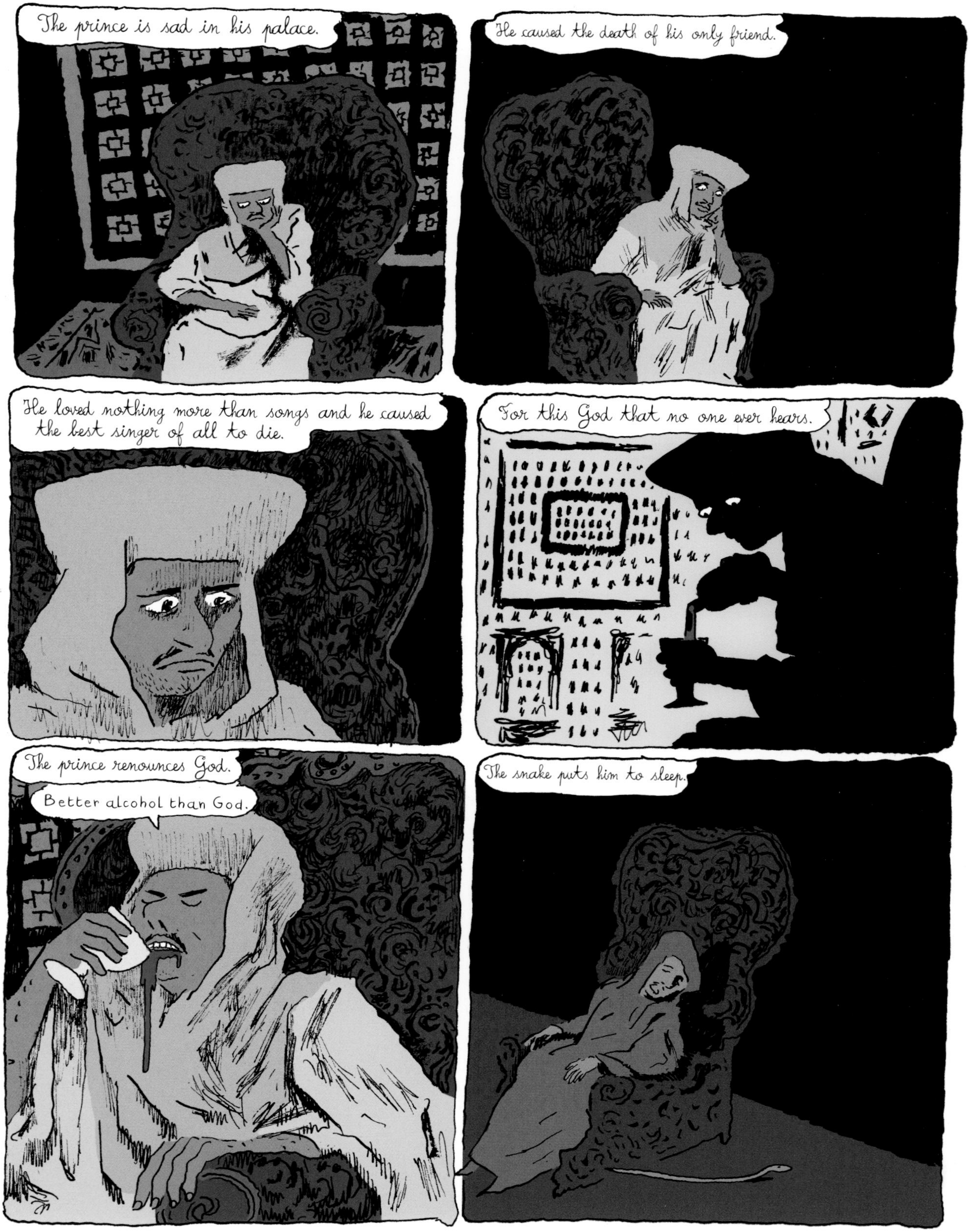
The prince is sad in his palace.
He caused the death of his only friend.
He loved nothing more than songs and he caused the best singer of all to die.
For this God that no one ever hears.
The prince renounces God.
Better alcohol than God.
The snake puts him to sleep.

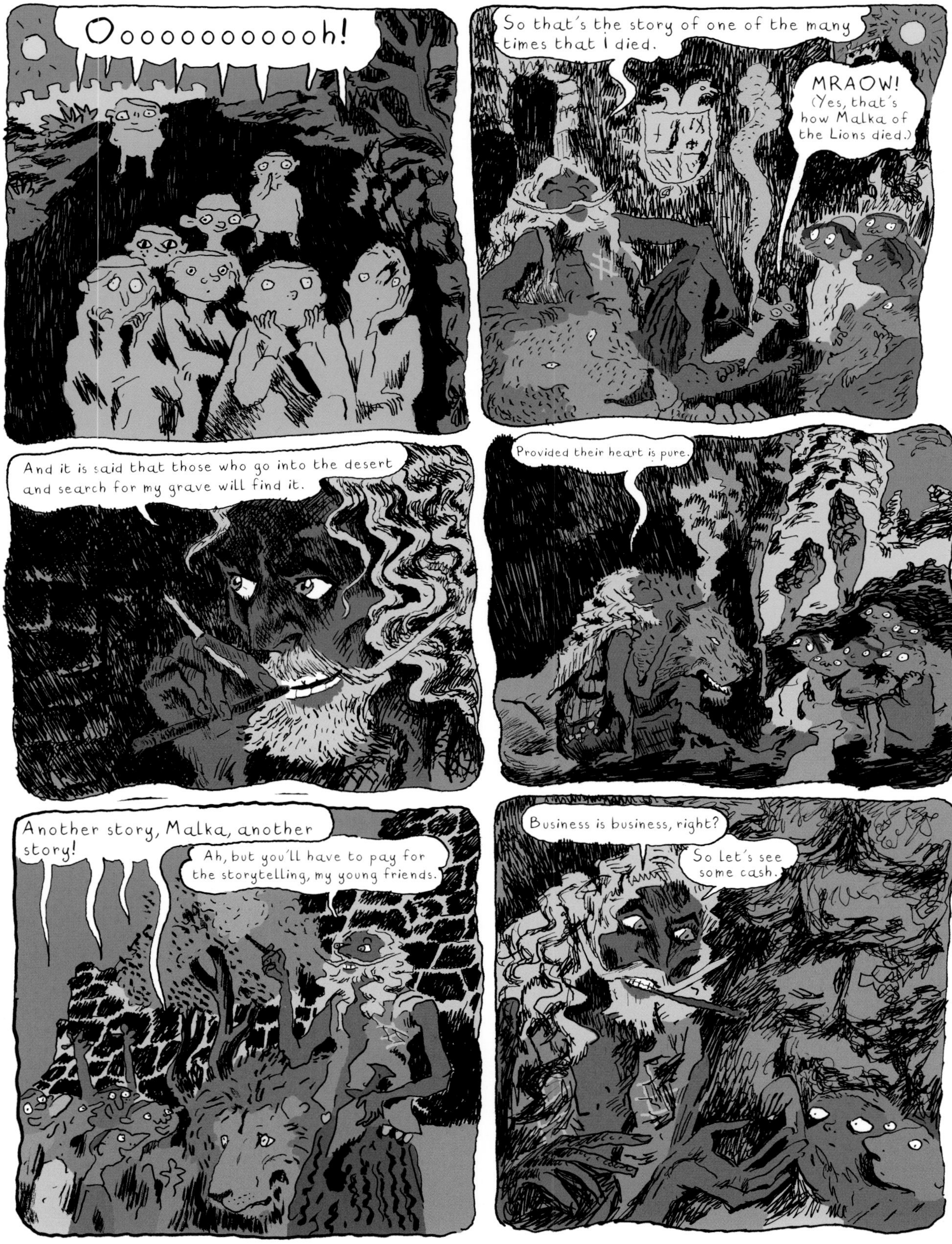
Ooooooooooooh!
So that's the story of one of the many times that I died.
MRAOW! (Yes, that's how Malka of the Lions died.)
And it is said that those who go into the desert and search for my grave will find it.
Provided their heart is pure.
Another story, Malka, another story!
Ah, but you'll have to pay for the storytelling, my young friends.
Business is business, right?
So let's see some cash.

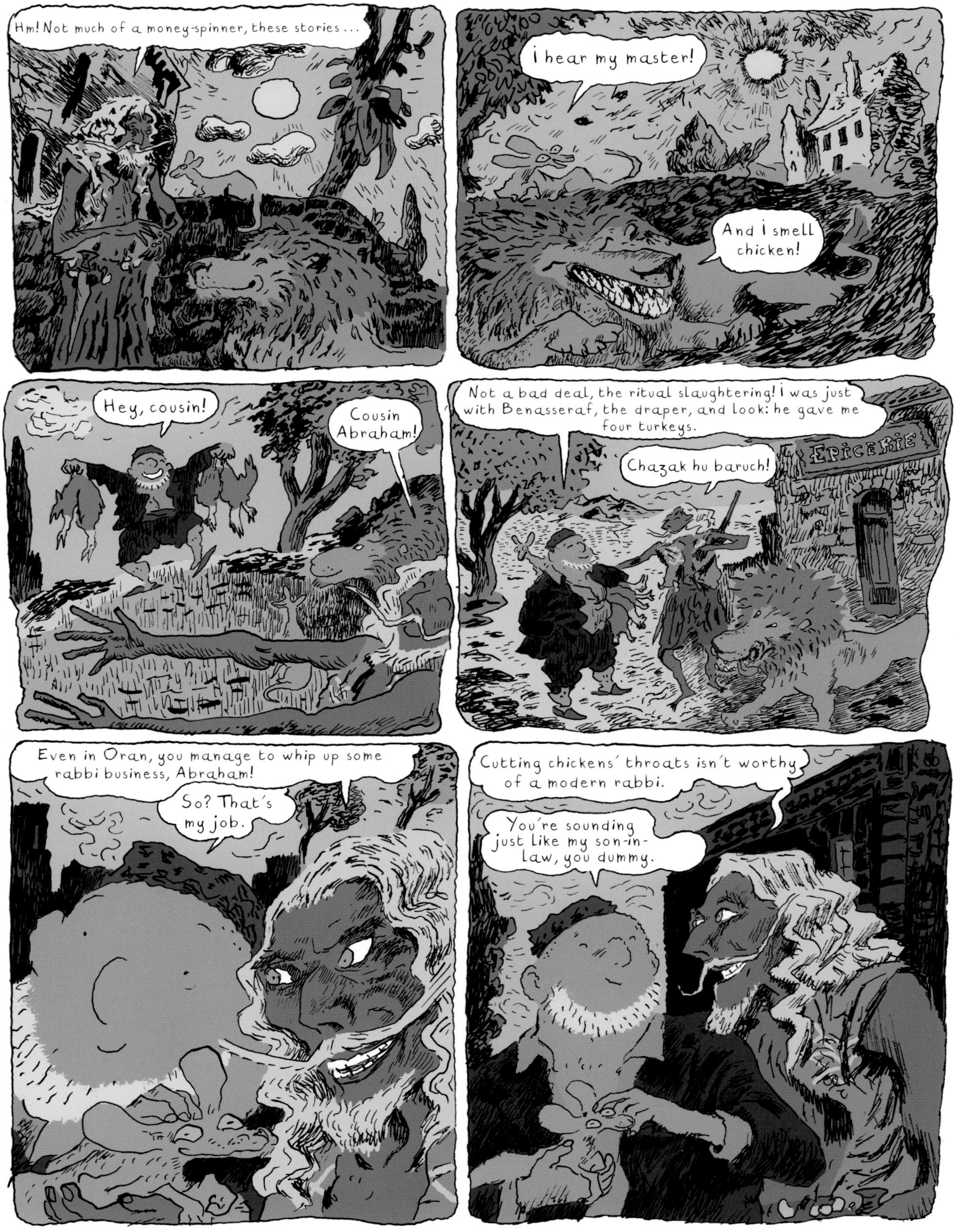
Hm! Not much of a money-spinner, these stories...
I hear my master!
And I smell chicken!
Hey, cousin!
Cousin Abraham!
Not a bad deal, the ritual slaughtering! I was just with Benasseraf, the draper, and look: he gave me four turkeys.
Chazak hu baruch!
EPICERIE
Even in Oran, you manage to whip up some rabbi business, Abraham!
So? That's my job.
Cutting chickens' throats isn't worthy of a modern rabbi.
You're sounding just like my son-in-law, you dummy.

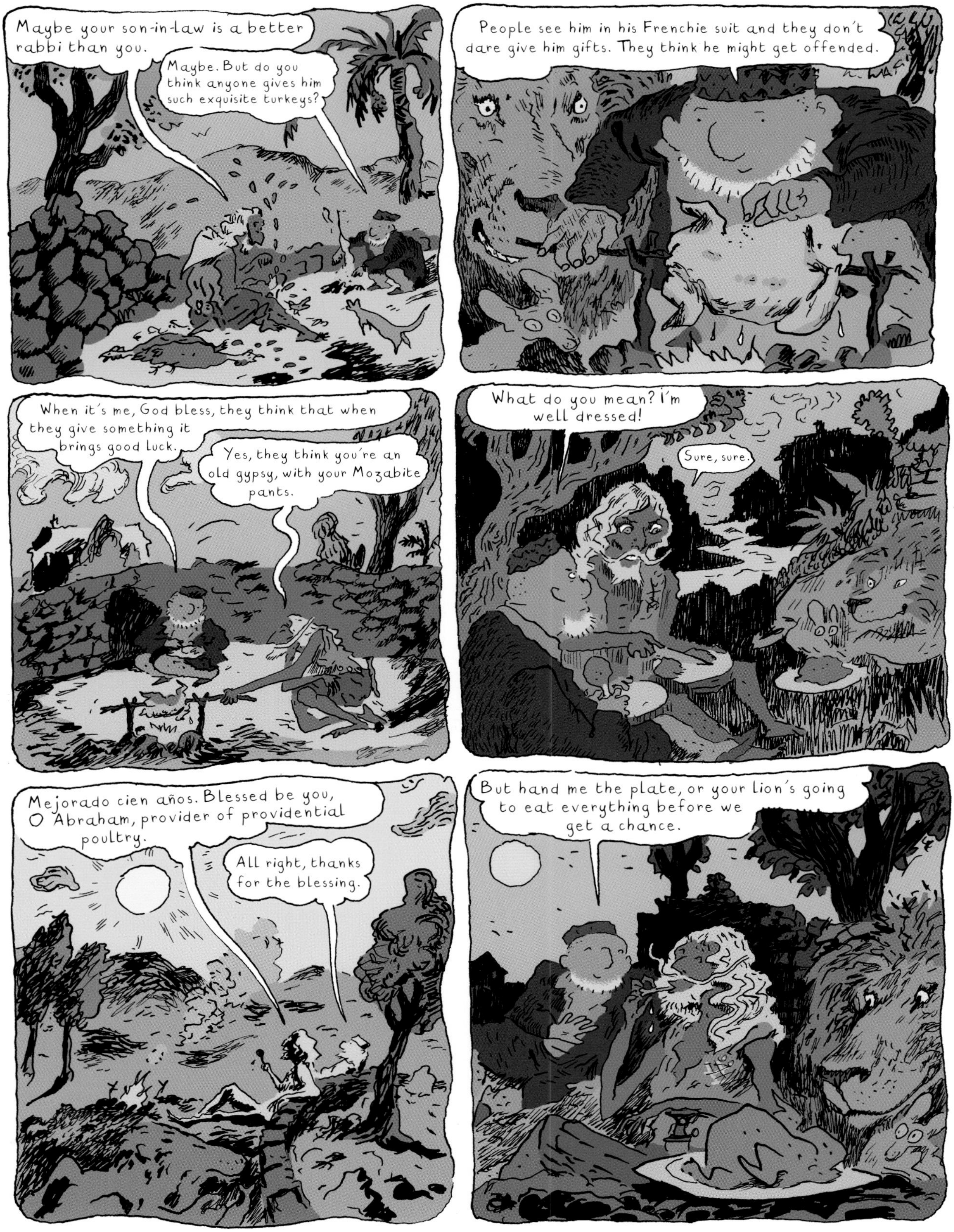
Maybe your son-in-law is a better rabbi than you.
Maybe. But do you think anyone gives him such exquisite turkeys?
People see him in his Frenchie suit and they don't dare give him gifts. They think he might get offended.
When it's me, God bless, they think that when they give something it brings good luck.
Yes, they think you're an old gypsy, with your Mozabite pants.
What do you mean? I'm well dressed!
Sure, sure.
Mejorado cien años. Blessed be you, O Abraham, provider of providential poultry.
All right, thanks for the blessing.
But hand me the plate, or your lion's going to eat everything before we get a chance.

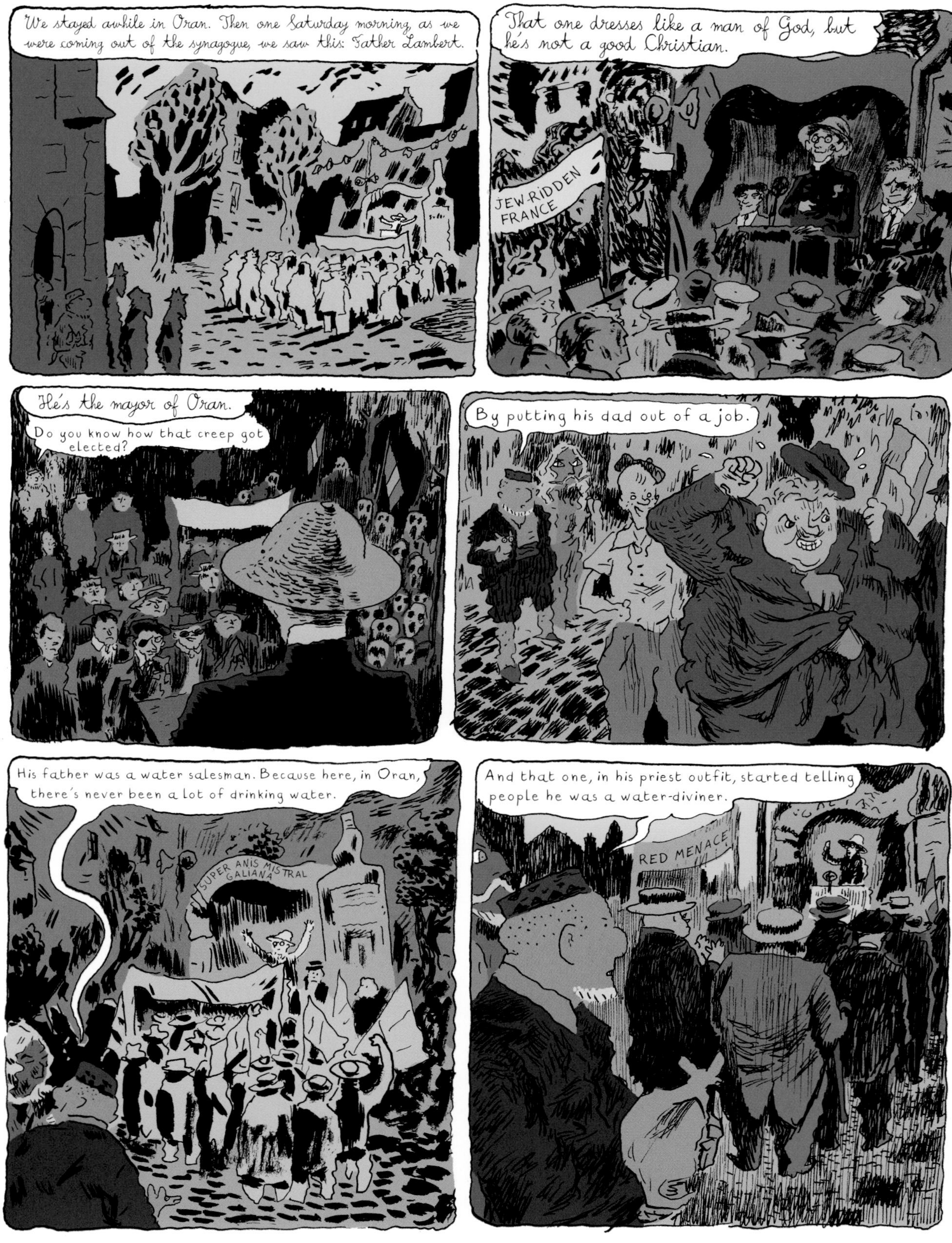

We stayed awhile in Oran. Then one Saturday morning, as we were coming out of the synagogue, we saw this: Father Lambert.
That one dresses like a man of God, but he's not a good Christian.
JEW-RIDDEN FRANCE
He's the mayor of Oran.
Do you know how that creep got elected?
By putting his dad out of a job.
His father was a water salesman. Because here, in Oran, there's never been a lot of drinking water.
SUPER ANIS MISTRAL GALIANA
And that one, in his priest outfit, started telling people he was a water-diviner.
RED MENACE

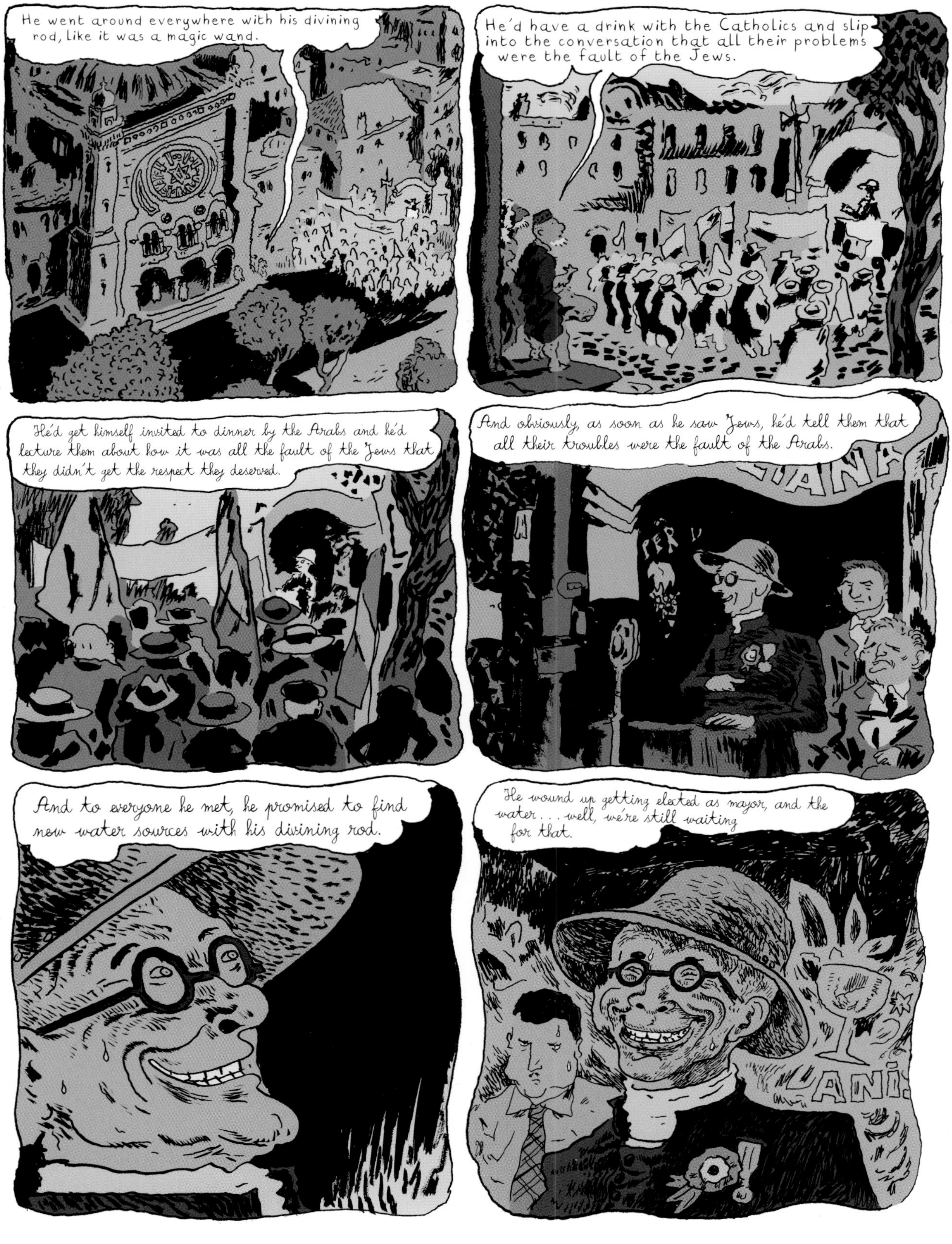

He went around everywhere with his divining rod, like it was a magic wand.
He'd have a drink with the Catholics and slip into the conversation that all their problems were the fault of the Jews.
He'd get himself invited to dinner by the Arabs and he'd lecture them about how it was all the fault of the Jews that they didn't get the respect they deserved.
And obviously, as soon as he saw Jews, he'd tell them that all their troubles were the fault of the Arabs.
And to everyone he met, he promised to find new water sources with his divining rod.
He wound up getting elected as mayor, and the water... well, we're still waiting for that.
ANI

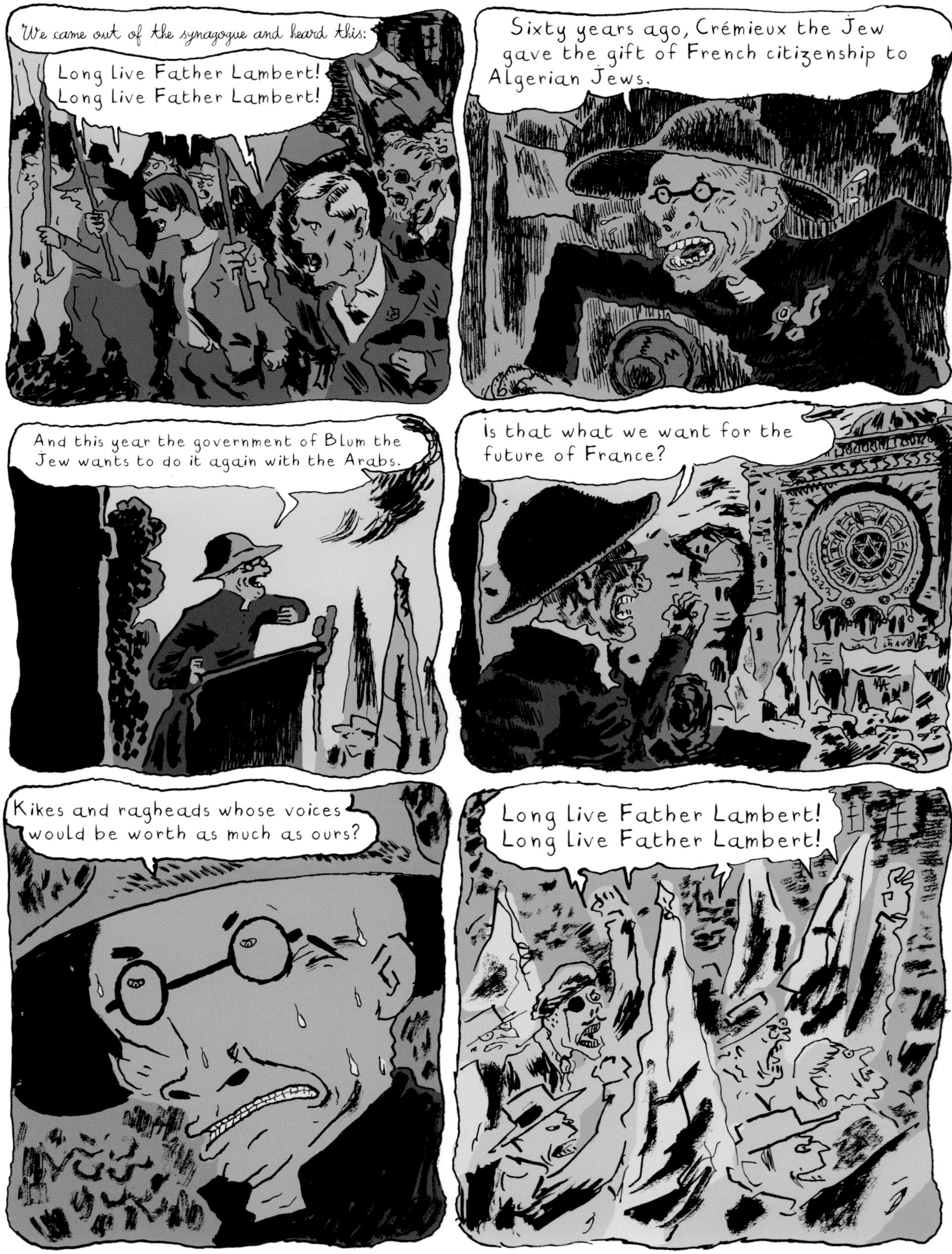
We came out of the synagogue and heard this:
Long live Father Lambert! Long live Father Lambert!
Sixty years ago, Crémieux the Jew gave the gift of French citizenship to Algerian Jews.
And this year the government of Blum the Jew wants to do it again with the Arabs.
Is that what we want for the future of France?
Kikes and ragheads whose voices would be worth as much as ours?
Long live Father Lambert! Long live Father Lambert!

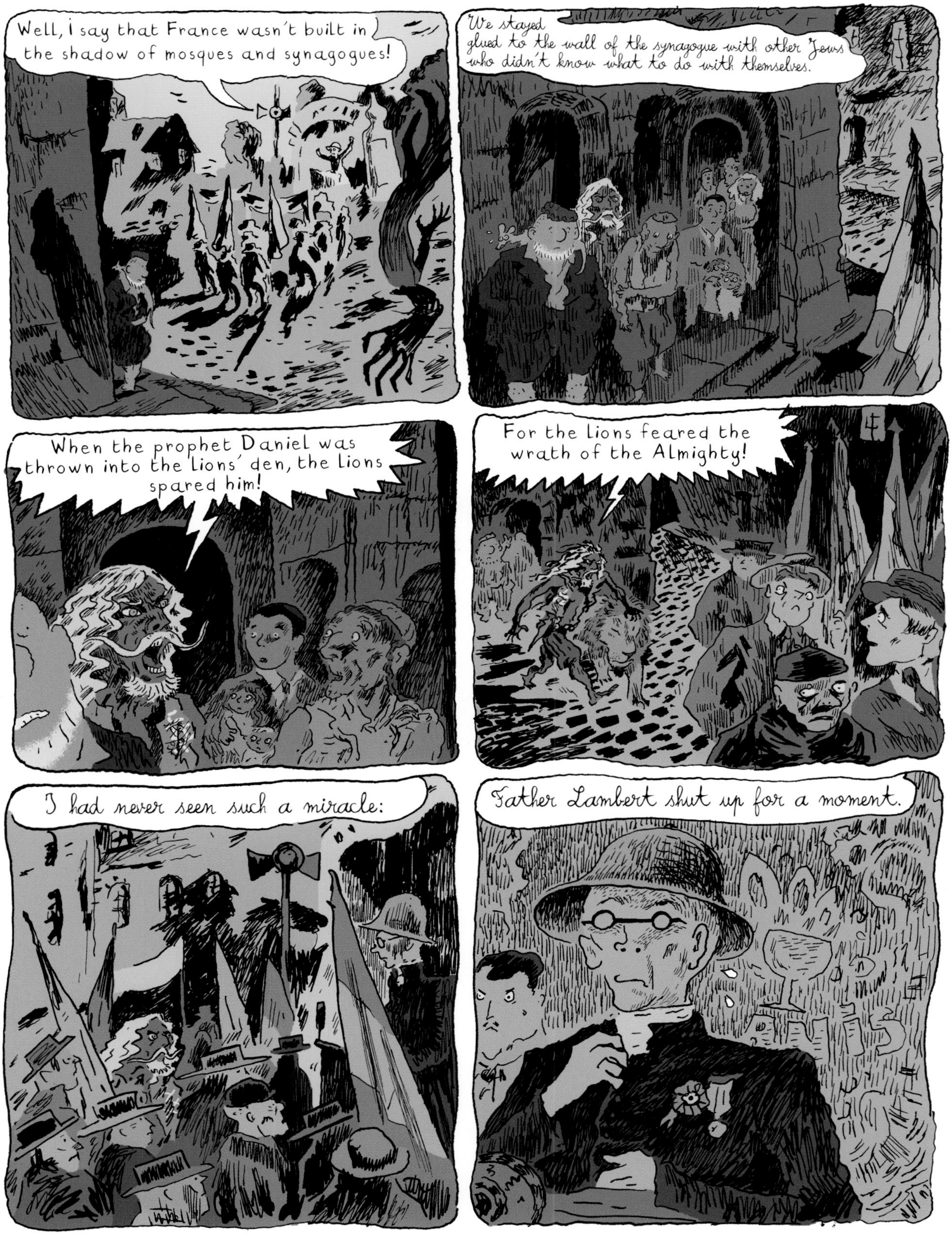
Well, I say that France wasn't built in the shadow of mosques and synagogues!
We stayed glued to the wall of the synagogue with other Jews who didn't know what to do with themselves.
When the prophet Daniel was thrown into the lions' den, the lions spared him!
For the lions feared the wrath of the Almighty!
I had never seen such a miracle:
Father Lambert shut up for a moment.

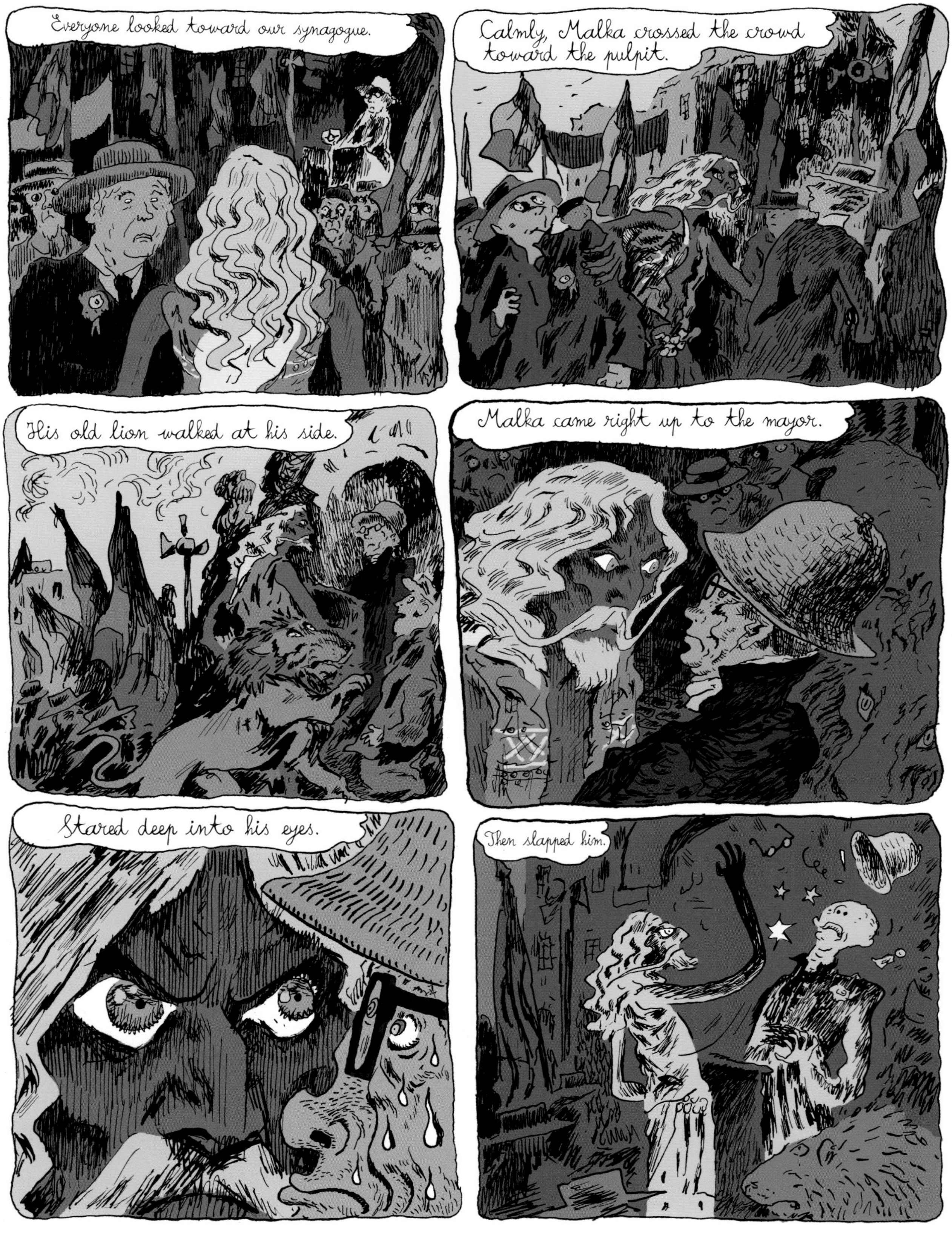
Everyone looked toward our synagogue.
Calmly, Malka crossed the crowd toward the pulpit.
His old lion walked at his side.
Malka came right up to the mayor.
Stared deep into his eyes.
Then slapped him.

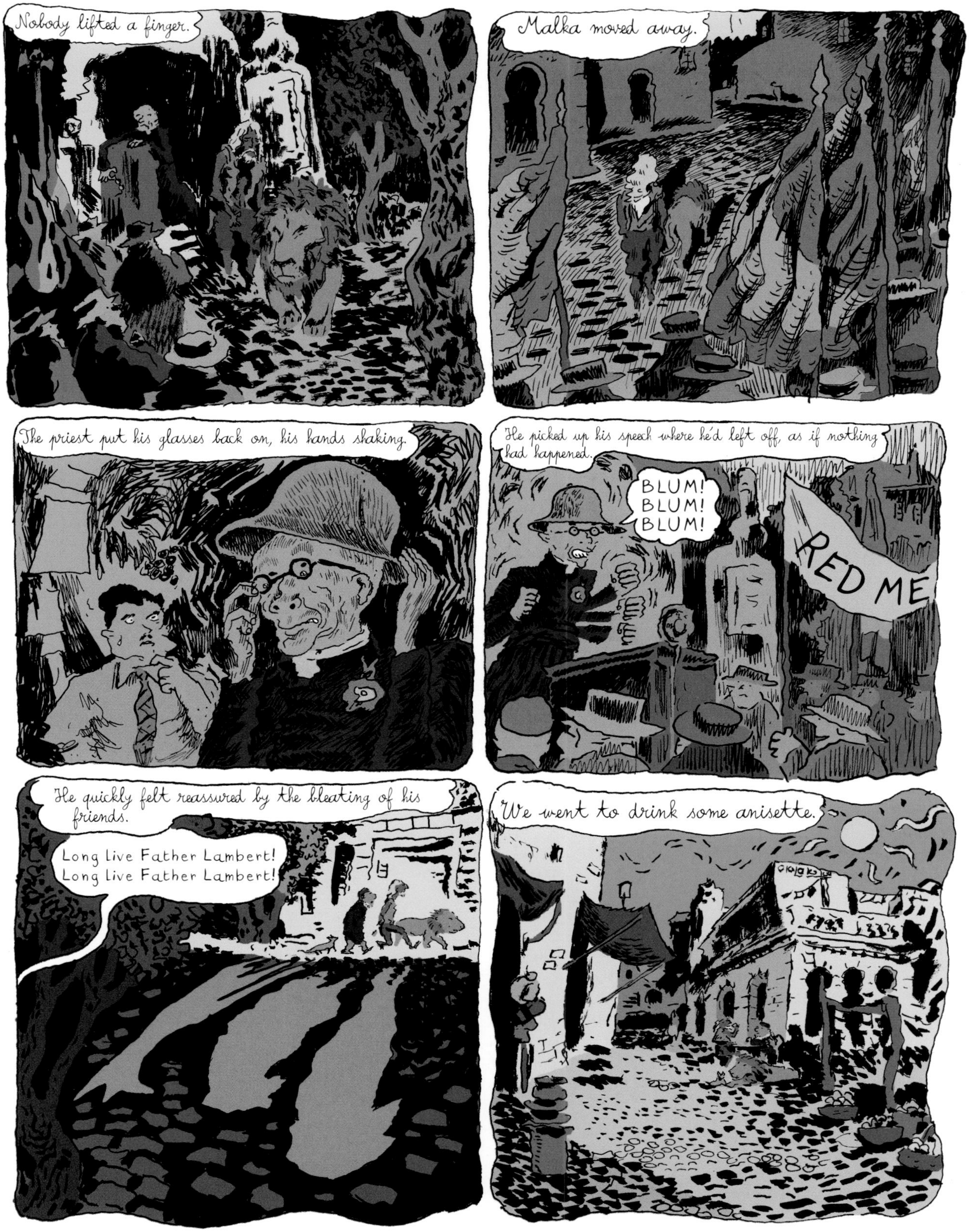

Nobody lifted a finger.
Malka moved away.
The priest put his glasses back on, his hands shaking.
He picked up his speech where he'd left off, as if nothing had happened.
BLUM! BLUM! BLUM!
RED ME
He quickly felt reassured by the bleating of his friends.
Long live Father Lambert! Long live Father Lambert!
We went to drink some anisette.

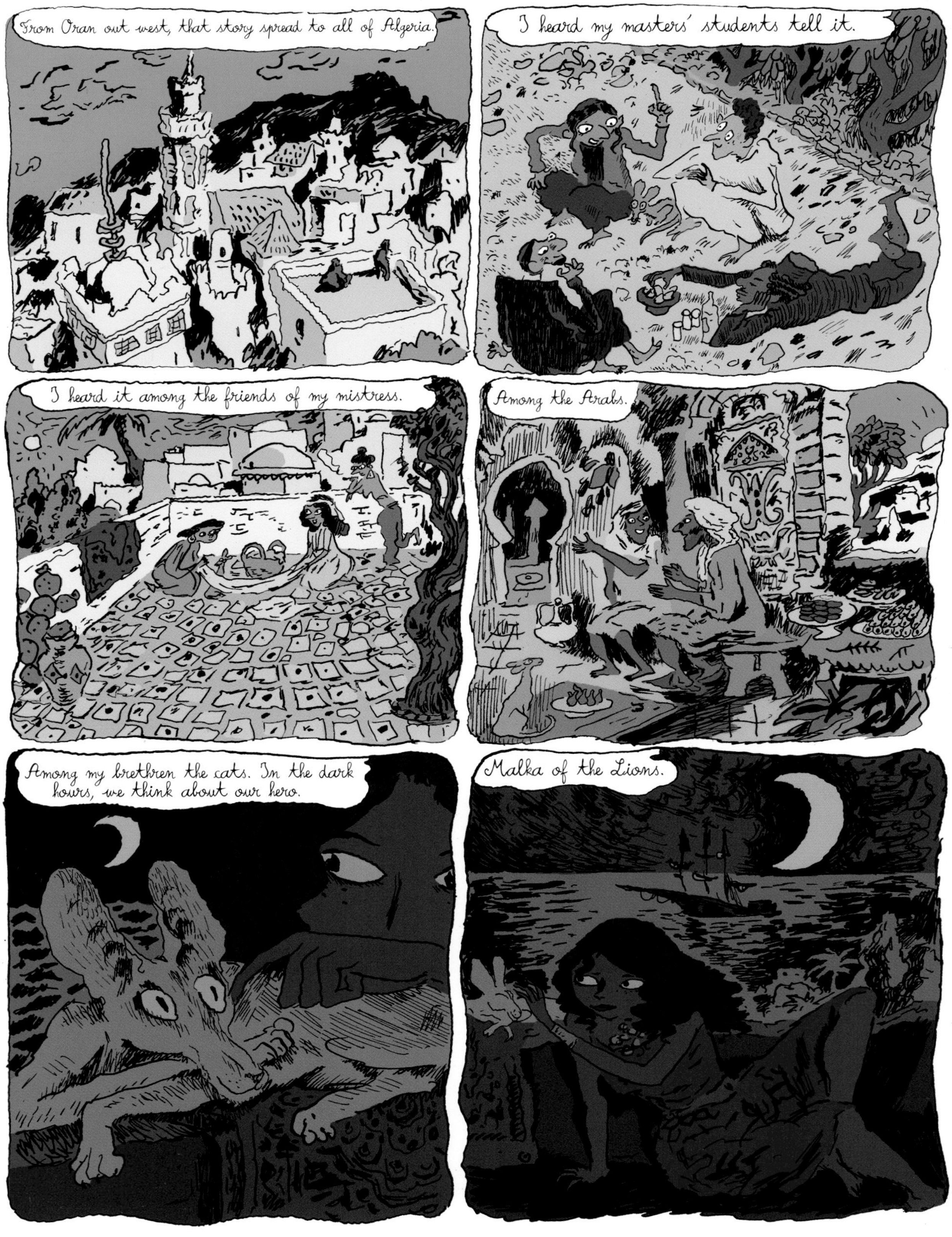
From Oran out west, that story spread to all of Algeria.
I heard my masters' students tell it.
I heard it among the friends of my mistress.
Among the Arabs.
Among my brethren the cats. In the dark hours, we think about our hero.
Malka of the Lions.

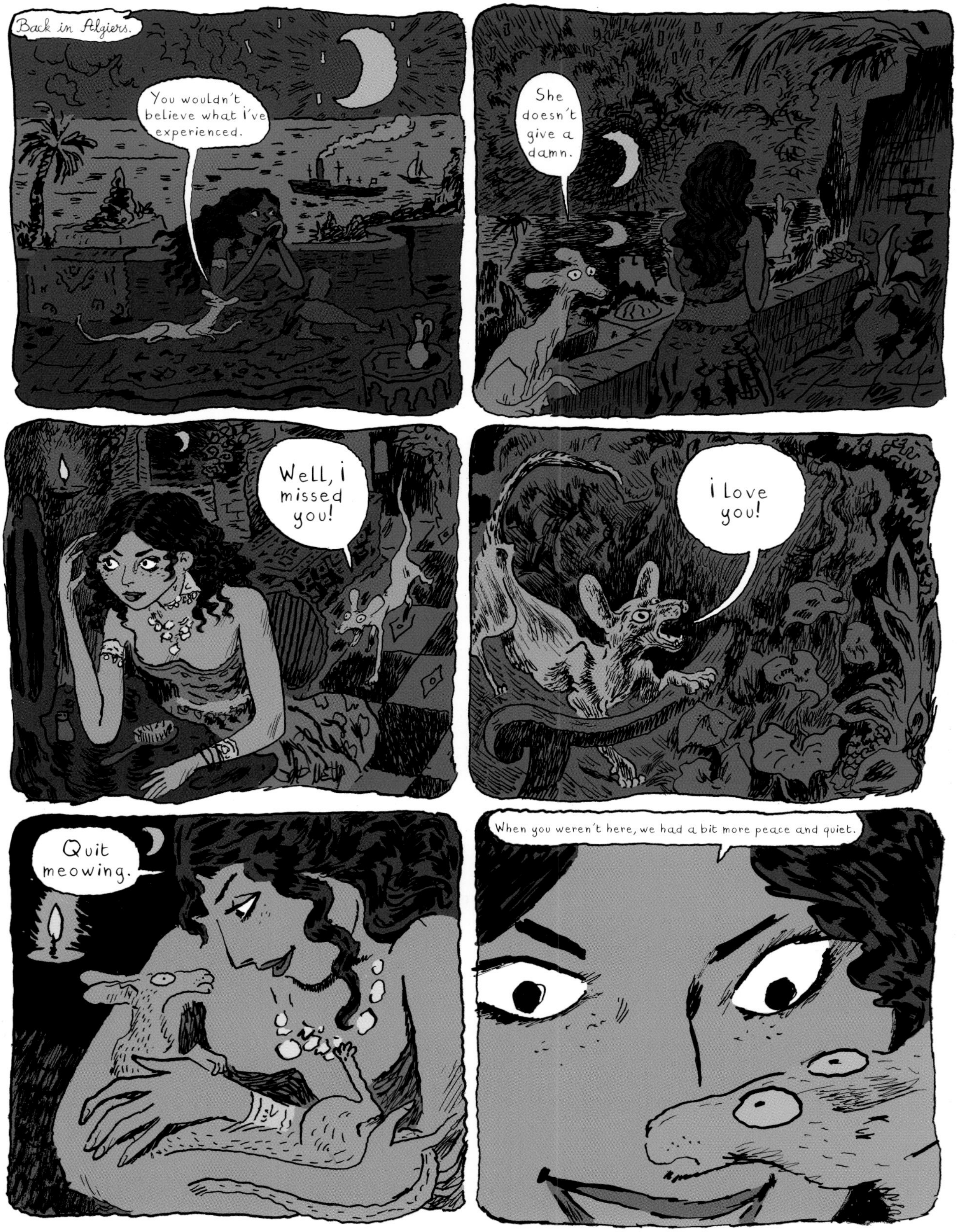
Back in Algiers.
You wouldn't believe what I've experienced.
She doesn't give a damn.
Well, I missed you!
I love you!
Quit meowing.
When you weren't here, we had a bit more peace and quiet.

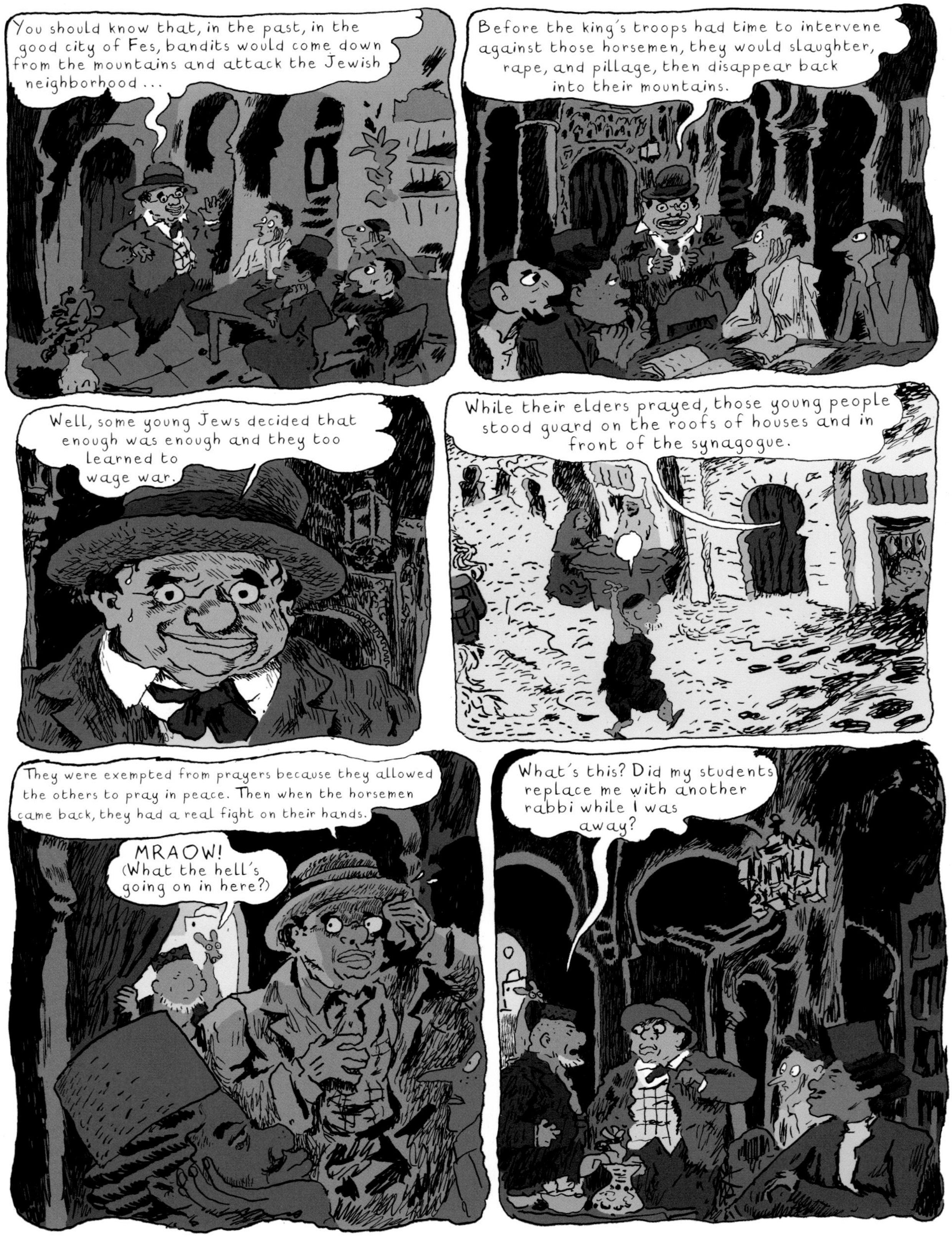
You should know that, in the past, in the good city of Fes, bandits would come down from the mountains and attack the Jewish neighborhood...
Before the king's troops had time to intervene against those horsemen, they would slaughter, rape, and pillage, then disappear back into their mountains.
Well, some young Jews decided that enough was enough and they too learned to wage war.
While their elders prayed, those young people stood guard on the roofs of houses and in front of the synagogue.
They were exempted from prayers because they allowed the others to pray in peace. Then when the horsemen came back, they had a real fight on their hands.
MRAOW! (What the hell's going on in here?)
What's this? Did my students replace me with another rabbi while I was away?

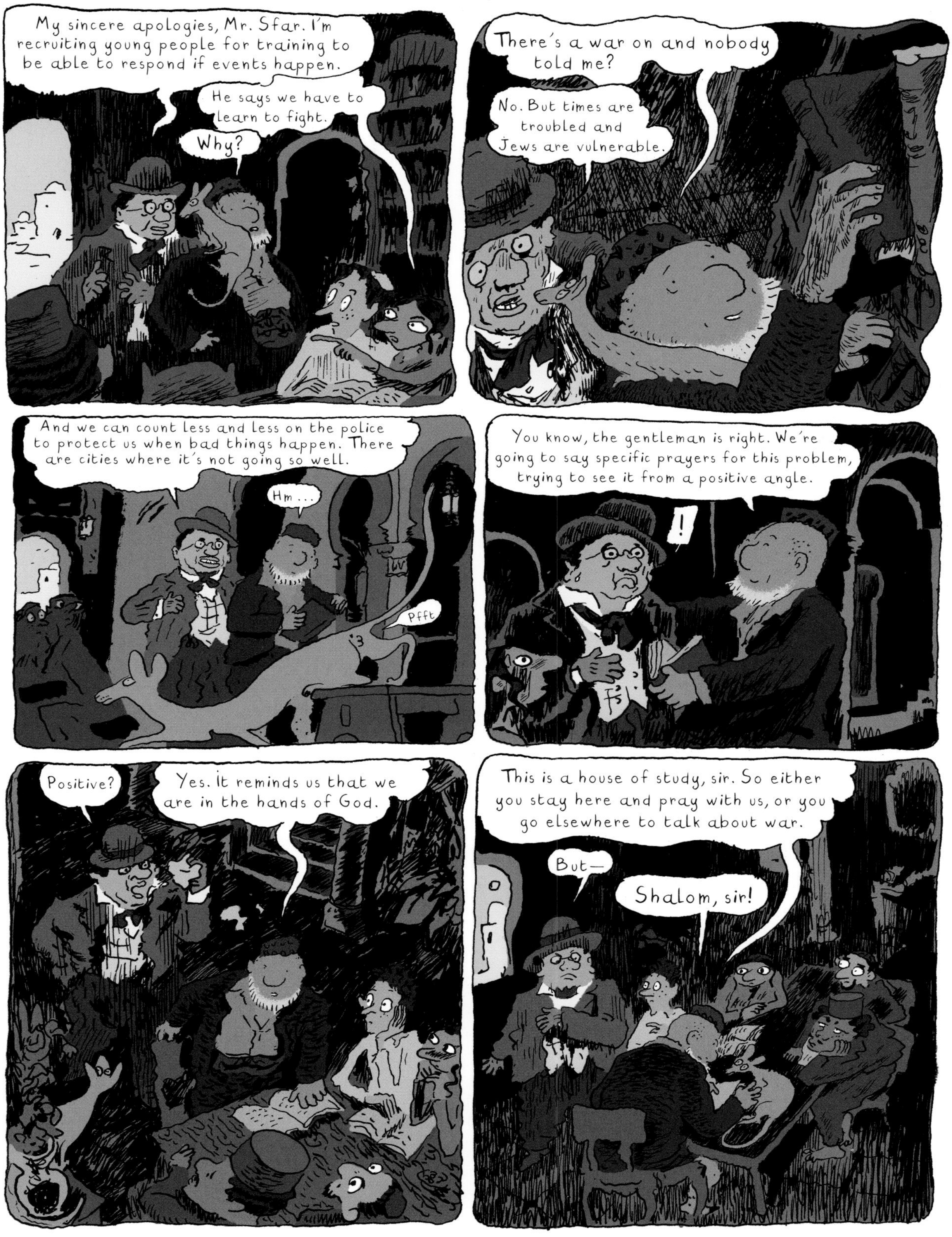

My sincere apologies, Mr. Sfar. I'm recruiting young people for training to be able to respond if events happen.
He says we have to learn to fight.
Why?
There's a war on and nobody told me?
No. But times are troubled and Jews are vulnerable.
And we can count less and less on the police to protect us when bad things happen. There are cities where it's not going so well.
Hm...
Pfft
You know, the gentleman is right. We're going to say specific prayers for this problem, trying to see it from a positive angle.
!
Positive?
Yes. It reminds us that we are in the hands of God.
This is a house of study, sir. So either you stay here and pray with us, or you go elsewhere to talk about war.
But—
Shalom, sir!

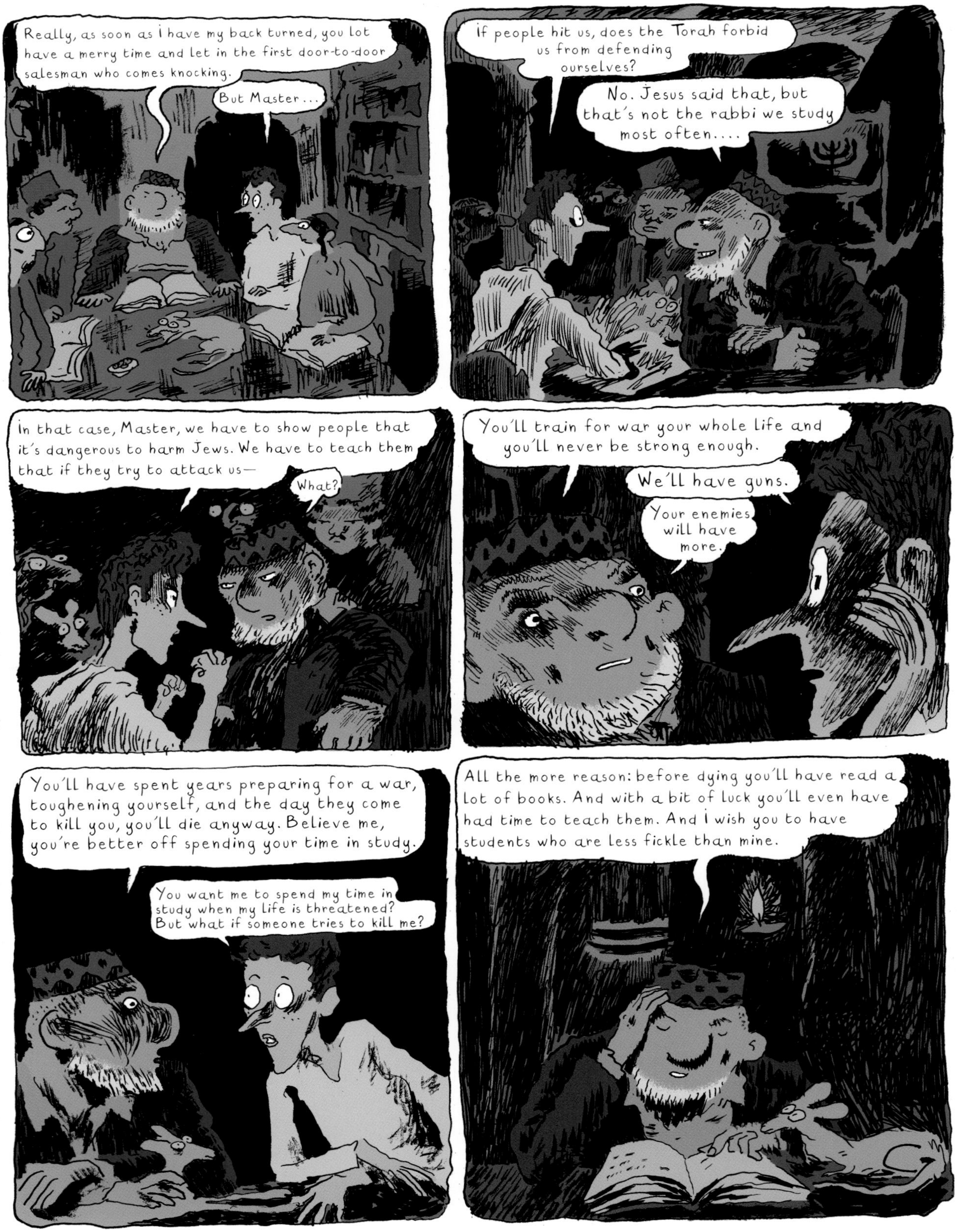
Really, as soon as i have my back turned, you lot have a merry time and let in the first door-to-door salesman who comes knocking.
But Master...
If people hit us, does the Torah forbid us from defending ourselves?
No. Jesus said that, but that's not the rabbi we study most often....
In that case, Master, we have to show people that it's dangerous to harm Jews. We have to teach them that if they try to attack us—
What?
You'll train for war your whole life and you'll never be strong enough.
We'll have guns.
Your enemies will have more.
You'll have spent years preparing for a war, toughening yourself, and the day they come to kill you, you'll die anyway. Believe me, you're better off spending your time in study.
You want me to spend my time in study when my life is threatened? But what if someone tries to kill me?
All the more reason: before dying you'll have read a lot of books. And with a bit of luck you'll even have had time to teach them. And i wish you to have students who are less fickle than mine.

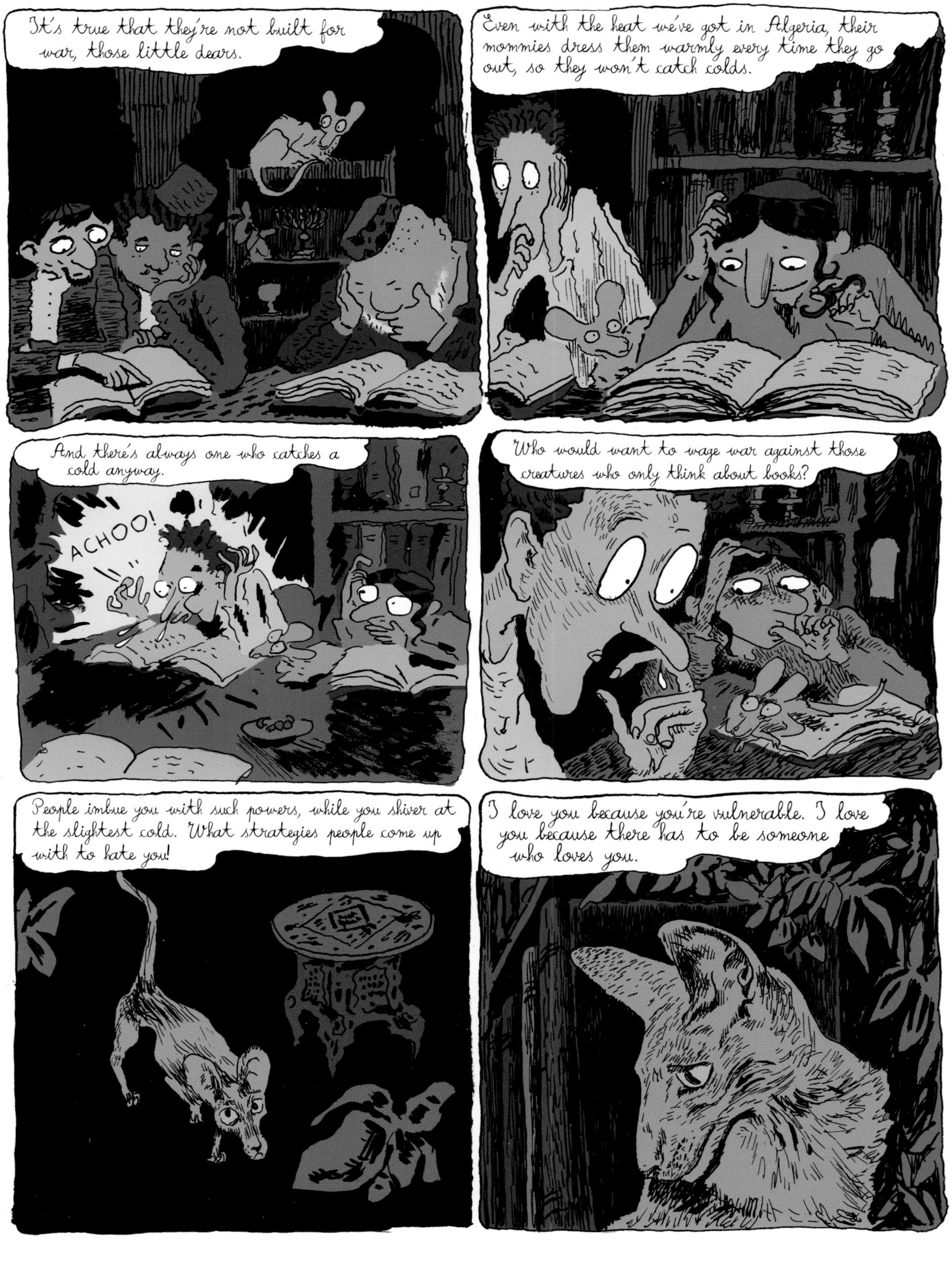
It's true that they're not built for war, those little dears.
Even with the heat we've got in Algeria, their mommies dress them warmly every time they go out, so they won't catch colds.
And there's always one who catches a cold anyway.
ACHOO!
Who would want to wage war against those creatures who only think about books?
People imbue you with such powers, while you shiver at the slightest cold. What strategies people come up with to hate you!
I love you because you're vulnerable. I love you because there has to be someone who loves you.

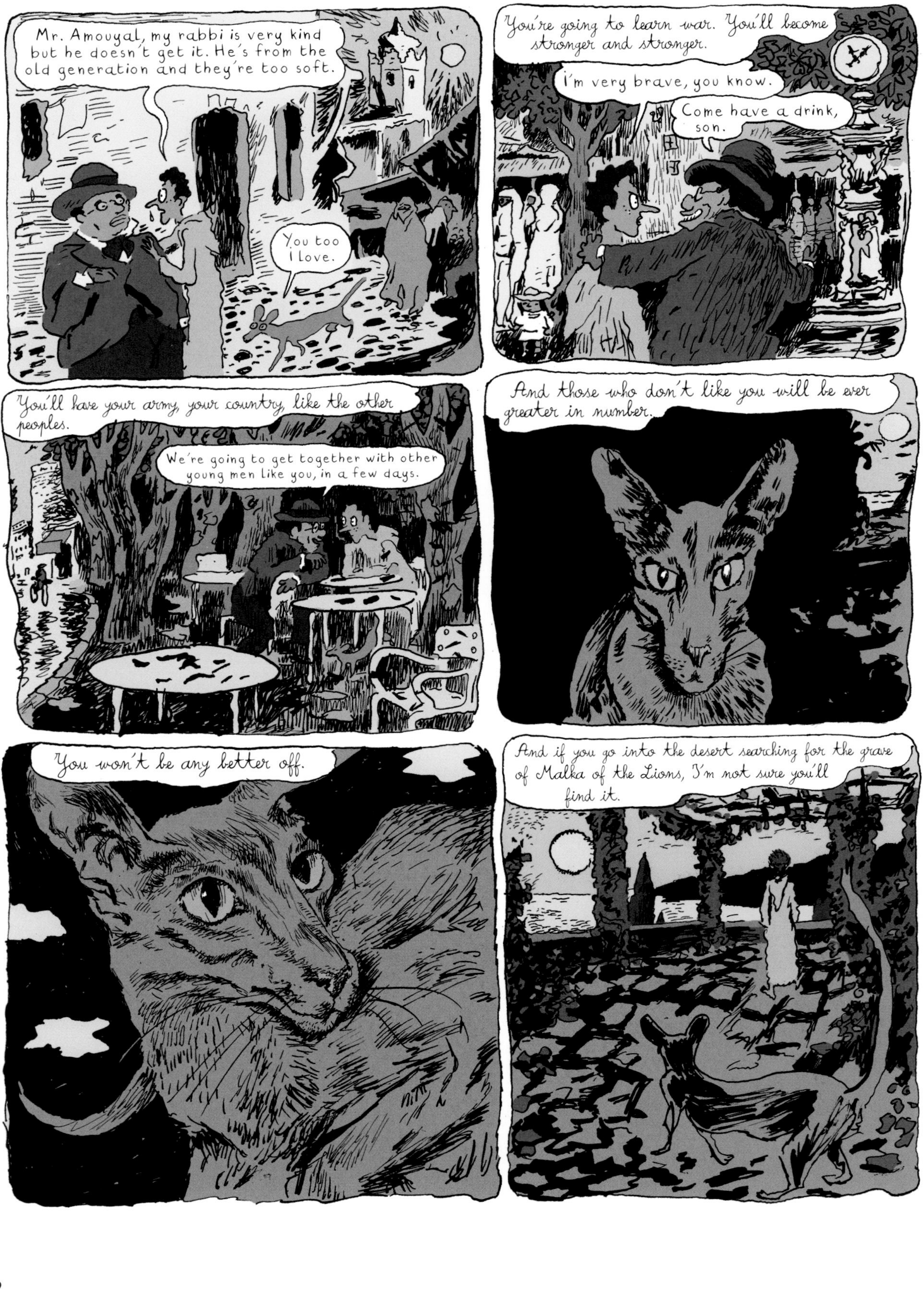
Mr. Amouyal, my rabbi is very kind but he doesn't get it. He's from the old generation and they're too soft.
You too I love.
You're going to learn war. You'll become stronger and stronger.
I'm very brave, you know.
Come have a drink, son.
You'll have your army, your country, like the other peoples.
We're going to get together with other young men like you, in a few days.
And those who don't like you will be ever greater in number.
You won't be any better off.
And if you go into the desert searching for the grave of Malka of the Lions, I'm not sure you'll find it.

II

AFRICA'S JERUSALEM

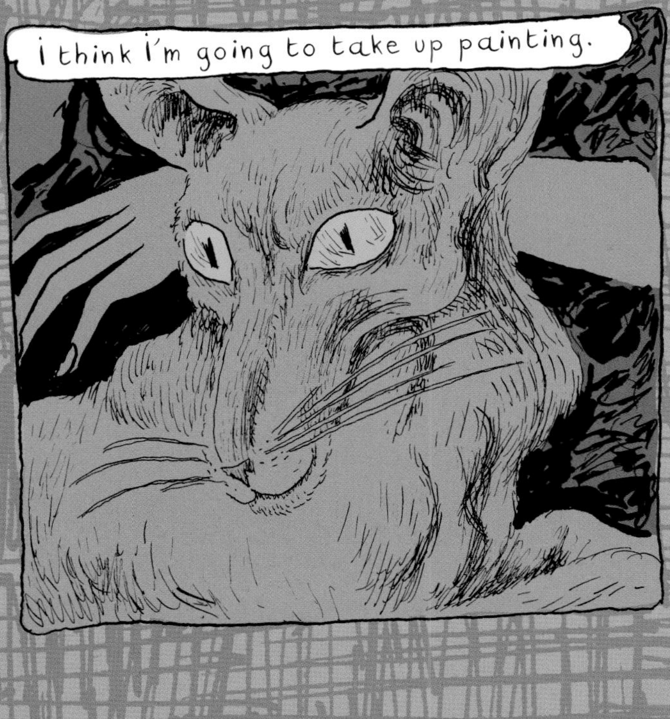
i think i'm going to take up painting.

Dedicated to my childhood friend Ivan Chiossone, who was the model for the character of the painter. I also drew the book in honor of my little nephew Avrone, whose mommy comes from North Africa while his daddy comes from black Africa.

For a long time I thought there was no point in doing a graphic novel against racism. That stance seemed so totally redundant that there was no need to flog a dying horse. Times are changing, apparently. Chances are everything's already been said, but since no one is paying attention you have to start all over again.

Among the huge number of works that were useful to the background research for this book, I would like to make special mention of the following:

- *Juifs en Érythrée* (*Jews in Eritrea*), by Marco Mensa and Marco Cavallarin, Editions Ethnos.
- *Croisières Citroën, carnets de routes africains* (*The Croisières Citroën Expeditions: Journals of African Road Trips*), by Eric Deschamps, E-T-A-I Editions.
- *Renault en Afrique* (*Renault in Africa*), by Marie-Christine Rouxel, E-T-A-I Editions.
- *La Croisière noire* (*The Croisière Noire Expedition*), by Ariane Audouin Dubreuil, Editions Glenat.
- *L'Afrique fantastique* (*Fantastical Africa*), by Jean-Marc Boutonnet-Tranier, Aethiopia Editions.
- *Le Cantique des cantiques* (*The Song of Songs*), illustrated by Kupka, MAHJ, Editions Cercle d'Art.

Many thanks also to Iryna Mylymuk and Antoni Yalap, the translators who allowed my characters to speak, respectively, Russian and Aramaic.

—JOANN SFAR

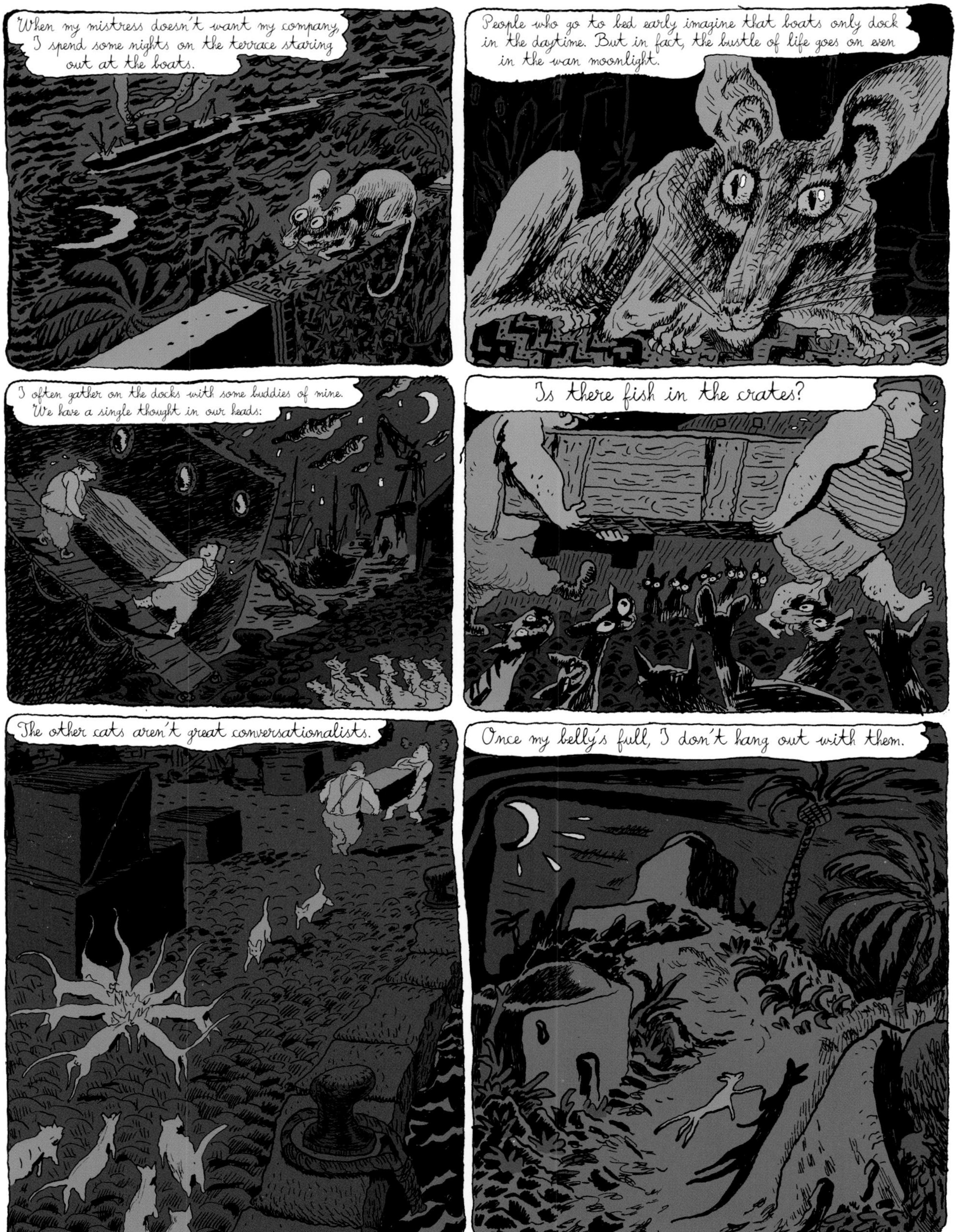
When my mistress doesn't want my company, I spend some nights on the terrace staring out at the boats.
People who go to bed early imagine that boats only dock in the daytime. But in fact, the bustle of life goes on even in the wan moonlight.
I often gather on the docks with some buddies of mine. We have a single thought in our heads:
Is there fish in the crates?
The other cats aren't great conversationalists.
Once my belly's full, I don't hang out with them.

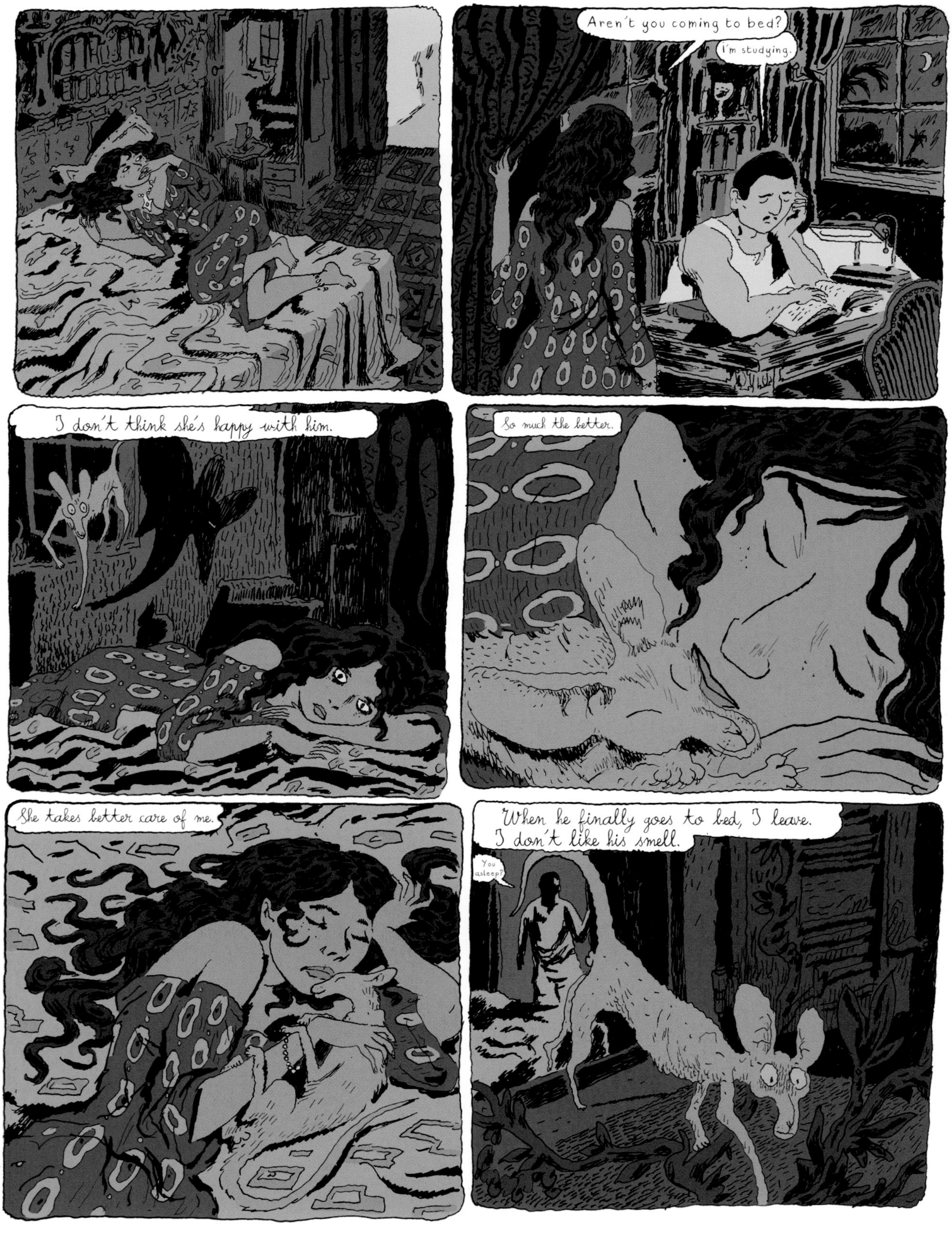

Aren't you coming to bed?
I'm studying.
I don't think she's happy with him.
So much the better.
She takes better care of me.
When he finally goes to bed, I leave. I don't like his smell.
You asleep?

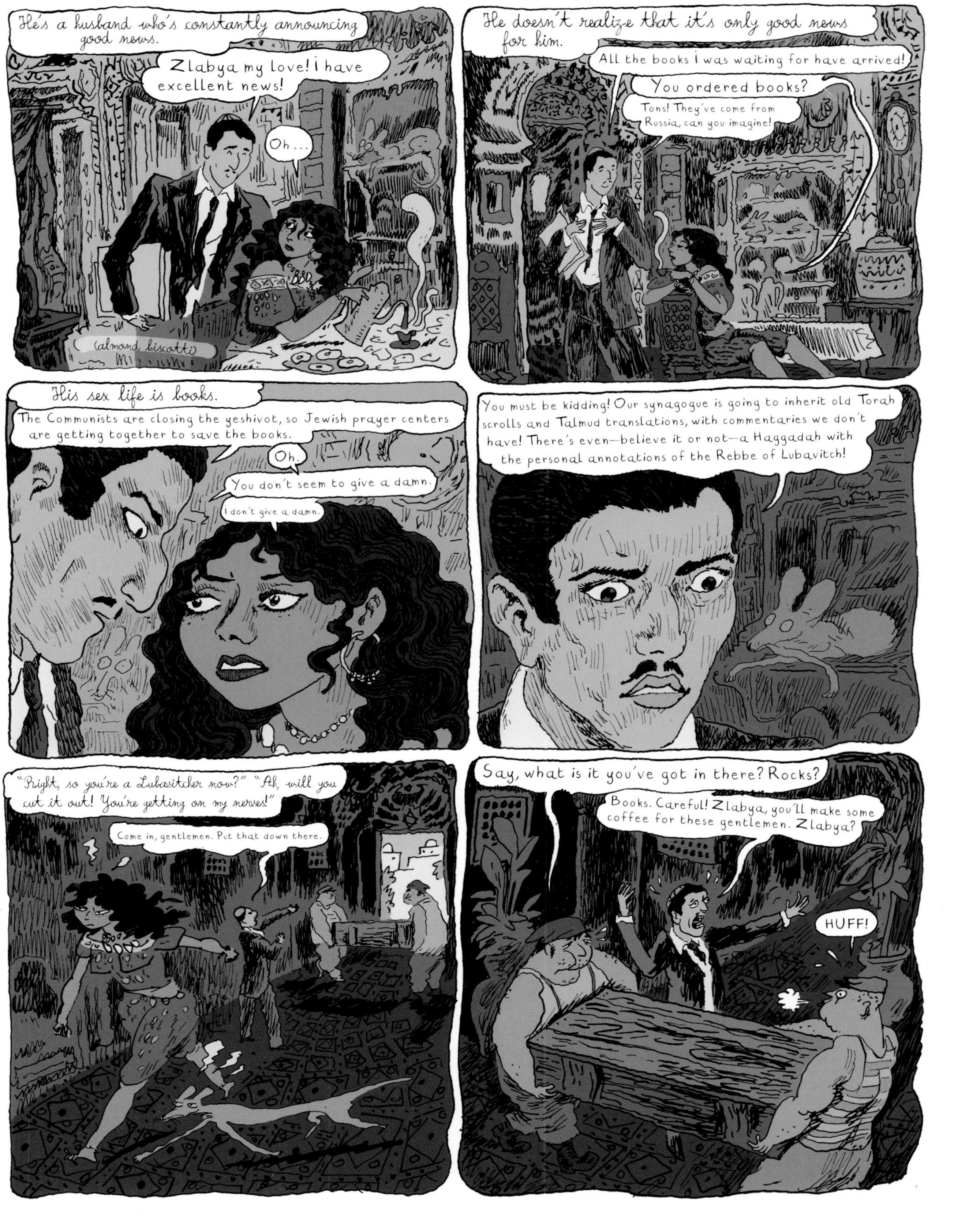
He's a husband who's constantly announcing good news.
Zlabya my love! I have excellent news!
Oh...
(almond biscotti)
He doesn't realize that it's only good news for him.
All the books I was waiting for have arrived!
You ordered books?
Tons! They've come from Russia, can you imagine!
His sex life is books.
The Communists are closing the yeshivot, so Jewish prayer centers are getting together to save the books.
Oh.
You don't seem to give a damn.
I don't give a damn.
You must be kidding! Our synagogue is going to inherit old Torah scrolls and Talmud translations, with commentaries we don't have! There's even—believe it or not—a Haggadah with the personal annotations of the Rebbe of Lubavitch!
"Right, so you're a Lubavitcher now?" "Ah, will you cut it out! You're getting on my nerves!"
Come in, gentlemen. Put that down there.
Say, what is it you've got in there? Rocks?
Books. Careful! Zlabya, you'll make some coffee for these gentlemen. Zlabya?
HUFF!

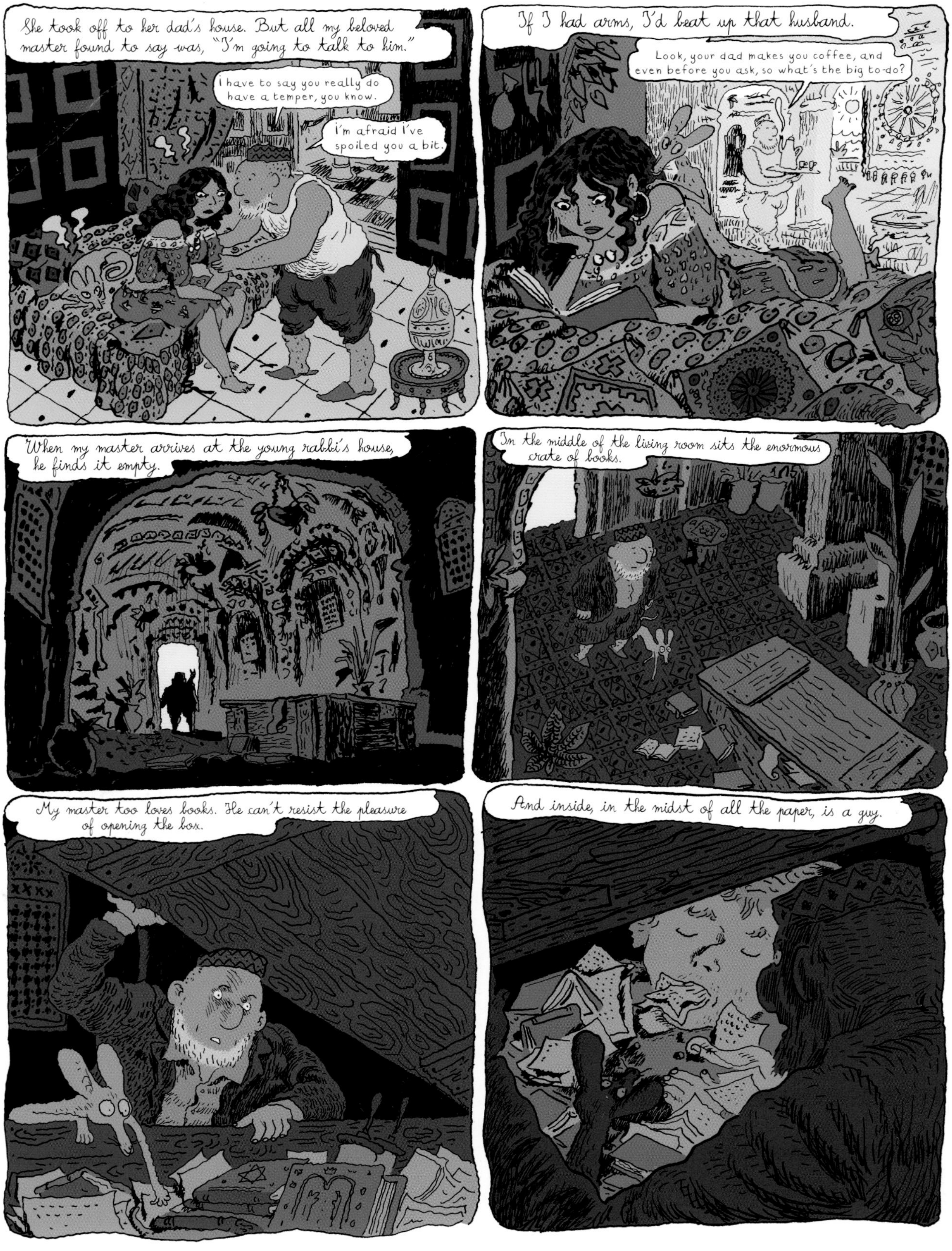
She took off to her dad's house. But all my beloved master found to say was, "I'm going to talk to him."
I have to say you really do have a temper, you know.
I'm afraid I've spoiled you a bit.
If I had arms, I'd beat up that husband.
Look, your dad makes you coffee, and even before you ask, so what's the big to-do?
When my master arrives at the young rabbi's house, he finds it empty.
In the middle of the living room sits the enormous crate of books.
My master too loves books. He can't resist the pleasure of opening the box.
And inside, in the midst of all the paper, is a guy.

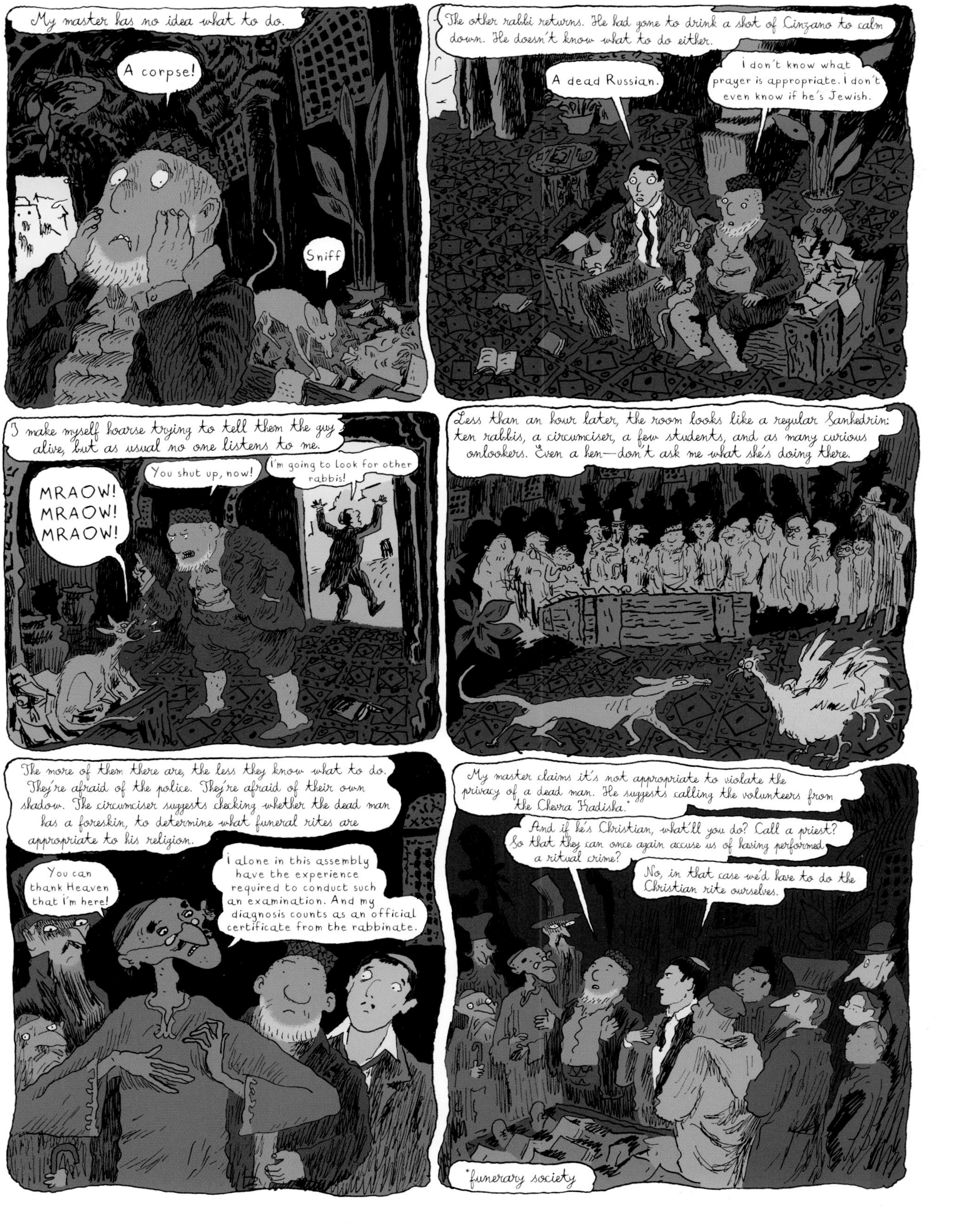

My master has no idea what to do.
A corpse!
Sniff
The other rabbi returns. He had gone to drink a shot of Cinzano to calm down. He doesn't know what to do either.
A dead Russian.
I don't know what prayer is appropriate. I don't even know if he's Jewish.
I make myself hoarse trying to tell them the guy is alive, but as usual no one listens to me.
MRAOW! MRAOW! MRAOW!
You shut up, now!
I'm going to look for other rabbis!
Less than an hour later, the room looks like a regular Sanhedrin: ten rabbis, a circumciser, a few students, and as many curious onlookers. Even a hen—don't ask me what she's doing there.
The more of them there are, the less they know what to do. They're afraid of the police. They're afraid of their own shadow. The circumciser suggests checking whether the dead man has a foreskin, to determine what funeral rites are appropriate to his religion.
You can thank Heaven that I'm here!
I alone in this assembly have the experience required to conduct such an examination. And my diagnosis counts as an official certificate from the rabbinate.
My master claims it's not appropriate to violate the privacy of a dead man. He suggests calling the volunteers from the Chevra Kadisha.*
And if he's Christian, what'll you do? Call a priest? So that they can once again accuse us of having performed a ritual crime?
No, in that case we'd have to do the Christian rite ourselves.
*funerary society

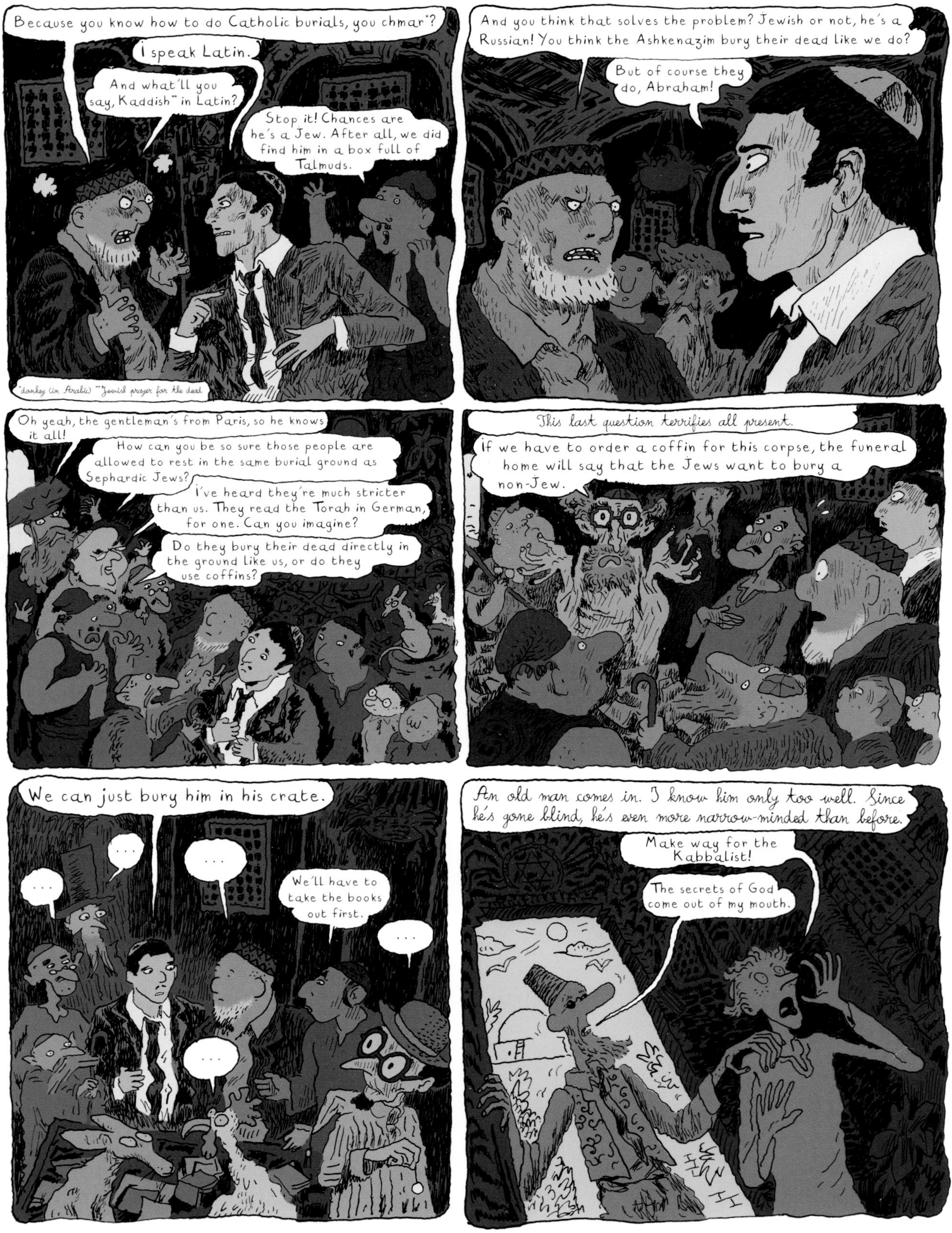
Because you know how to do Catholic burials, you chmar*?
I speak Latin.
And what'll you say, Kaddish** in Latin?
Stop it! Chances are he's a Jew. After all, we did find him in a box full of Talmuds.
*donkey (in Arabic) **Jewish prayer for the dead
And you think that solves the problem? Jewish or not, he's a Russian! You think the Ashkenazim bury their dead like we do?
But of course they do, Abraham!
Oh yeah, the gentleman's from Paris, so he knows it all!
How can you be so sure those people are allowed to rest in the same burial ground as Sephardic Jews?
I've heard they're much stricter than us. They read the Torah in German, for one. Can you imagine?
Do they bury their dead directly in the ground like us, or do they use coffins?
This last question terrifies all present.
If we have to order a coffin for this corpse, the funeral home will say that the Jews want to bury a non-Jew.
We can just bury him in his crate.
...
...
...
We'll have to take the books out first.
...
...
An old man comes in. I know him only too well. Since he's gone blind, he's even more narrow-minded than before.
Make way for the Kabbalist!
The secrets of God come out of my mouth.

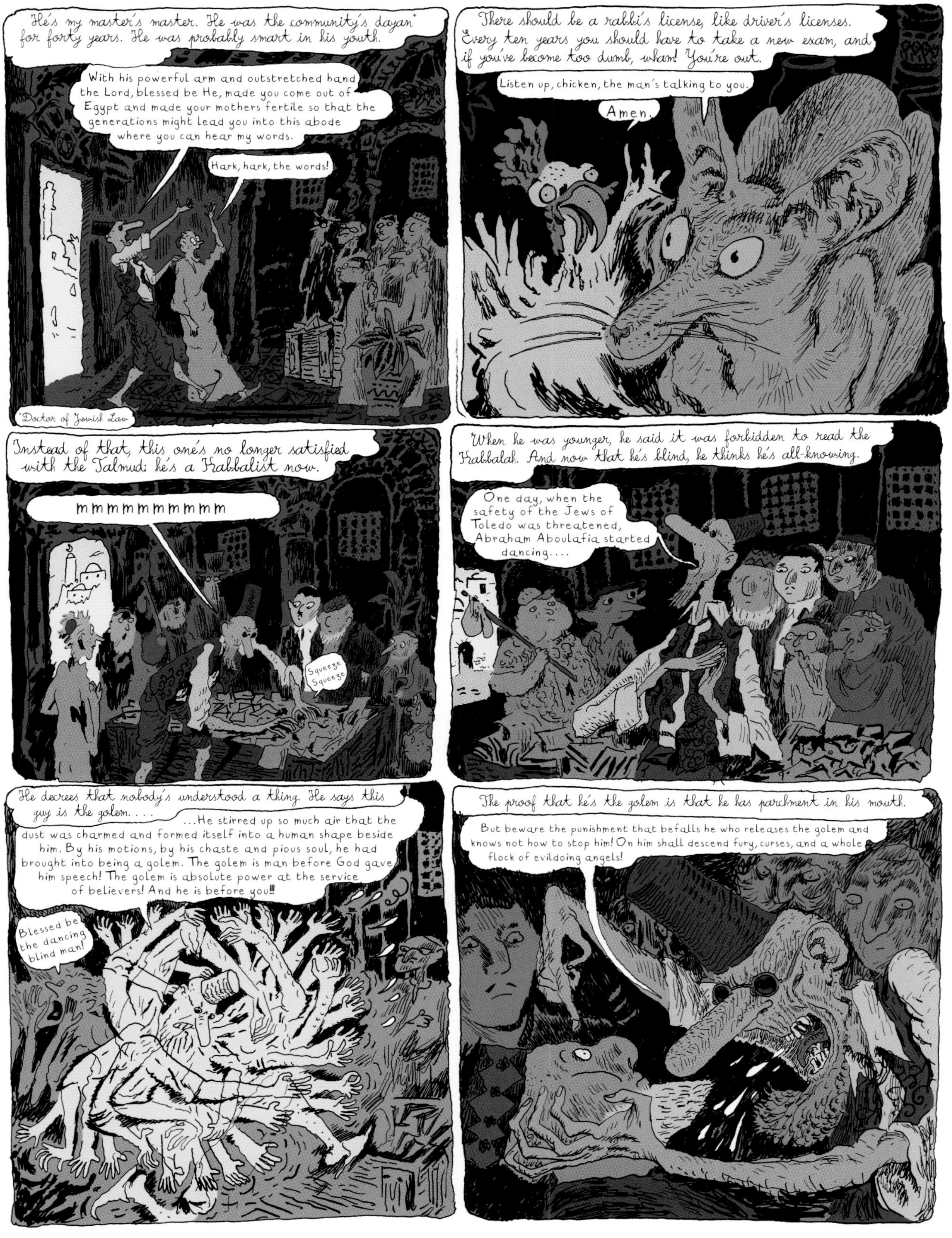
He's my master's master. He was the community's dayan* for forty years. He was probably smart in his youth.
With his powerful arm and outstretched hand the Lord, blessed be He, made you come out of Egypt and made your mothers fertile so that the generations might lead you into this abode where you can hear my words.
Hark, hark, the words!
*Doctor of Jewish Law
There should be a rabbi's license, like driver's licenses. Every ten years you should have to take a new exam, and if you've become too dumb, wham! You're out.
Listen up, chicken, the man's talking to you.
Amen.
Instead of that, this one's no longer satisfied with the Talmud: he's a Kabbalist now.
mmmmmmmmmm
Squeeze Squeeze
When he was younger, he said it was forbidden to read the Kabbalah. And now that he's blind, he thinks he's all-knowing.
One day, when the safety of the Jews of Toledo was threatened, Abraham Aboulafia started dancing....
He decrees that nobody's understood a thing. He says this guy is the golem. . . .
...He stirred up so much air that the dust was charmed and formed itself into a human shape beside him. By his motions, by his chaste and pious soul, he had brought into being a golem. The golem is man before God gave him speech! The golem is absolute power at the service of believers! And he is before you!!!
Blessed be the dancing blind man!
The proof that he's the golem is that he has parchment in his mouth.
But beware the punishment that befalls he who releases the golem and knows not how to stop him! On him shall descend fury, curses, and a whole flock of evildoing angels!

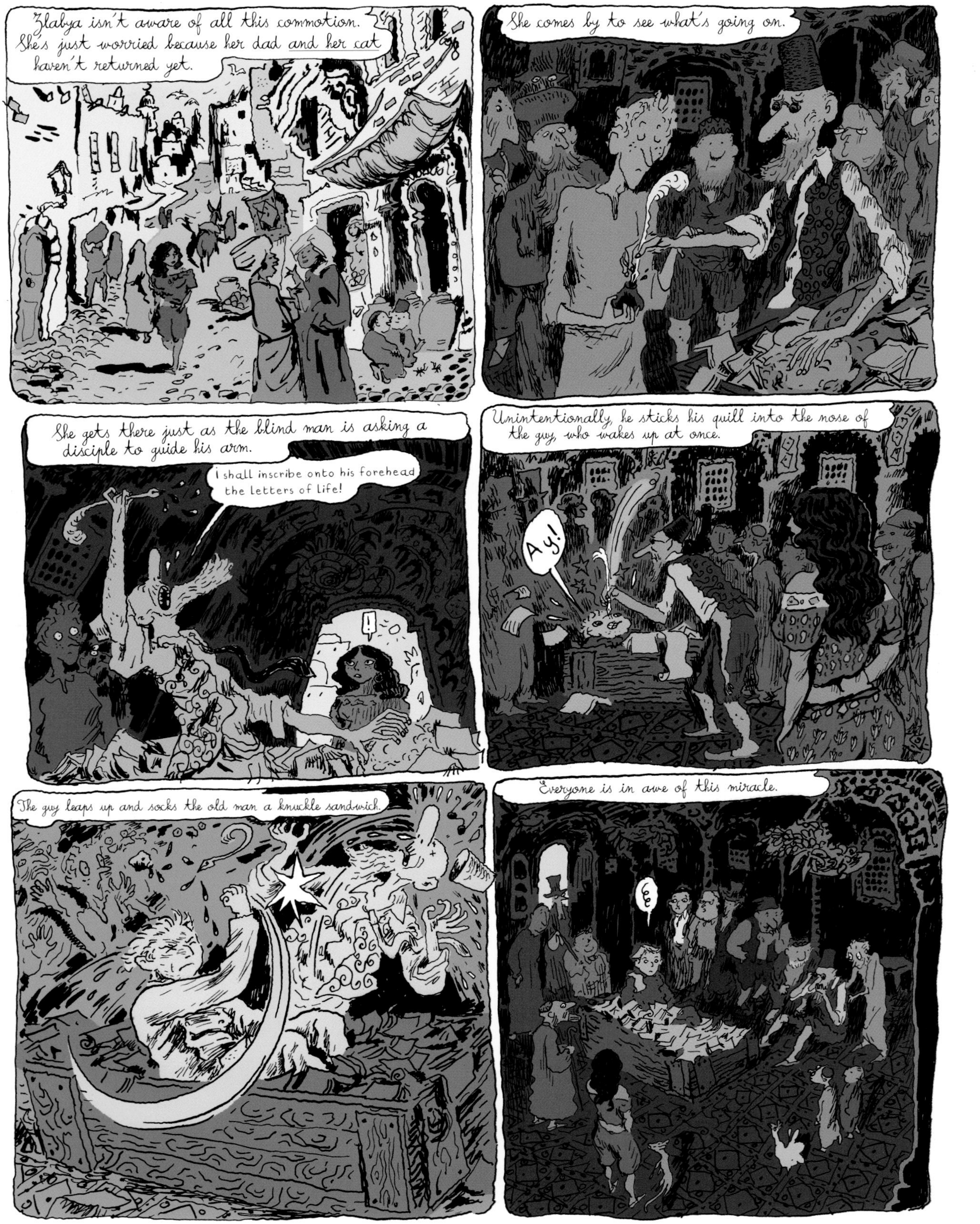
Zlabya isn't aware of all this commotion. She's just worried because her dad and her cat haven't returned yet.
She comes by to see what's going on.
She gets there just as the blind man is asking a disciple to guide his arm.
I shall inscribe onto his forehead the letters of life!
!
Unintentionally, he sticks his quill into the nose of the guy, who wakes up at once.
Ay!
The guy leaps up and socks the old man a knuckle sandwich.
Everyone is in awe of this miracle.

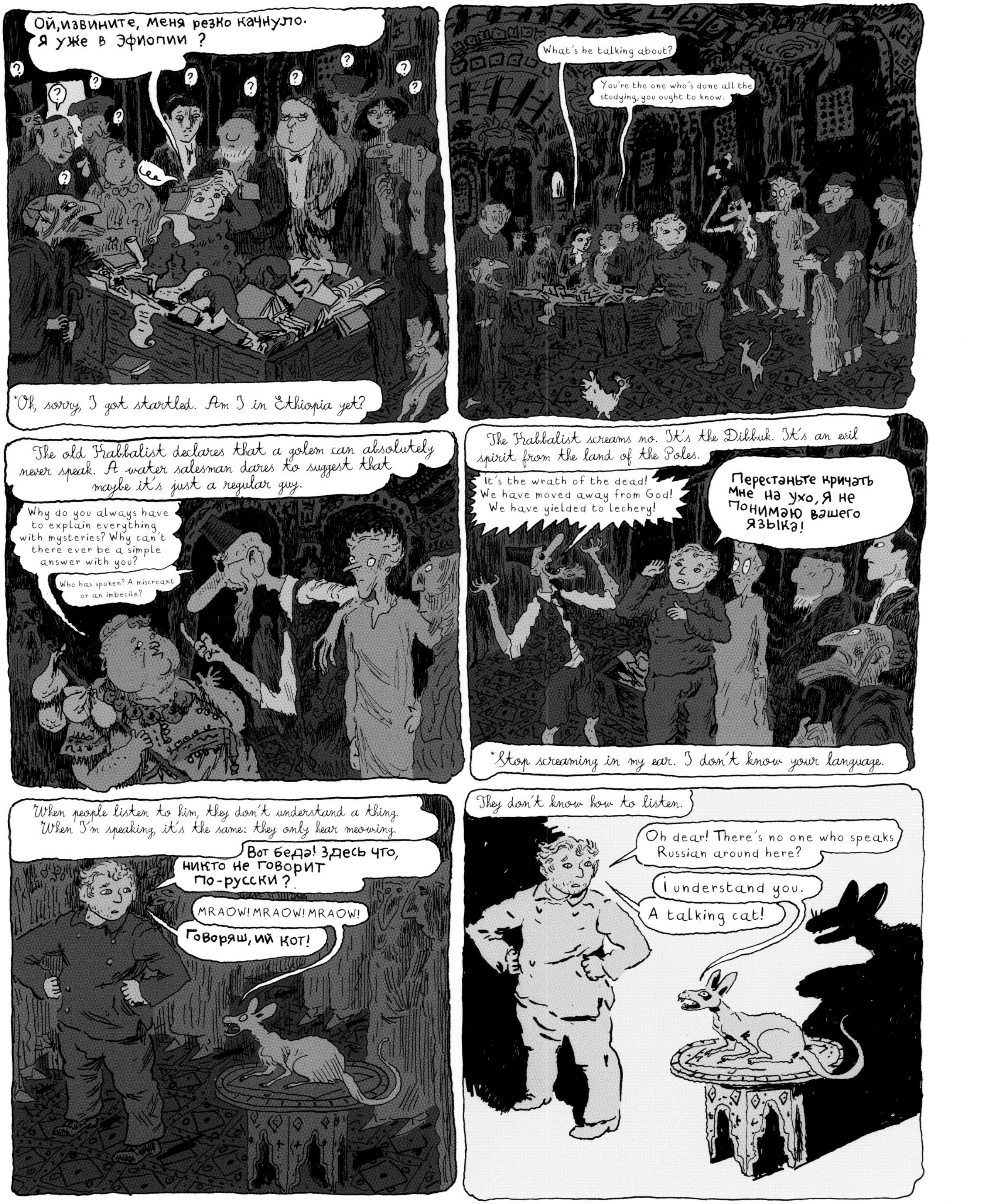

Ой,извините, меня резко качнуло. Я уже в Эфиопии ?
*Oh, sorry, I got startled. Am I in Ethiopia yet?
What's he talking about?
You're the one who's done all the studying, you ought to know.
The old Kabbalist declares that a golem can absolutely never speak. A water salesman dares to suggest that maybe it's just a regular guy.
Why do you always have to explain everything with mysteries? Why can't there ever be a simple answer with you?
Who has spoken? A miscreant or an imbecile?
The Kabbalist screams no. It's the Dibbuk. It's an evil spirit from the land of the Poles.
It's the wrath of the dead! We have moved away from God! We have yielded to lechery!
Перестаньте кричать мне на ухо, Я не понимаю вашего языка!
*Stop screaming in my ear. I don't know your language.
When people listen to him, they don't understand a thing. When I'm speaking, it's the same: they only hear meowing.
Вот беда! Здесь что, никто не говорит по-русски?
MRAOW! MRAOW! MRAOW!
Говоряш,ий кот!
They don't know how to listen.
Oh dear! There's no one who speaks Russian around here?
I understand you.
A talking cat!

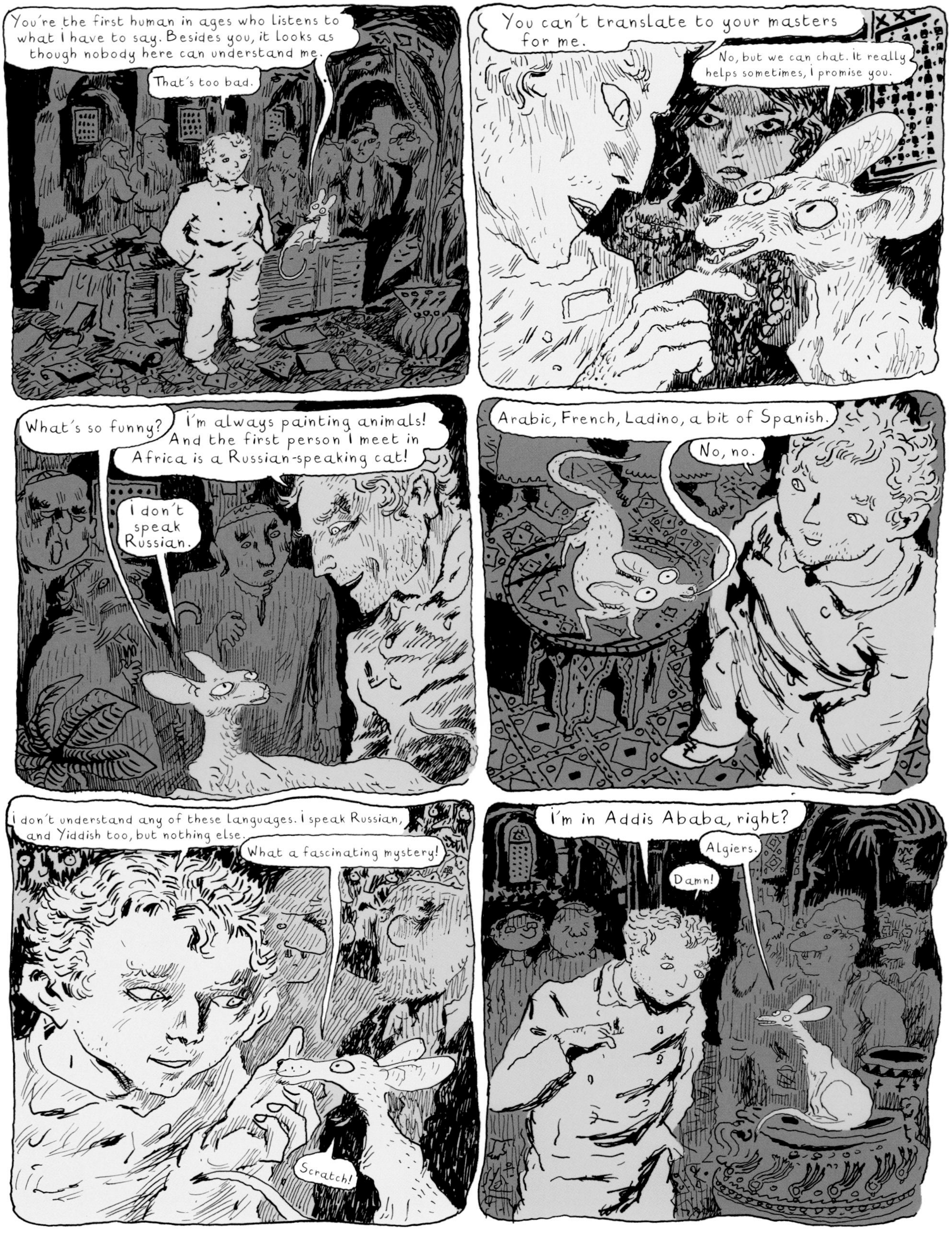
You're the first human in ages who listens to what I have to say. Besides you, it looks as though nobody here can understand me.
That's too bad.
You can't translate to your masters for me.
No, but we can chat. It really helps sometimes, I promise you.
What's so funny?
I'm always painting animals! And the first person I meet in Africa is a Russian-speaking cat!
I don't speak Russian.
Arabic, French, Ladino, a bit of Spanish.
No, no.
I don't understand any of these languages. I speak Russian, and Yiddish too, but nothing else.
What a fascinating mystery!
Scratch!
I'm in Addis Ababa, right?
Algiers.
Damn!

The Russian is exhausted. Zlabya gets all the onlookers out and takes him to her father's place. She gives him something to drink. He starts perking up.

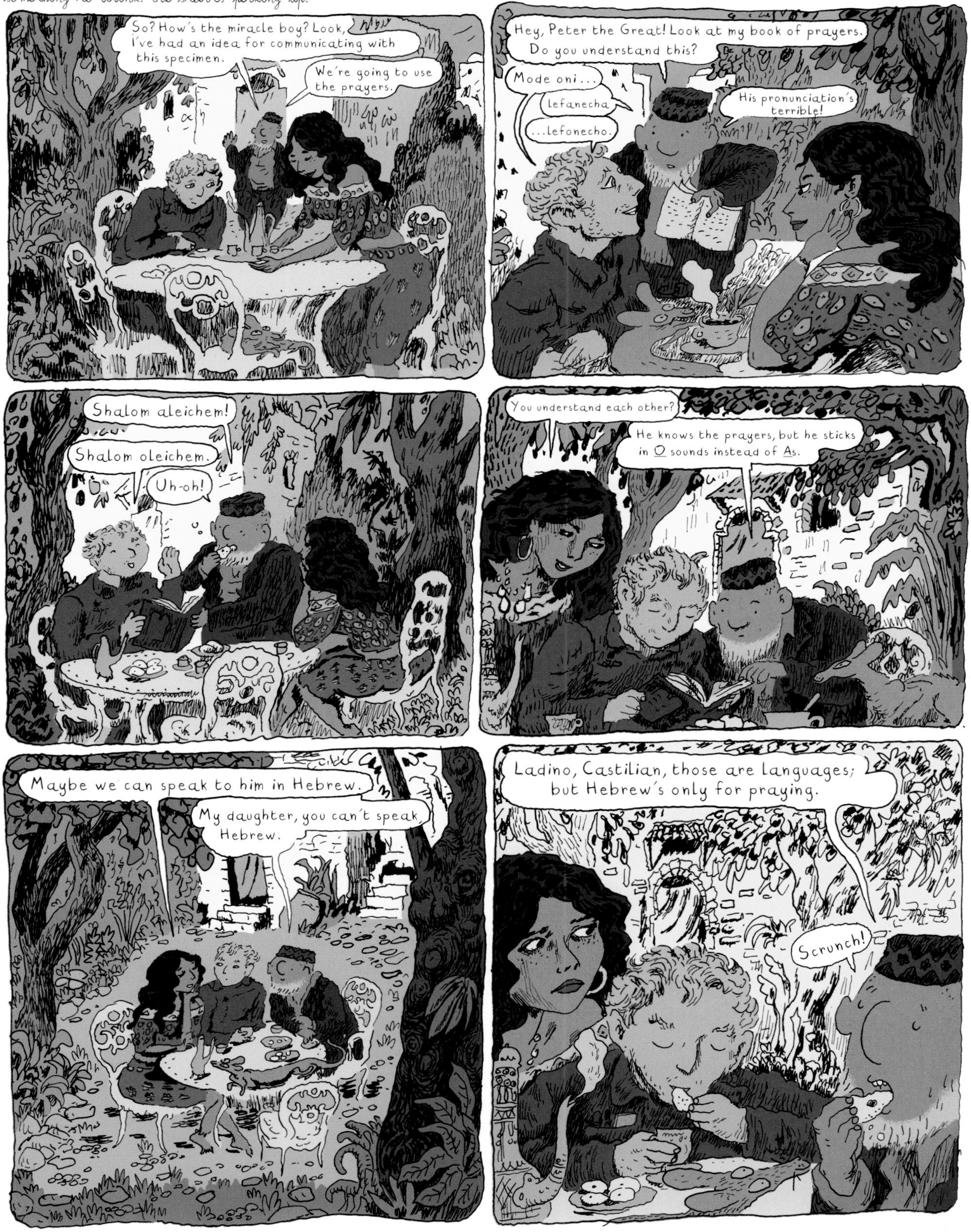
So? How's the miracle boy? Look, I've had an idea for communicating with this specimen.
We're going to use the prayers.
Hey, Peter the Great! Look at my book of prayers. Do you understand this?
Mode oni...
lefanecha
...lefonecho.
His pronunciation's terrible!
Shalom aleichem!
Shalom oleichem.
Uh-oh!
You understand each other?
He knows the prayers, but he sticks in O sounds instead of As.
Maybe we can speak to him in Hebrew.
My daughter, you can't speak Hebrew.
Ladino, Castilian, those are languages; but Hebrew's only for praying.
Scrunch!

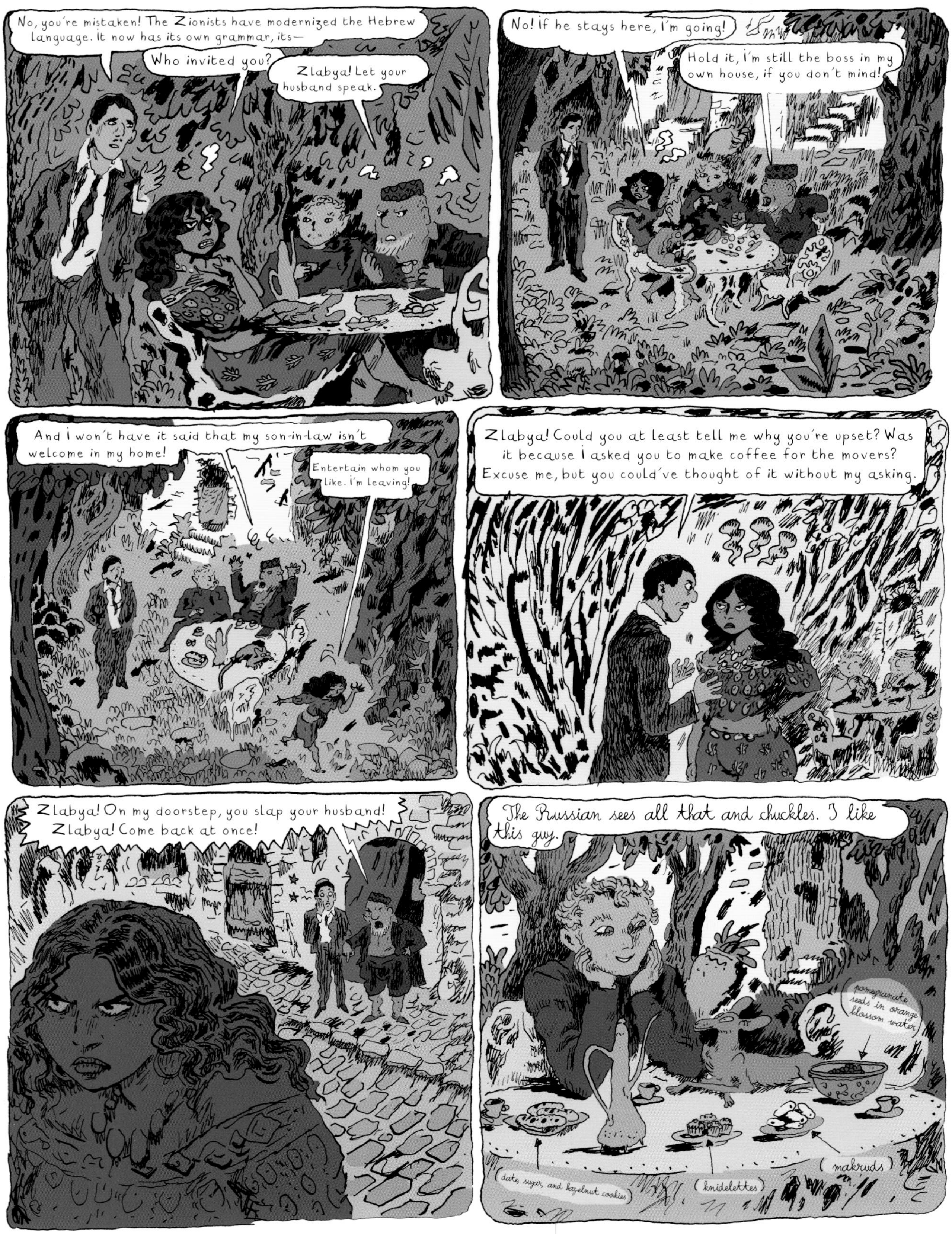
No, you're mistaken! The Zionists have modernized the Hebrew language. It now has its own grammar, its—
Who invited you?
Zlabya! Let your husband speak.
No! If he stays here, I'm going!
Hold it, I'm still the boss in my own house, if you don't mind!
And I won't have it said that my son-in-law isn't welcome in my home!
Entertain whom you like. I'm leaving!
Zlabya! Could you at least tell me why you're upset? Was it because I asked you to make coffee for the movers? Excuse me, but you could've thought of it without my asking.
Zlabya! On my doorstep, you slap your husband! Zlabya! Come back at once!
The Russian sees all that and chuckles. I like this guy.
pomegranate seeds in orange blossom water
(makruds)
(dates, sugar, and hazelnut cookies)
(knidelettes)

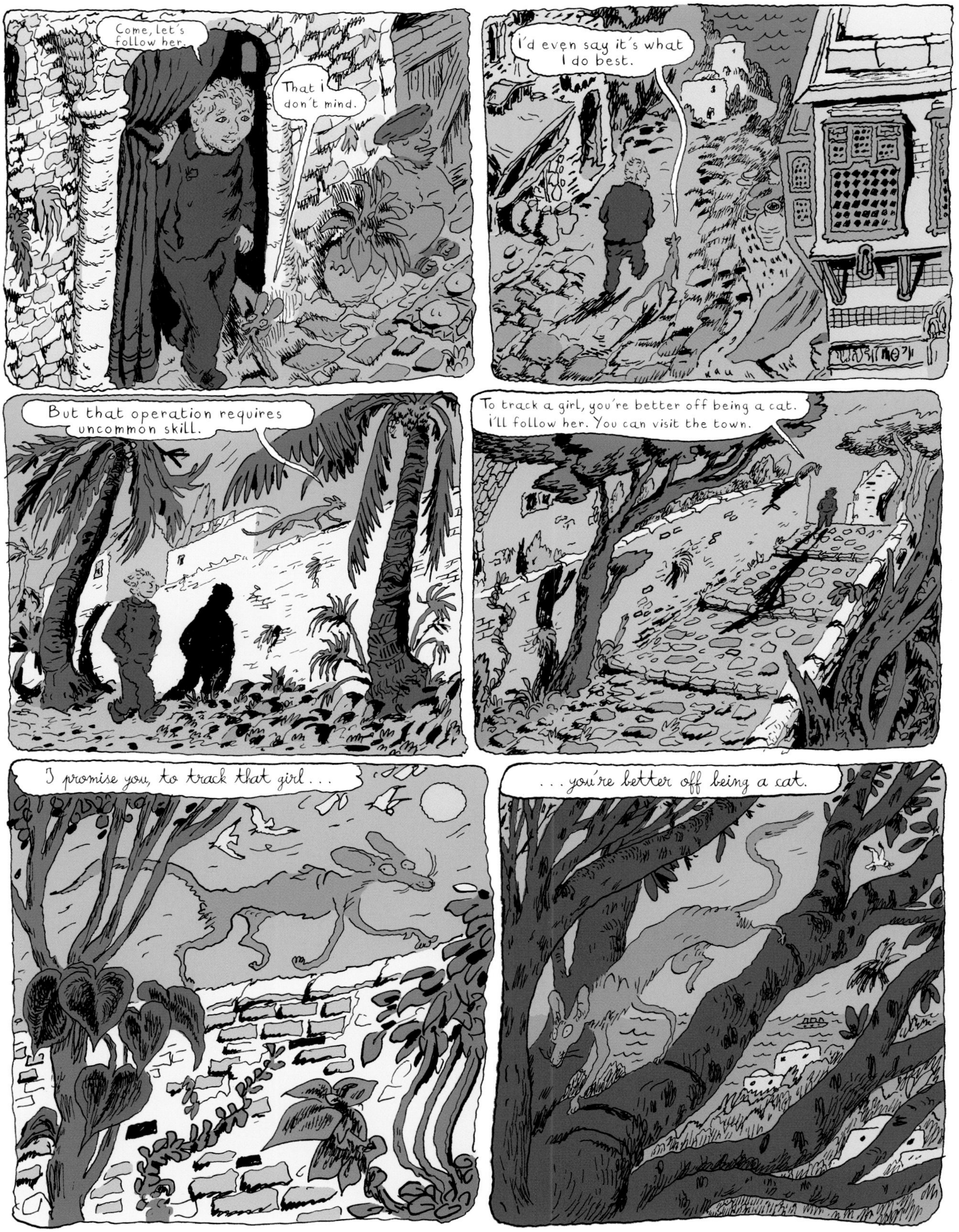
Come, let's follow her.
That I don't mind.
I'd even say it's what I do best.
But that operation requires uncommon skill.
To track a girl, you're better off being a cat. I'll follow her. You can visit the town.
I promise you, to track that girl . . .
. . . you're better off being a cat.

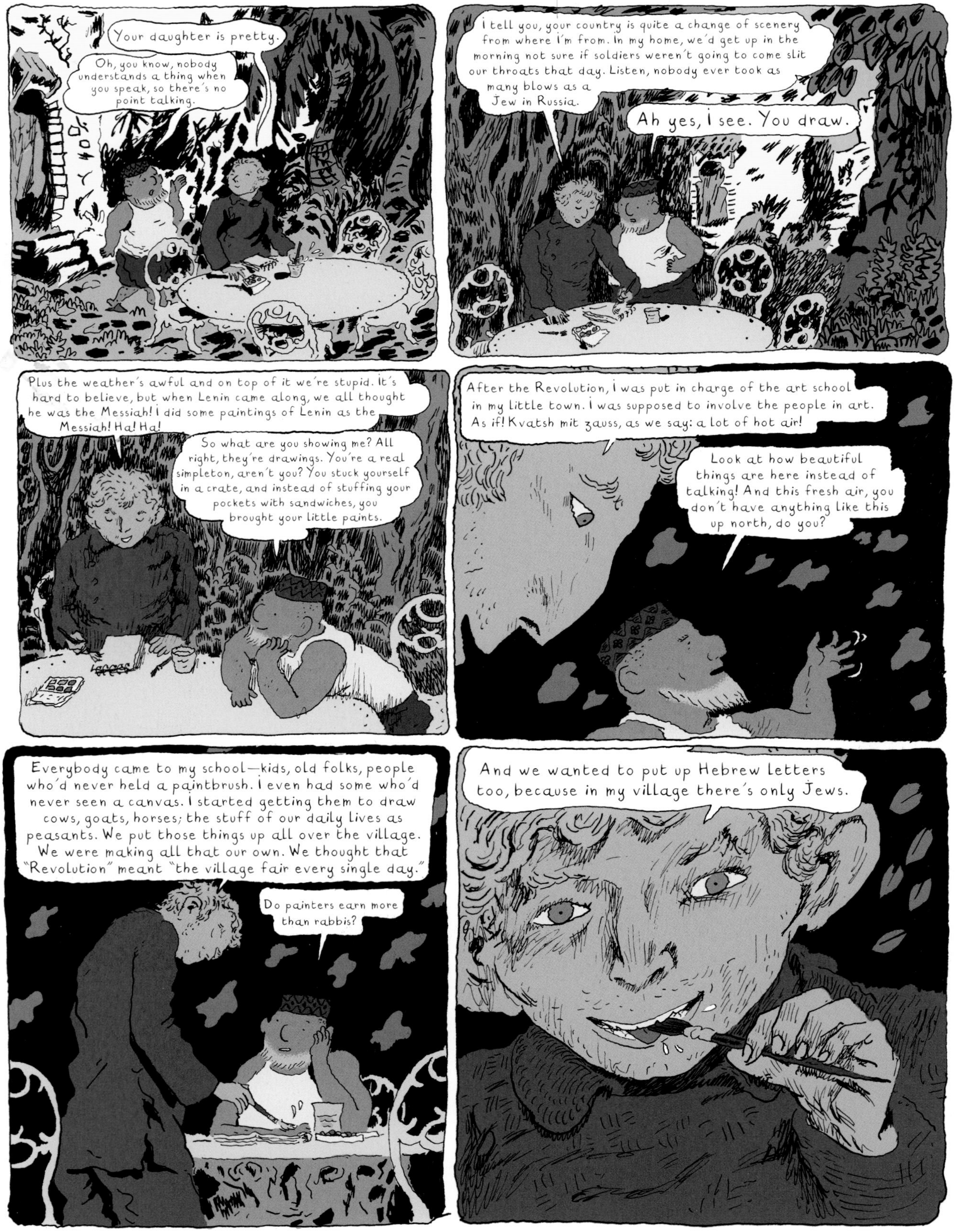
Your daughter is pretty.
Oh, you know, nobody understands a thing when you speak, so there's no point talking.
I tell you, your country is quite a change of scenery from where I'm from. In my home, we'd get up in the morning not sure if soldiers weren't going to come slit our throats that day. Listen, nobody ever took as many blows as a Jew in Russia.
Ah yes, I see. You draw.
Plus the weather's awful and on top of it we're stupid. It's hard to believe, but when Lenin came along, we all thought he was the Messiah! I did some paintings of Lenin as the Messiah! Ha! Ha!
So what are you showing me? All right, they're drawings. You're a real simpleton, aren't you? You stuck yourself in a crate, and instead of stuffing your pockets with sandwiches, you brought your little paints.
After the Revolution, I was put in charge of the art school in my little town. I was supposed to involve the people in art. As if! Kvatsh mit zauss, as we say: a lot of hot air!
Look at how beautiful things are here instead of talking! And this fresh air, you don't have anything like this up north, do you?
Everybody came to my school—kids, old folks, people who'd never held a paintbrush. I even had some who'd never seen a canvas. I started getting them to draw cows, goats, horses; the stuff of our daily lives as peasants. We put those things up all over the village. We were making all that our own. We thought that "Revolution" meant "the village fair every single day."
Do painters earn more than rabbis?
And we wanted to put up Hebrew letters too, because in my village there's only Jews.

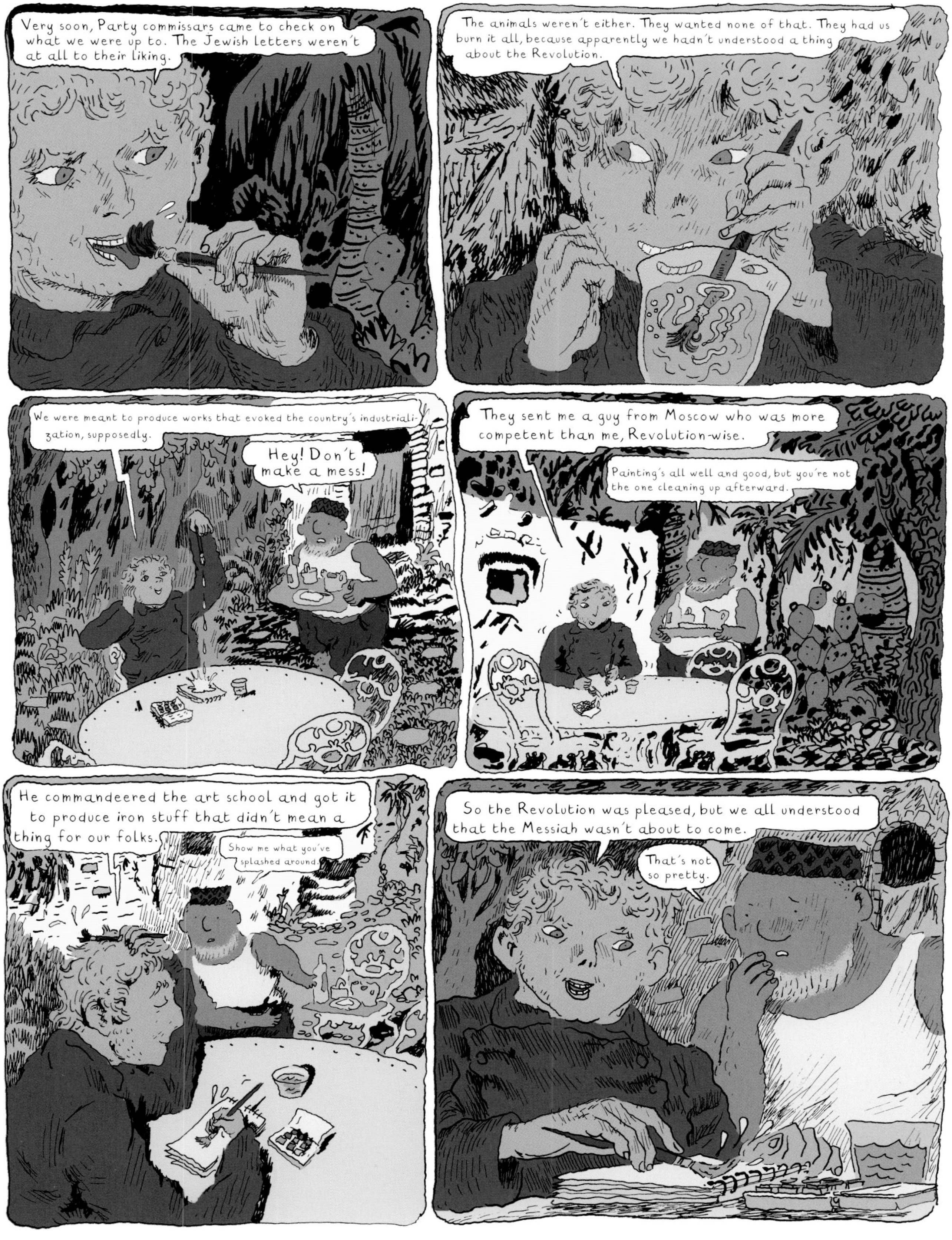
Very soon, Party commissars came to check on what we were up to. The Jewish letters weren't at all to their liking.
The animals weren't either. They wanted none of that. They had us burn it all, because apparently we hadn't understood a thing about the Revolution.
We were meant to produce works that evoked the country's industrialization, supposedly.
Hey! Don't make a mess!
They sent me a guy from Moscow who was more competent than me, Revolution-wise.
Painting's all well and good, but you're not the one cleaning up afterward.
He commandeered the art school and got it to produce iron stuff that didn't mean a thing for our folks.
Show me what you've splashed around.
So the Revolution was pleased, but we all understood that the Messiah wasn't about to come.
That's not so pretty.

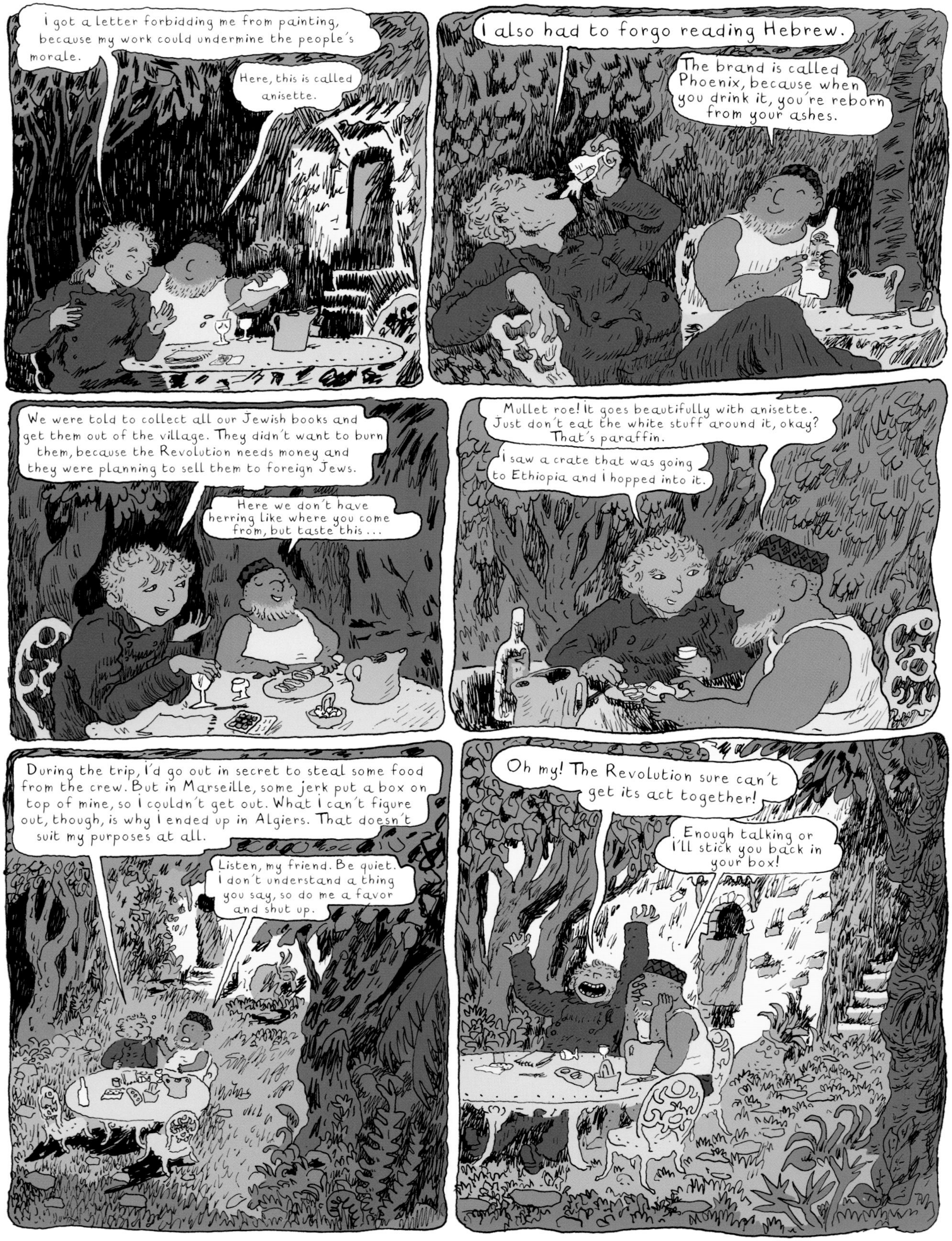

I got a letter forbidding me from painting, because my work could undermine the people's morale.
Here, this is called anisette.
I also had to forgo reading Hebrew.
The brand is called Phoenix, because when you drink it, you're reborn from your ashes.
We were told to collect all our Jewish books and get them out of the village. They didn't want to burn them, because the Revolution needs money and they were planning to sell them to foreign Jews.
Here we don't have herring like where you come from, but taste this . . .
Mullet roe! It goes beautifully with anisette. Just don't eat the white stuff around it, okay? That's paraffin.
I saw a crate that was going to Ethiopia and I hopped into it.
During the trip, I'd go out in secret to steal some food from the crew. But in Marseille, some jerk put a box on top of mine, so I couldn't get out. What I can't figure out, though, is why I ended up in Algiers. That doesn't suit my purposes at all.
Listen, my friend. Be quiet. I don't understand a thing you say, so do me a favor and shut up.
Oh my! The Revolution sure can't get its act together!
Enough talking or I'll stick you back in your box!

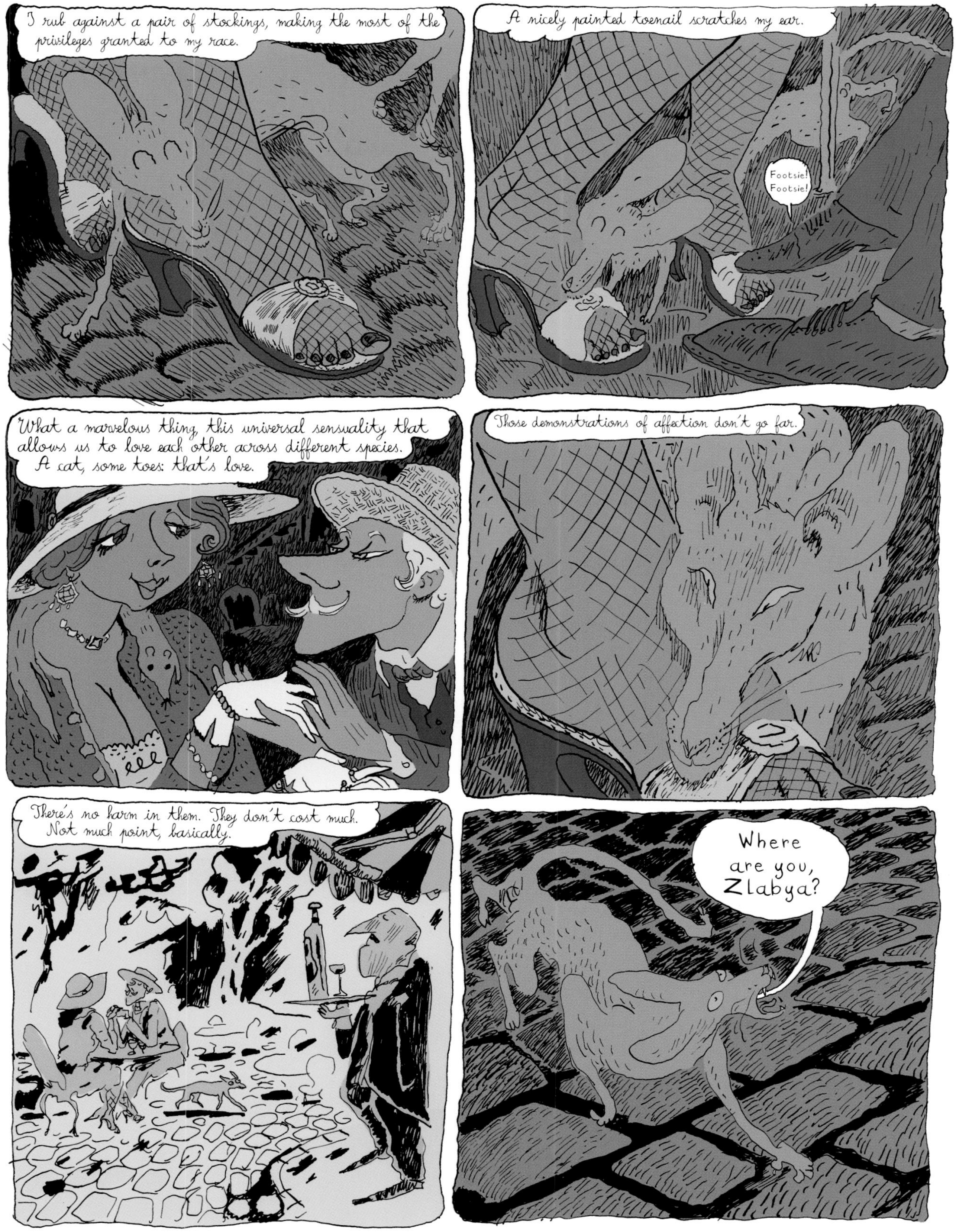
I rub against a pair of stockings, making the most of the privileges granted to my race.
A nicely painted toenail scratches my ear.
Footsie! Footsie!
What a marvelous thing, this universal sensuality that allows us to love each other across different species. A cat, some toes: that's love.
Those demonstrations of affection don't go far.
There's no harm in them. They don't cost much. Not much point, basically.
Where are you, Zlabya?

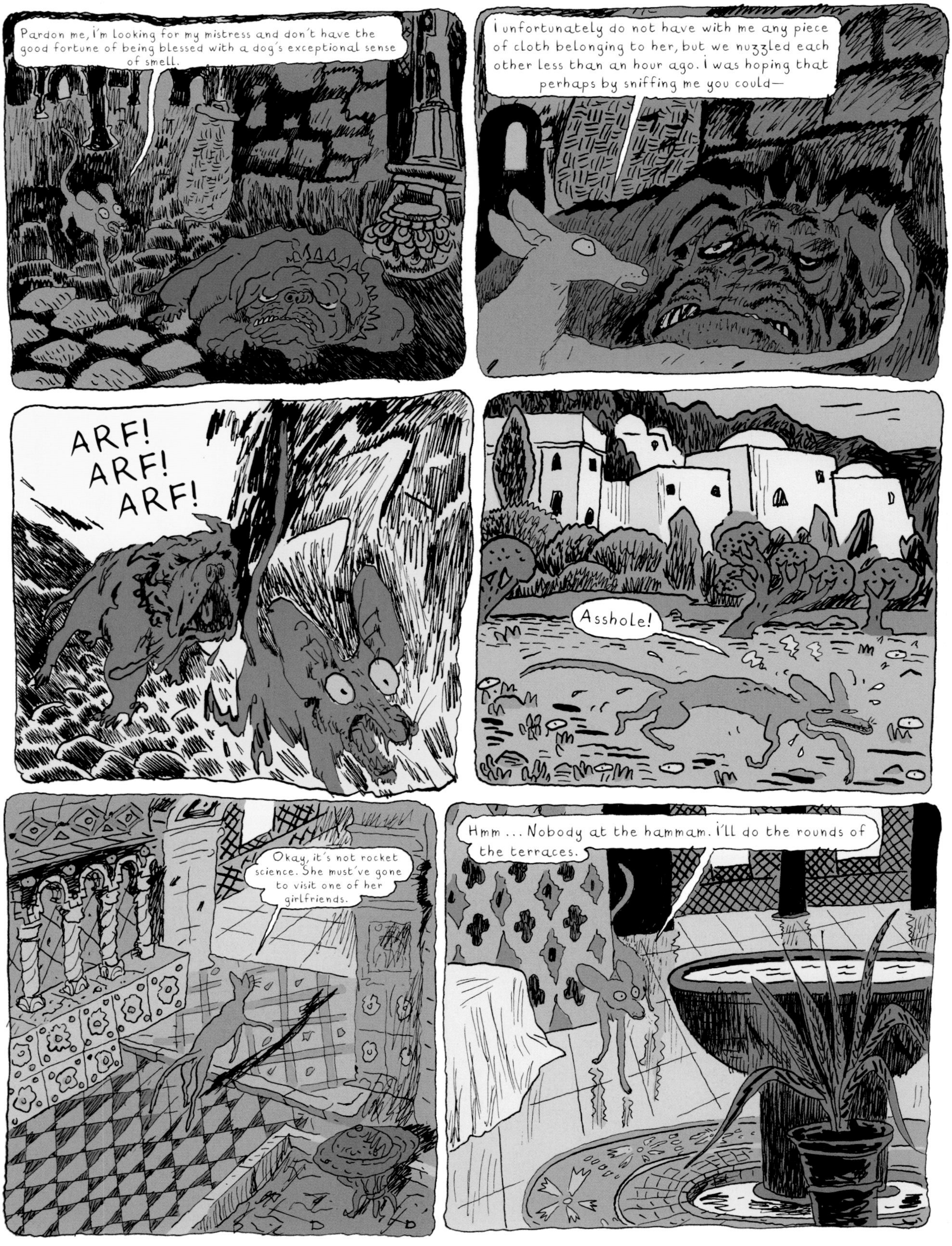
Pardon me, I'm looking for my mistress and don't have the good fortune of being blessed with a dog's exceptional sense of smell.
I unfortunately do not have with me any piece of cloth belonging to her, but we nuzzled each other less than an hour ago. I was hoping that perhaps by sniffing me you could—
ARF! ARF! ARF!
Asshole!
Okay, it's not rocket science. She must've gone to visit one of her girlfriends.
Hmm ... Nobody at the hammam. I'll do the rounds of the terraces.

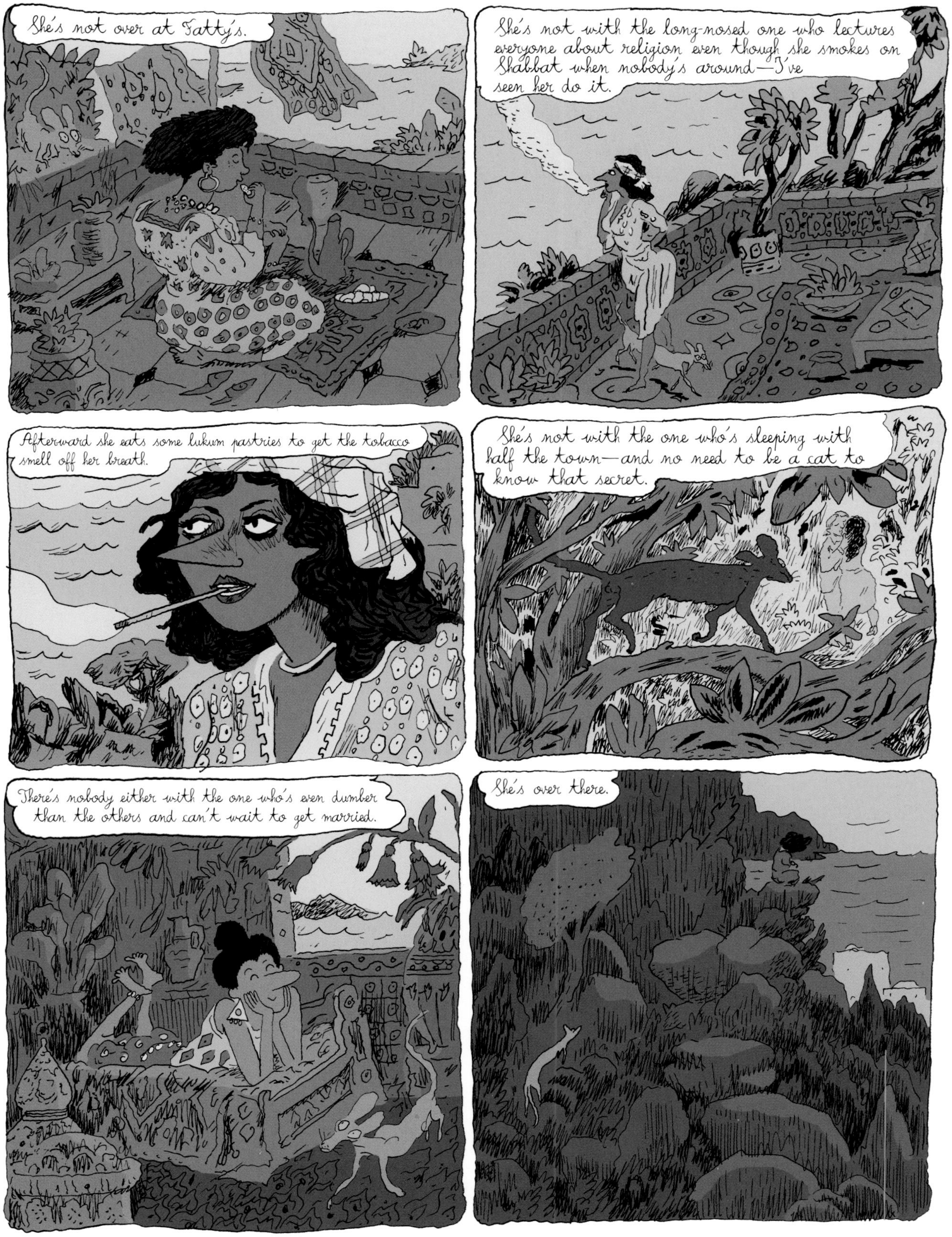
She's not over at Tatty's.
She's not with the long-nosed one who lectures everyone about religion even though she smokes on Shabbat when nobody's around—I've seen her do it.
Afterward she eats some lukum pastries to get the tobacco smell off her breath.
She's not with the one who's sleeping with half the town—and no need to be a cat to know that secret.
There's nobody either with the one who's even dumber than the others and can't wait to get married.
She's over there.

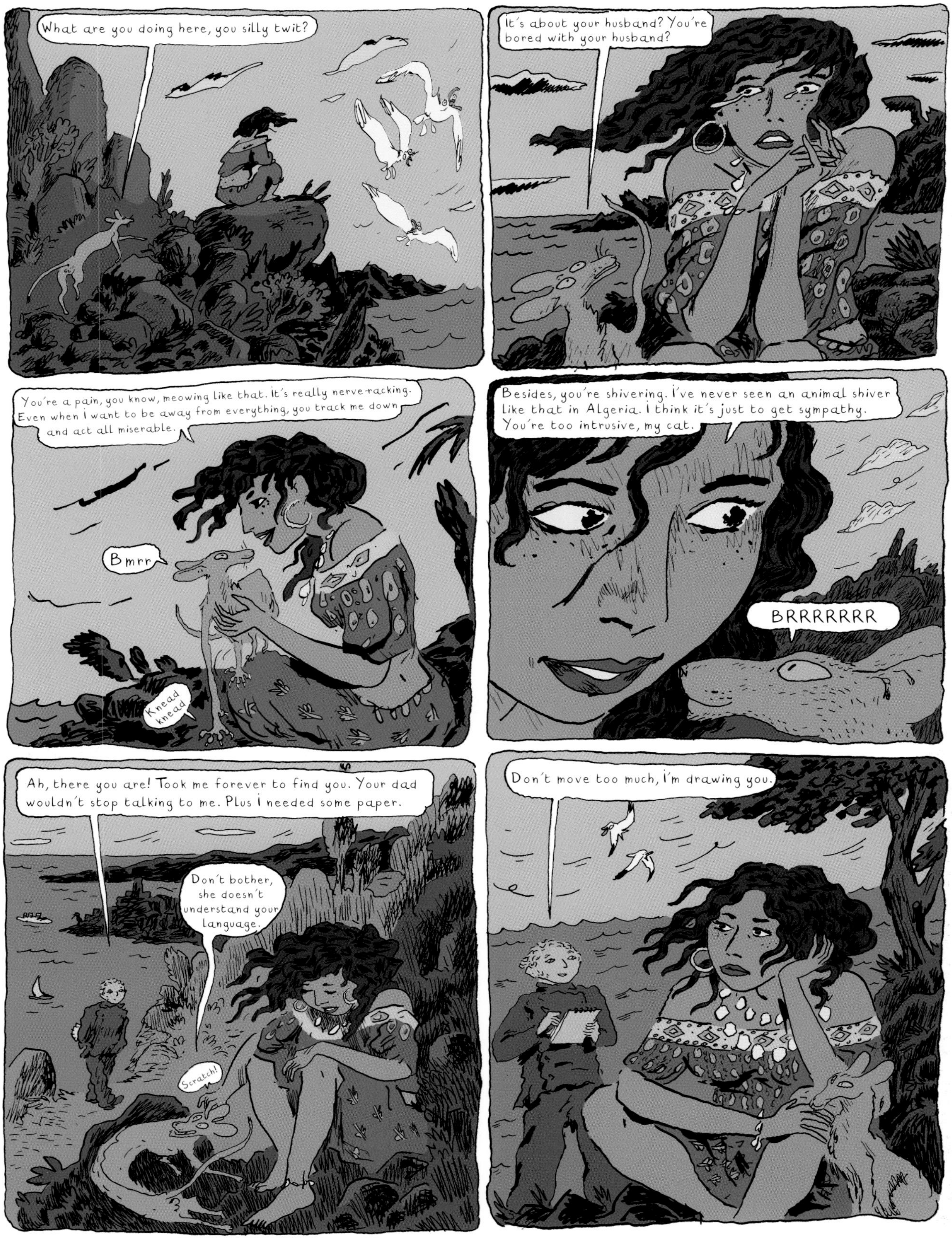

What are you doing here, you silly twit?
It's about your husband? You're bored with your husband?
You're a pain, you know, meowing like that. It's really nerve-racking. Even when I want to be away from everything, you track me down and act all miserable.
Bmrr
Knead knead
Besides, you're shivering. I've never seen an animal shiver like that in Algeria. I think it's just to get sympathy. You're too intrusive, my cat.
BRRRRRRR
Ah, there you are! Took me forever to find you. Your dad wouldn't stop talking to me. Plus I needed some paper.
Don't bother, she doesn't understand your language.
Scratch!
Don't move too much, I'm drawing you.

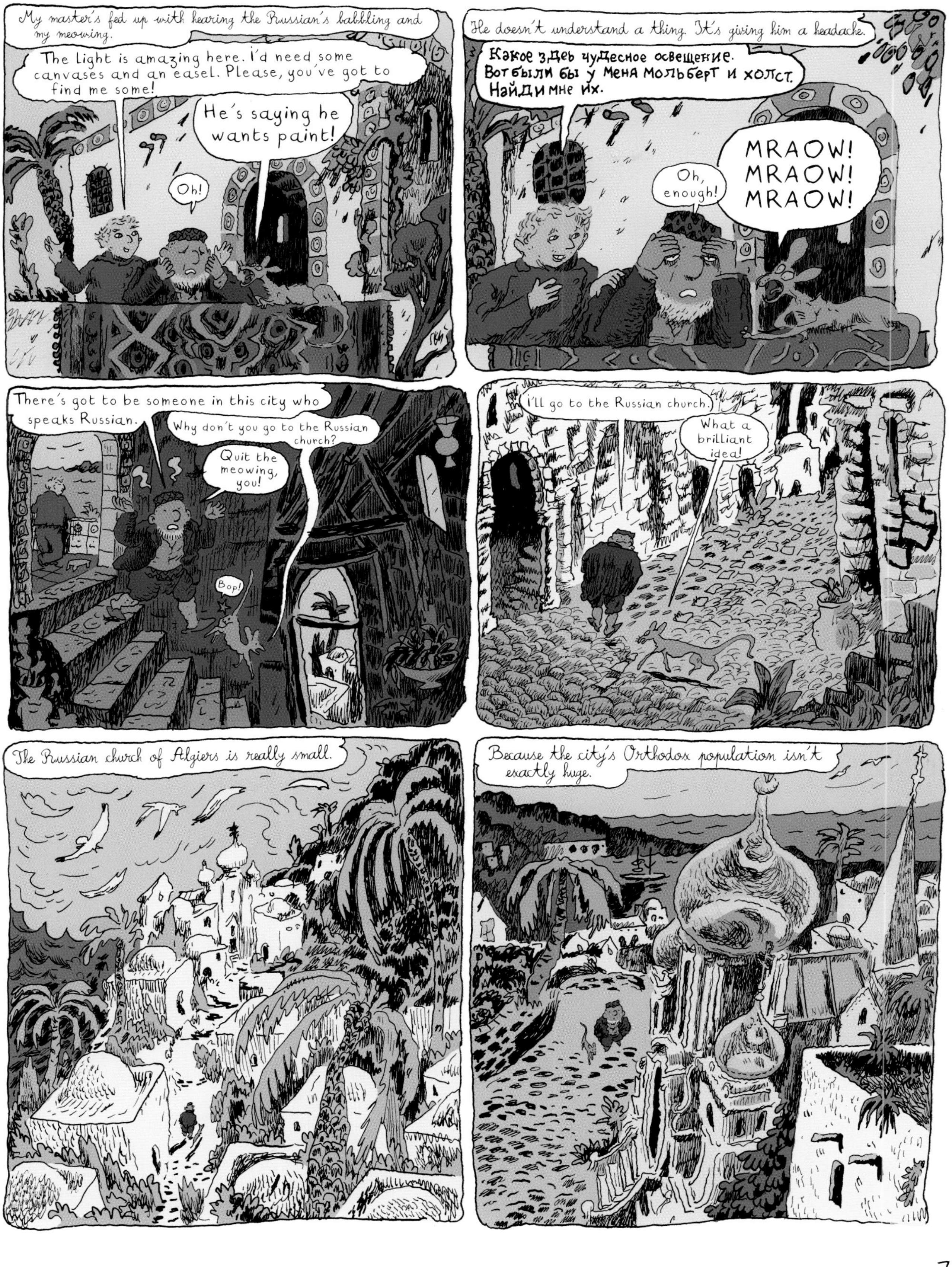

My master's fed up with hearing the Russian's babbling and my meowing.
The light is amazing here. I'd need some canvases and an easel. Please, you've got to find me some!
He's saying he wants paint!
Oh!
He doesn't understand a thing. It's giving him a headache.
Какое здесь чудесное освещение. Вот были бы у мена мольберт и холст. Найди мне их.
Oh, enough!
MRAOW! MRAOW! MRAOW!
There's got to be someone in this city who speaks Russian.
Why don't you go to the Russian church?
Quit the meowing, you!
Bop!
I'll go to the Russian church.
What a brilliant idea!
The Russian church of Algiers is really small.
Because the city's Orthodox population isn't exactly huge.

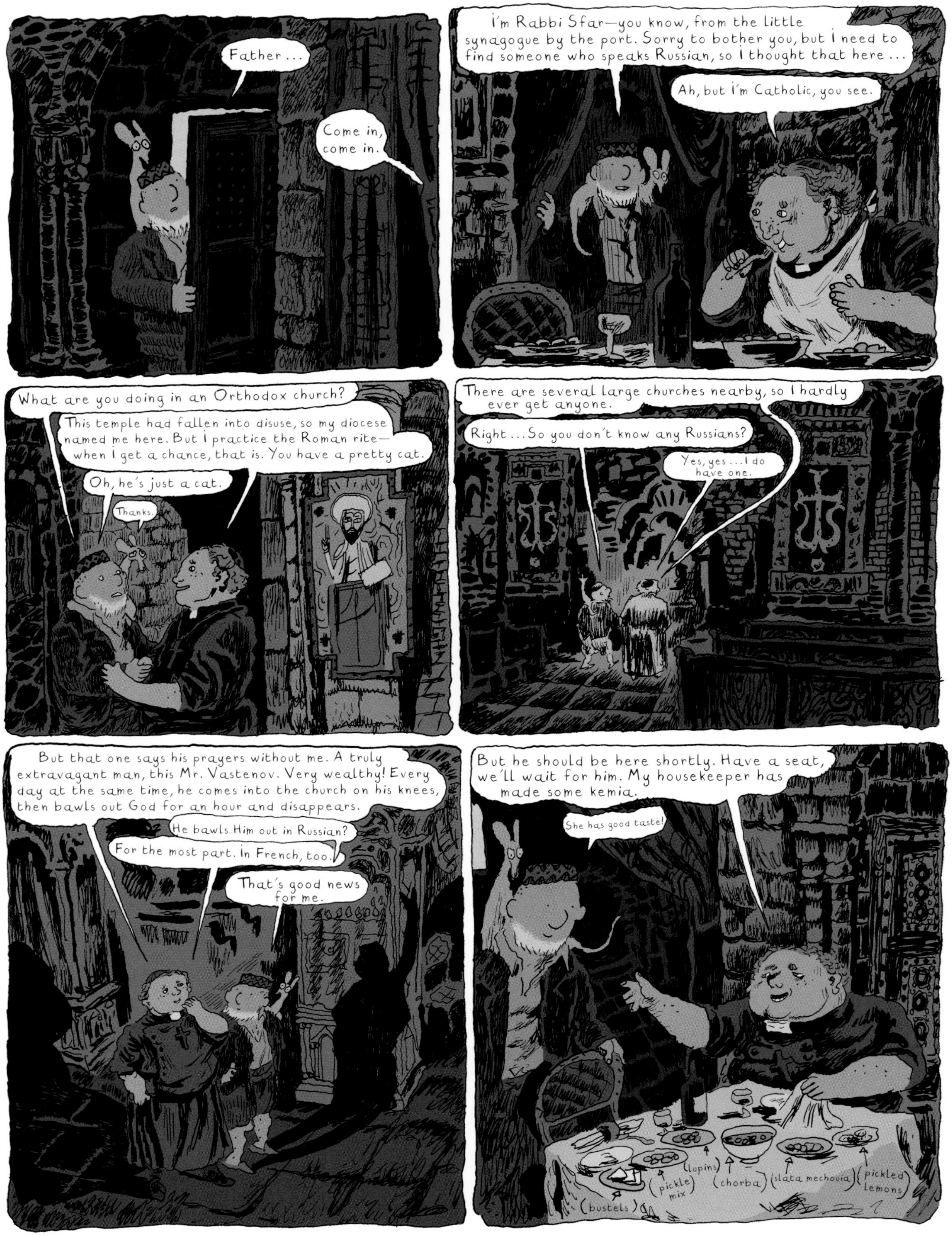

Father ...
Come in, come in.
I'm Rabbi Sfar—you know, from the little synagogue by the port. Sorry to bother you, but I need to find someone who speaks Russian, so I thought that here ...
Ah, but I'm Catholic, you see.
What are you doing in an Orthodox church?
This temple had fallen into disuse, so my diocese named me here. But I practice the Roman rite—when I get a chance, that is. You have a pretty cat.
Oh, he's just a cat.
Thanks.
There are several large churches nearby, so I hardly ever get anyone.
Right ... So you don't know any Russians?
Yes, yes ... I do have one.
But that one says his prayers without me. A truly extravagant man, this Mr. Vastenov. Very wealthy! Every day at the same time, he comes into the church on his knees, then bawls out God for an hour and disappears.
He bawls Him out in Russian?
For the most part. In French, too.
That's good news for me.
But he should be here shortly. Have a seat, we'll wait for him. My housekeeper has made some kemia.
She has good taste!
(bustels)
(pickle mix)
(lupins)
(chorba)
(slata mechouia)
(pickled lemons)

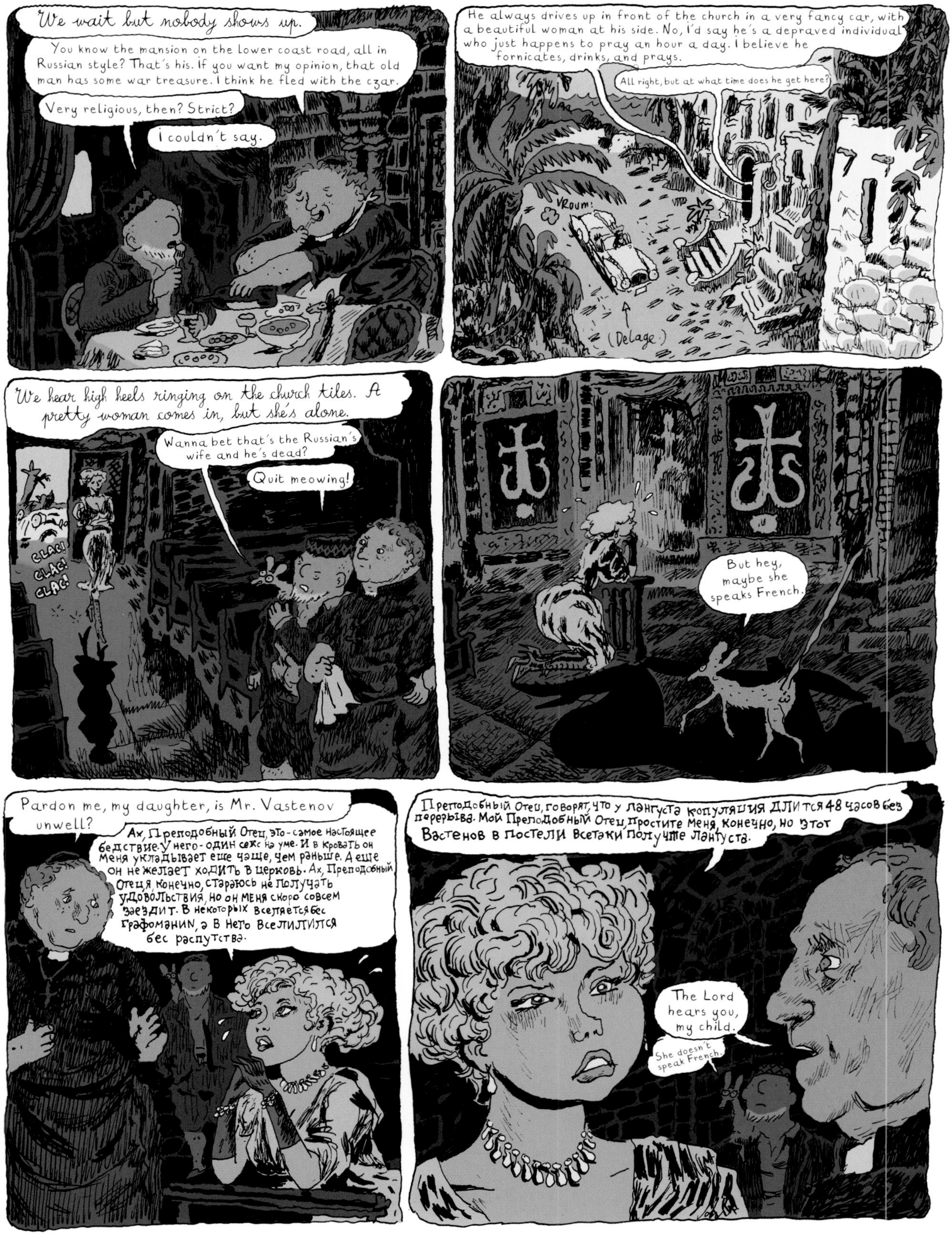
We wait but nobody shows up.
You know the mansion on the lower coast road, all in Russian style? That's his. If you want my opinion, that old man has some war treasure. I think he fled with the czar.
Very religious, then? Strict?
I couldn't say.
He always drives up in front of the church in a very fancy car, with a beautiful woman at his side. No, I'd say he's a depraved individual who just happens to pray an hour a day. I believe he fornicates, drinks, and prays.
All right, but at what time does he get here?
VROUM!
(Delage.)
We hear high heels ringing on the church tiles. A pretty woman comes in, but she's alone.
Wanna bet that's the Russian's wife and he's dead?
Quit meowing!
CLAC! CLAC! CLAC!
But hey, maybe she speaks French.
Pardon me, my daughter, is Mr. Vastenov unwell?
Ах, Преподобный Отец, это - самое настоящее бедствие. У него - один секс на уме. И в кровать он меня укладывает еще чаще, чем раньше. А еще он не желает ходить в церковь. Ах, Преподобный Отец, я, конечно, стараюсь не получать удовольствия, но он меня скоро совсем заездит. В некоторых вселяется бес графоманиn, а в него вселилился бес распутства.
Преподобный Отец, говорят, что у лангуста копуляция длится 48 часов без перерыва. Мой Преподобный Отец, простите меня, конечно, но этот Вастенов в постели всетаки получше лангуста.
The Lord hears you, my child.
She doesn't speak French.

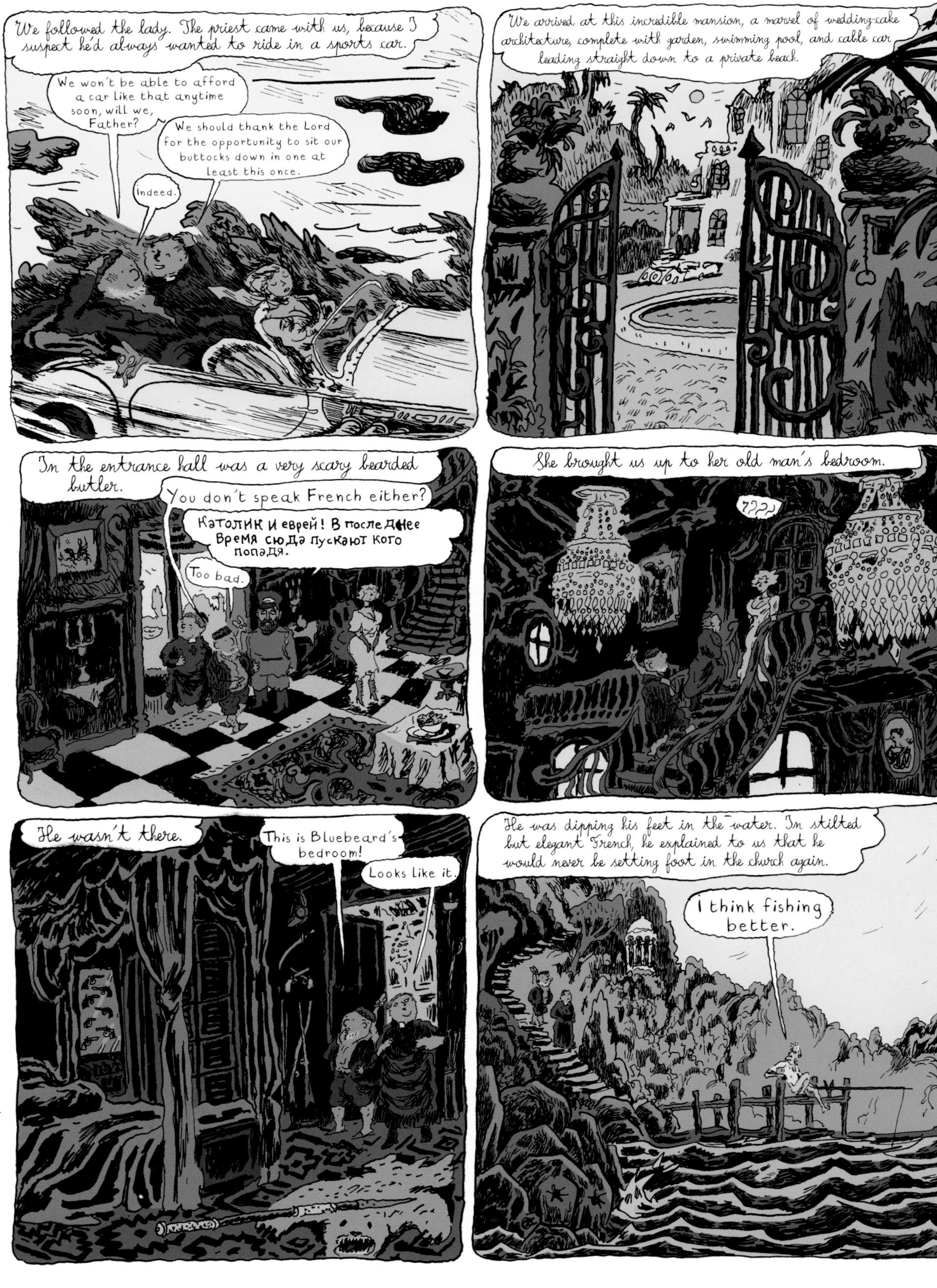
We followed the lady. The priest came with us, because I suspect he'd always wanted to ride in a sports car.
We won't be able to afford a car like that anytime soon, will we, Father?
We should thank the Lord for the opportunity to sit our buttocks down in one at least this once.
Indeed.
We arrived at this incredible mansion, a marvel of wedding-cake architecture, complete with garden, swimming pool, and cable car leading straight down to a private beach.
In the entrance hall was a very scary bearded butler.
You don't speak French either?
Католик и еврей! В последнее время сюда пускают кого попадя.
Too bad.
She brought us up to her old man's bedroom.
????
He wasn't there.
This is Bluebeard's bedroom!
Looks like it.
He was dipping his feet in the water. In stilted but elegant French, he explained to us that he would never be setting foot in the church again.
I think fishing better.

My rabbi pointed out that he too preferred fishing to praying but that the two activities were not incompatible.

God I see never. Fish, at least, it bite sometimes.

That is a fact.

"But not that often, mind you," my master answered, "because this is more of a sea urchin spot." My master knows his stuff. He waded in a bit and picked up some sea urchins.

Watch out, they're prickly!

Ha! Ha! Bravo! This is useful man! You are what profession?

I serve God.

While a late breakfast was being prepared, the priest pointed out to my master that Jews are not supposed to eat seafood. My rabbi answered that there's no obligation to eat what you fish.

When I was young, my buddies were Catholic, so when we went fishing, I would do like them and catch crabs, sea urchins, shellfish...

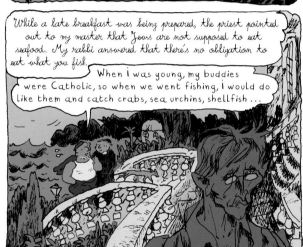

...but when mealtimes came around, I would never eat any of it.

Liar!

I promise you, I've always strictly kept kosher. And it was by no means easy! My late grandmother, who tasted everything, kept telling me that crawfish are so good that they can only be allowed by God.

So? Why you never taste?

I don't know...

...I like going through life telling myself that there are some good things I won't have.

I'm the same way about sports cars.

Hum...

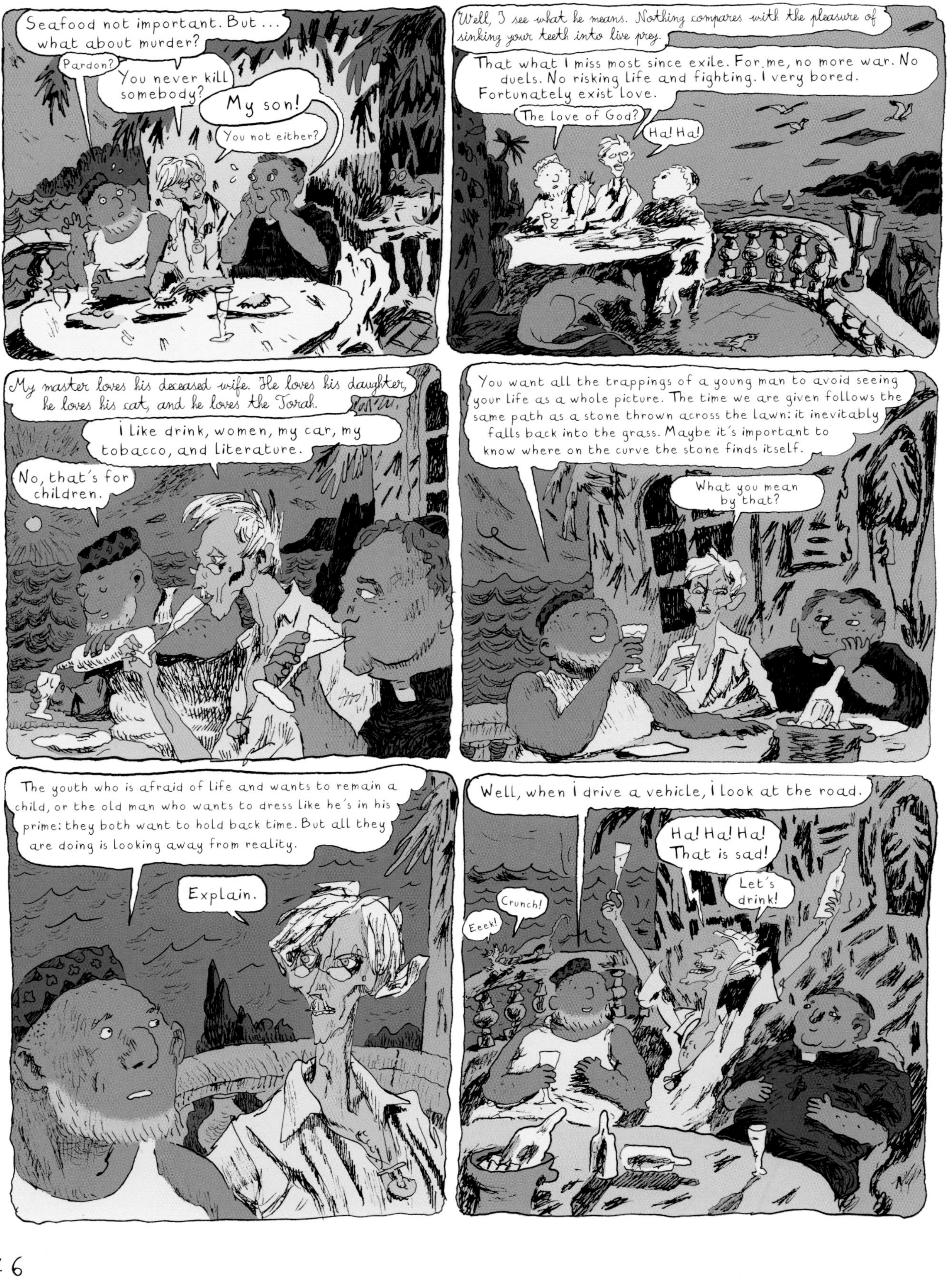

Seafood not important. But . . . what about murder?
Pardon?
You never kill somebody?
My son!
You not either?
Well, I see what he means. Nothing compares with the pleasure of sinking your teeth into live prey.
That what I miss most since exile. For me, no more war. No duels. No risking life and fighting. I very bored. Fortunately exist love.
The love of God?
Ha! Ha!
My master loves his deceased wife. He loves his daughter, he loves his cat, and he loves the Torah.
I like drink, women, my car, my tobacco, and literature.
No, that's for children.
You want all the trappings of a young man to avoid seeing your life as a whole picture. The time we are given follows the same path as a stone thrown across the lawn: it inevitably falls back into the grass. Maybe it's important to know where on the curve the stone finds itself.
What you mean by that?
The youth who is afraid of life and wants to remain a child, or the old man who wants to dress like he's in his prime: they both want to hold back time. But all they are doing is looking away from reality.
Explain.
Well, when I drive a vehicle, I look at the road.
Ha! Ha! Ha! That is sad!
Let's drink!
Crunch!
Eeek!

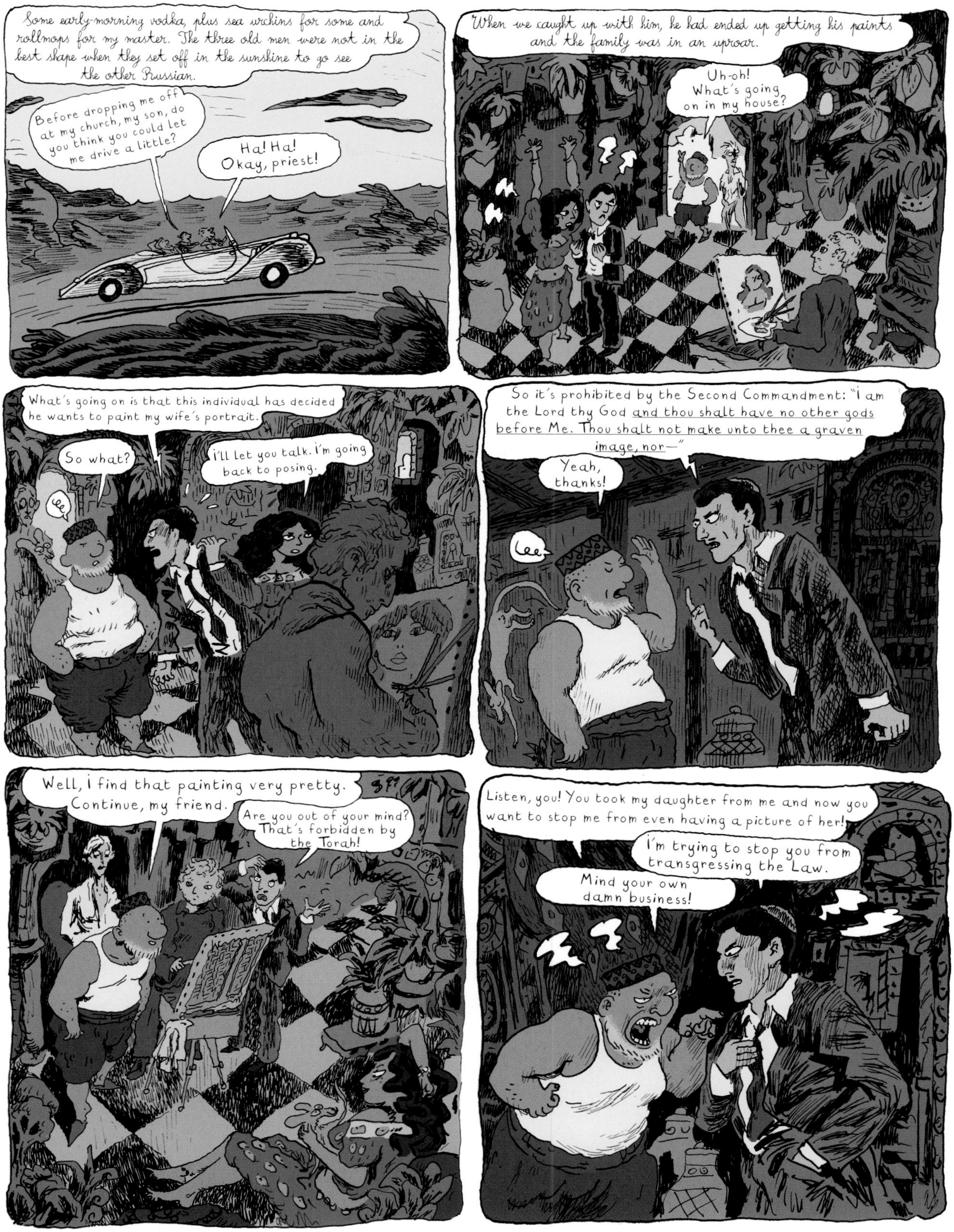
Some early-morning vodka, plus sea urchins for some and rollmops for my master. The three old men were not in the best shape when they set off in the sunshine to go see the other Russian.
Before dropping me off at my church, my son, do you think you could let me drive a little?
Ha! Ha! Okay, priest!
When we caught up with him, he had ended up getting his paints and the family was in an uproar.
Uh-oh! What's going on in my house?
What's going on is that this individual has decided he wants to paint my wife's portrait.
So what?
I'll let you talk. I'm going back to posing.
So it's prohibited by the Second Commandment: "I am the Lord thy God and thou shalt have no other gods before Me. Thou shalt not make unto thee a graven image, nor—"
Yeah, thanks!
Well, I find that painting very pretty. Continue, my friend.
Are you out of your mind? That's forbidden by the Torah!
Listen, you! You took my daughter from me and now you want to stop me from even having a picture of her!
I'm trying to stop you from transgressing the Law.
Mind your own damn business!

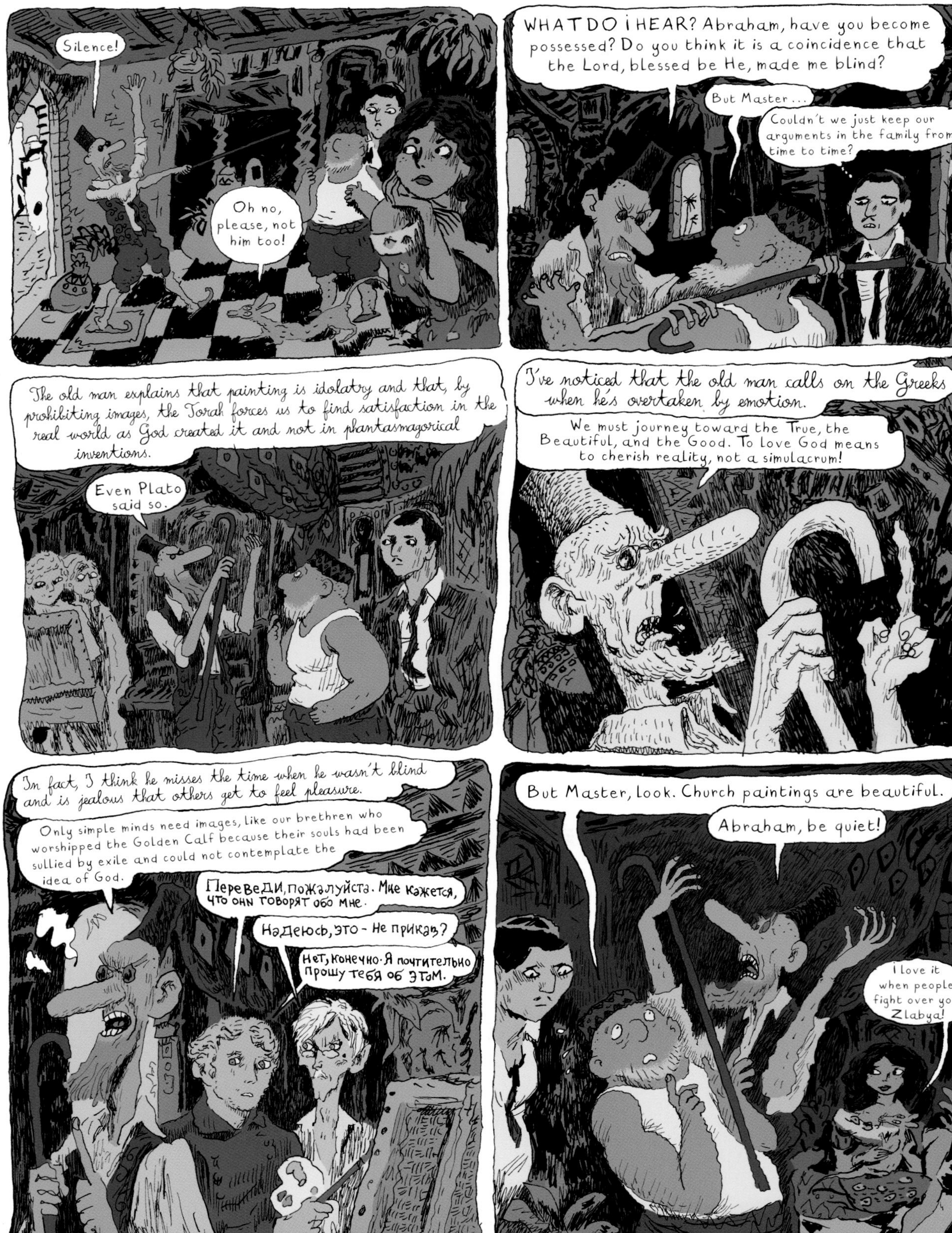
Silence!
Oh no, please, not him too!
WHAT DO I HEAR? Abraham, have you become possessed? Do you think it is a coincidence that the Lord, blessed be He, made me blind?
But Master...
Couldn't we just keep our arguments in the family from time to time?
The old man explains that painting is idolatry and that, by prohibiting images, the Torah forces us to find satisfaction in the real world as God created it and not in phantasmagorical inventions.
Even Plato said so.
I've noticed that the old man calls on the Greeks when he's overtaken by emotion.
We must journey toward the True, the Beautiful, and the Good. To love God means to cherish reality, not a simulacrum!
In fact, I think he misses the time when he wasn't blind and is jealous that others get to feel pleasure.
Only simple minds need images, like our brethren who worshipped the Golden Calf because their souls had been sullied by exile and could not contemplate the idea of God.
Переведи, пожалуйста. Мне кажется, что они говорят обо мне.
Надеюсь, это - не приказ?
Нет, конечно. Я почтительно прошу тебя об этом.
But Master, look. Church paintings are beautiful.
Abraham, be quiet!
I love it when people fight over you, Zlabya!

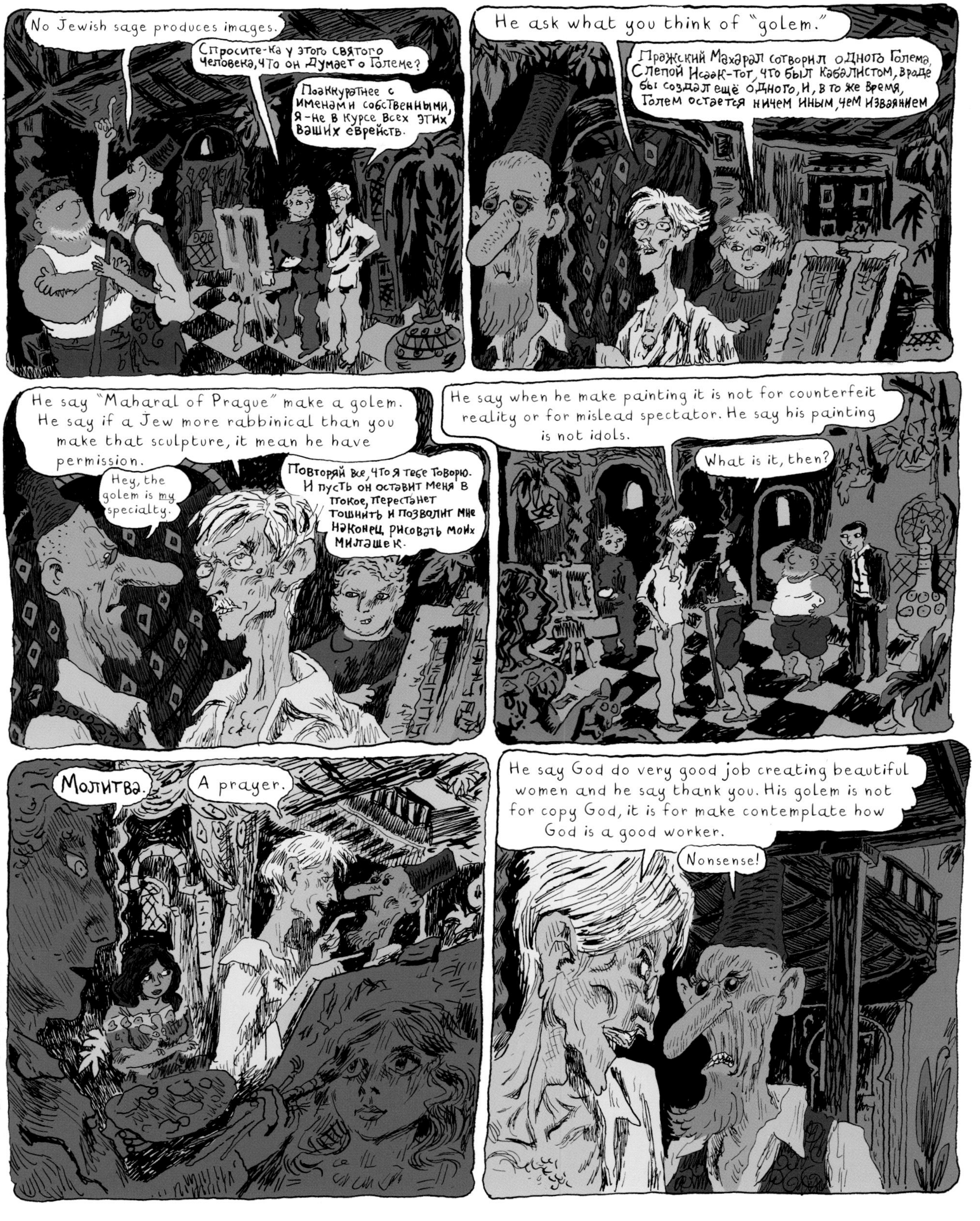

No Jewish sage produces images.
Спросите-ка у этого святого человека, что он думает о Големе?
Поаккуратнее с именами собственными, я-не в курсе всех этих ваших еврейств.
He ask what you think of "golem."
Пражский Махарал сотворил одного Голема, Слепой Исаак-тот, что был Кабалистом, вроде бы создал ещё одного, и, в то же время, Голем остается ничем иным, чем изваянием
He say "Maharal of Prague" make a golem. He say if a Jew more rabbinical than you make that sculpture, it mean he have permission.
Hey, the golem is my specialty.
Повторяй все, что я тебе говорю. И пусть он оставит меня в покое, перестанет тошнить и позволит мне наконец рисовать моих милашек.
He say when he make painting it is not for counterfeit reality or for mislead spectator. He say his painting is not idols.
What is it, then?
Молитва.
A prayer.
He say God do very good job creating beautiful women and he say thank you. His golem is not for copy God, it is for make contemplate how God is a good worker.
Nonsense!

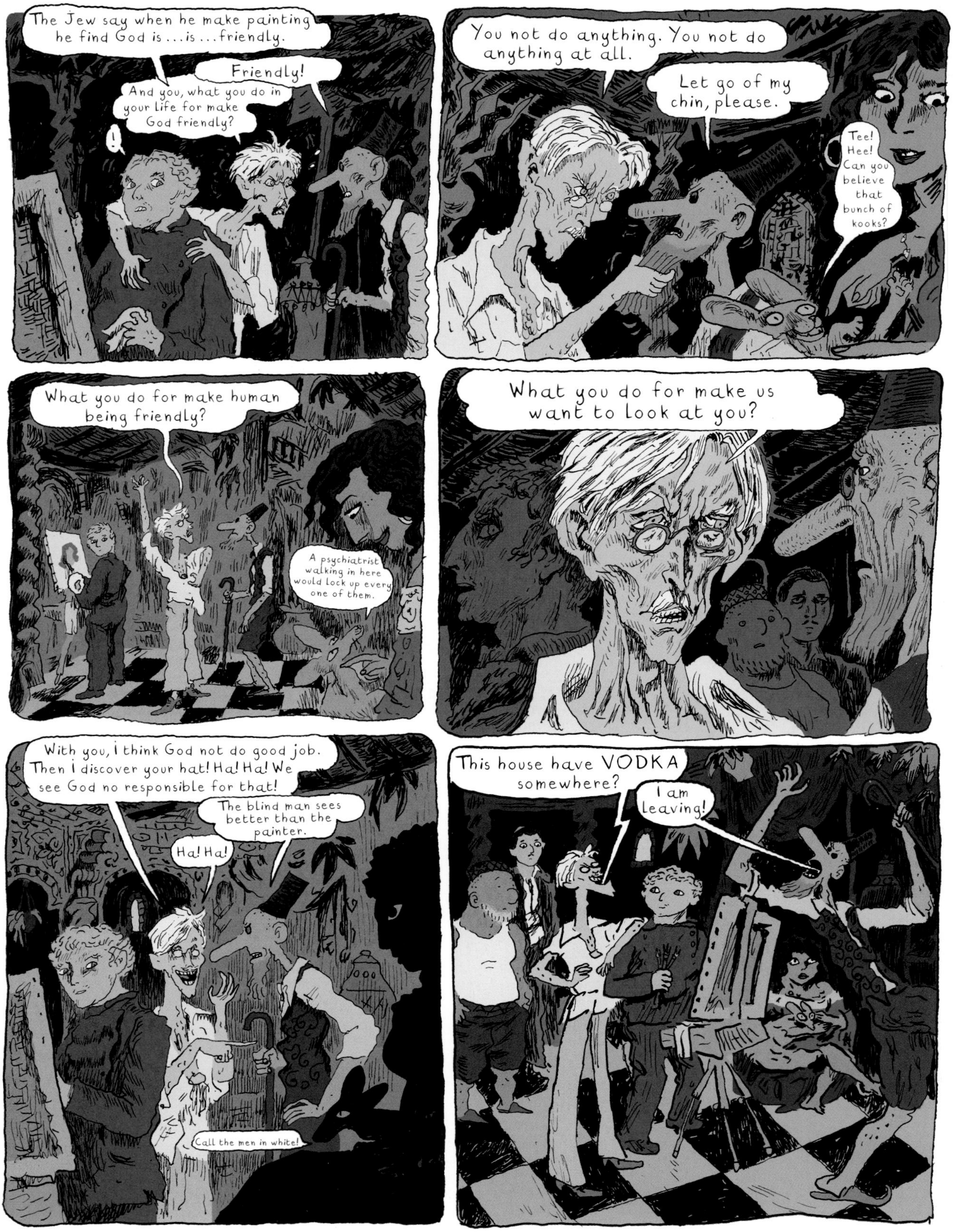
The Jew say when he make painting he find God is . . . is . . . friendly.
Friendly!
And you, what you do in your life for make God friendly?
!
You not do anything. You not do anything at all.
Let go of my chin, please.
Tee! Hee! Can you believe that bunch of kooks?
What you do for make human being friendly?
A psychiatrist walking in here would lock up every one of them.
What you do for make us want to look at you?
With you, I think God not do good job. Then I discover your hat! Ha! Ha! We see God no responsible for that!
The blind man sees better than the painter.
Ha! Ha!
Call the men in white!
This house have VODKA somewhere?
I am leaving!

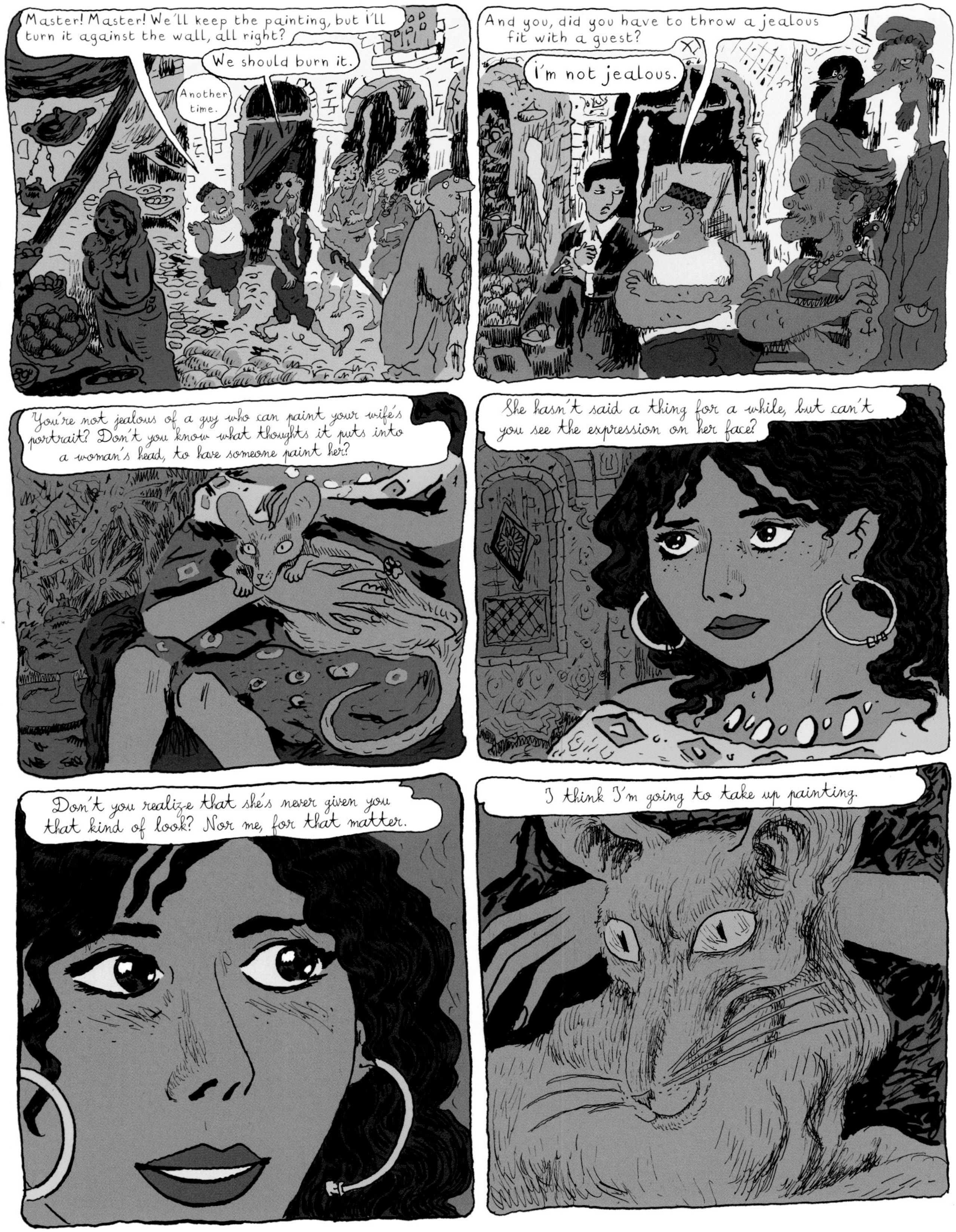
Master! Master! We'll keep the painting, but I'll turn it against the wall, all right?
We should burn it.
Another time.
And you, did you have to throw a jealous fit with a guest?
I'm not jealous.
You're not jealous of a guy who can paint your wife's portrait? Don't you know what thoughts it puts into a woman's head, to have someone paint her?
She hasn't said a thing for a while, but can't you see the expression on her face?
Don't you realize that she's never given you that kind of look? Nor me, for that matter.
I think I'm going to take up painting.

One thing Russians and Algerians have in common is steam baths.

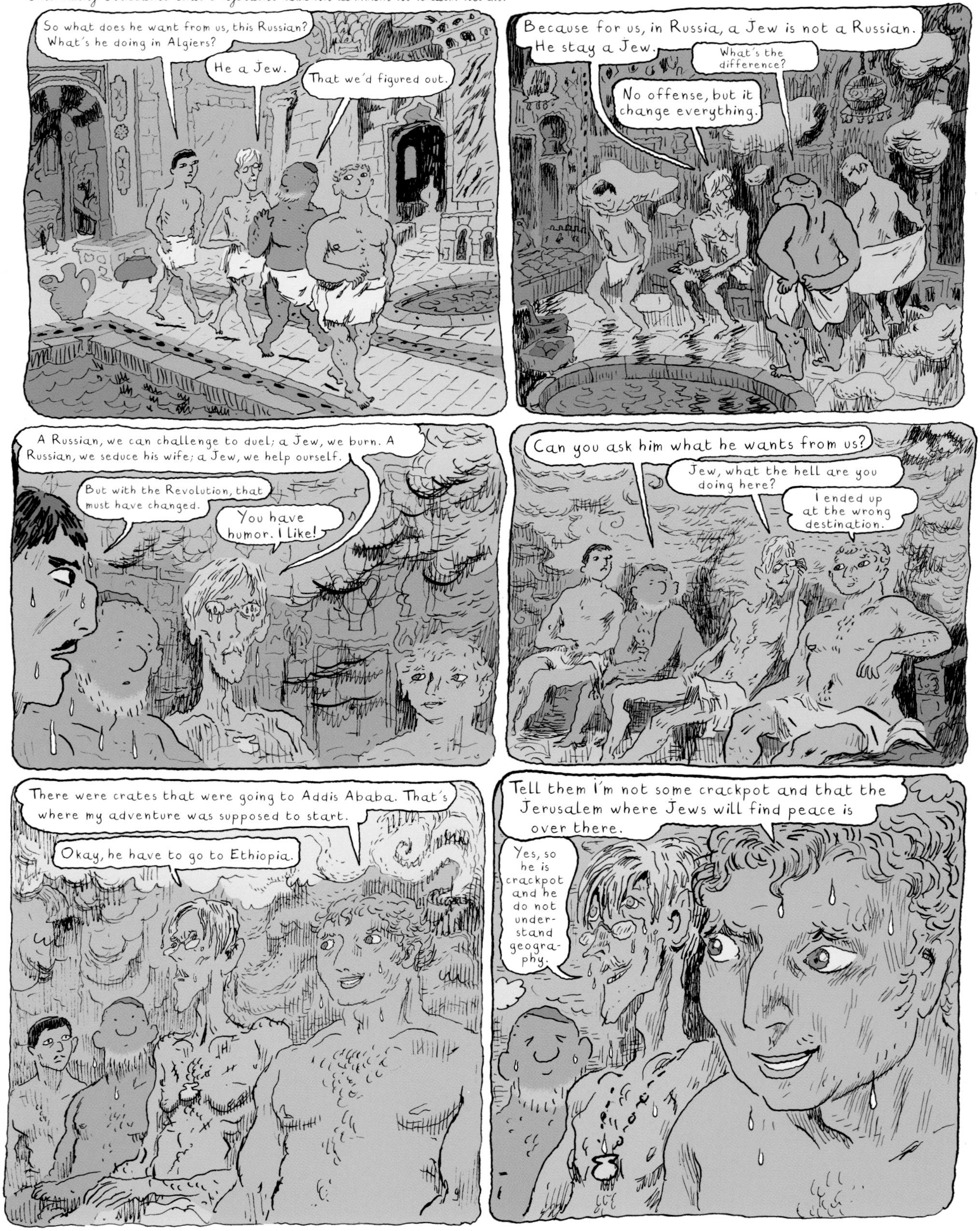
So what does he want from us, this Russian? What's he doing in Algiers?
He a Jew.
That we'd figured out.
Because for us, in Russia, a Jew is not a Russian. He stay a Jew.
What's the difference?
No offense, but it change everything.
A Russian, we can challenge to duel; a Jew, we burn. A Russian, we seduce his wife; a Jew, we help ourself.
But with the Revolution, that must have changed.
You have humor. I like!
Can you ask him what he wants from us?
Jew, what the hell are you doing here?
I ended up at the wrong destination.
There were crates that were going to Addis Ababa. That's where my adventure was supposed to start.
Okay, he have to go to Ethiopia.
Tell them I'm not some crackpot and that the Jerusalem where Jews will find peace is over there.
Yes, so he is crackpot and he do not understand geography.

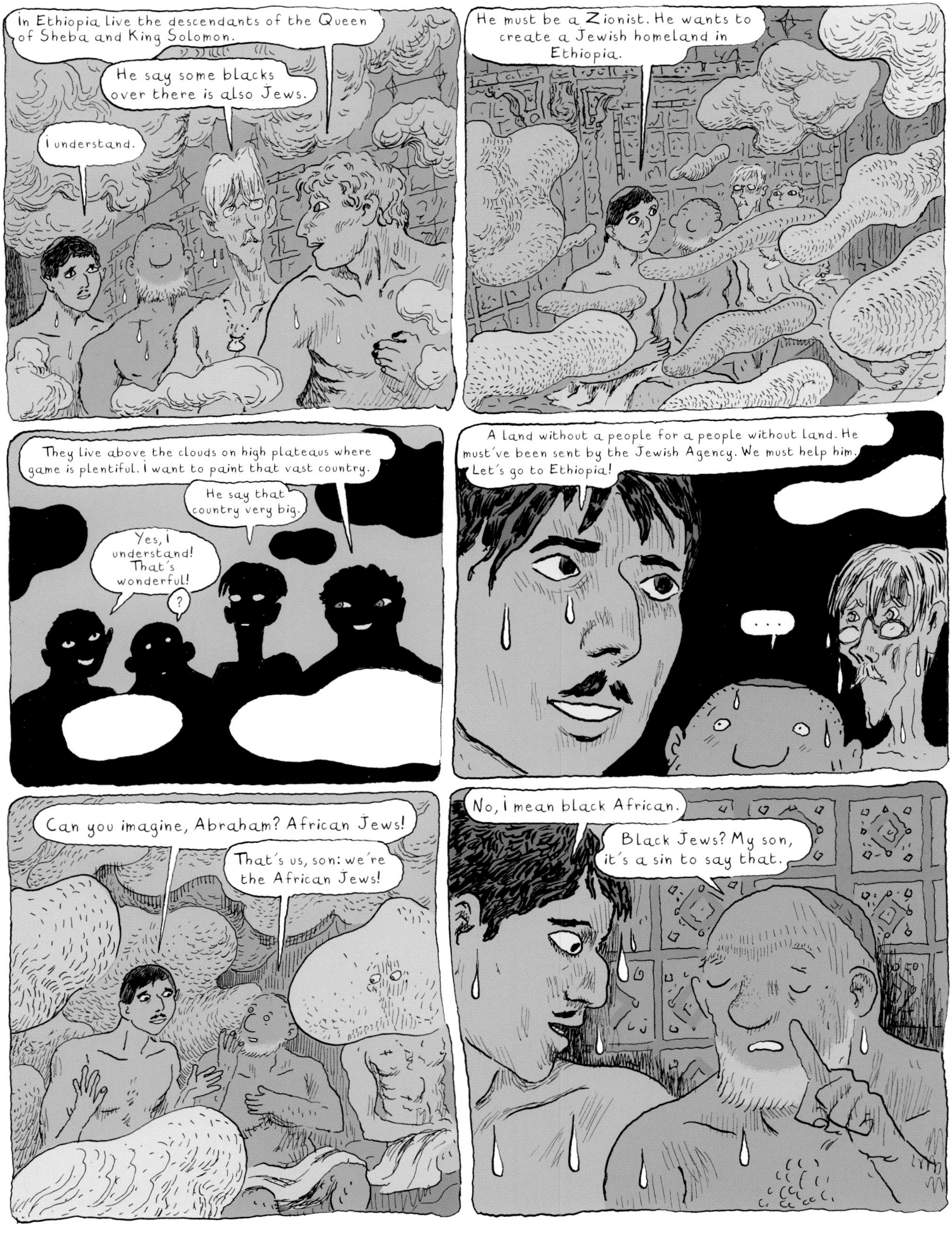
In Ethiopia live the descendants of the Queen of Sheba and King Solomon.
He say some blacks over there is also Jews.
I understand.
He must be a Zionist. He wants to create a Jewish homeland in Ethiopia.
They live above the clouds on high plateaus where game is plentiful. I want to paint that vast country.
He say that country very big.
Yes, I understand! That's wonderful!
?
A land without a people for a people without land. He must've been sent by the Jewish Agency. We must help him. Let's go to Ethiopia!
...
Can you imagine, Abraham? African Jews!
That's us, son: we're the African Jews!
No, I mean black African.
Black Jews? My son, it's a sin to say that.

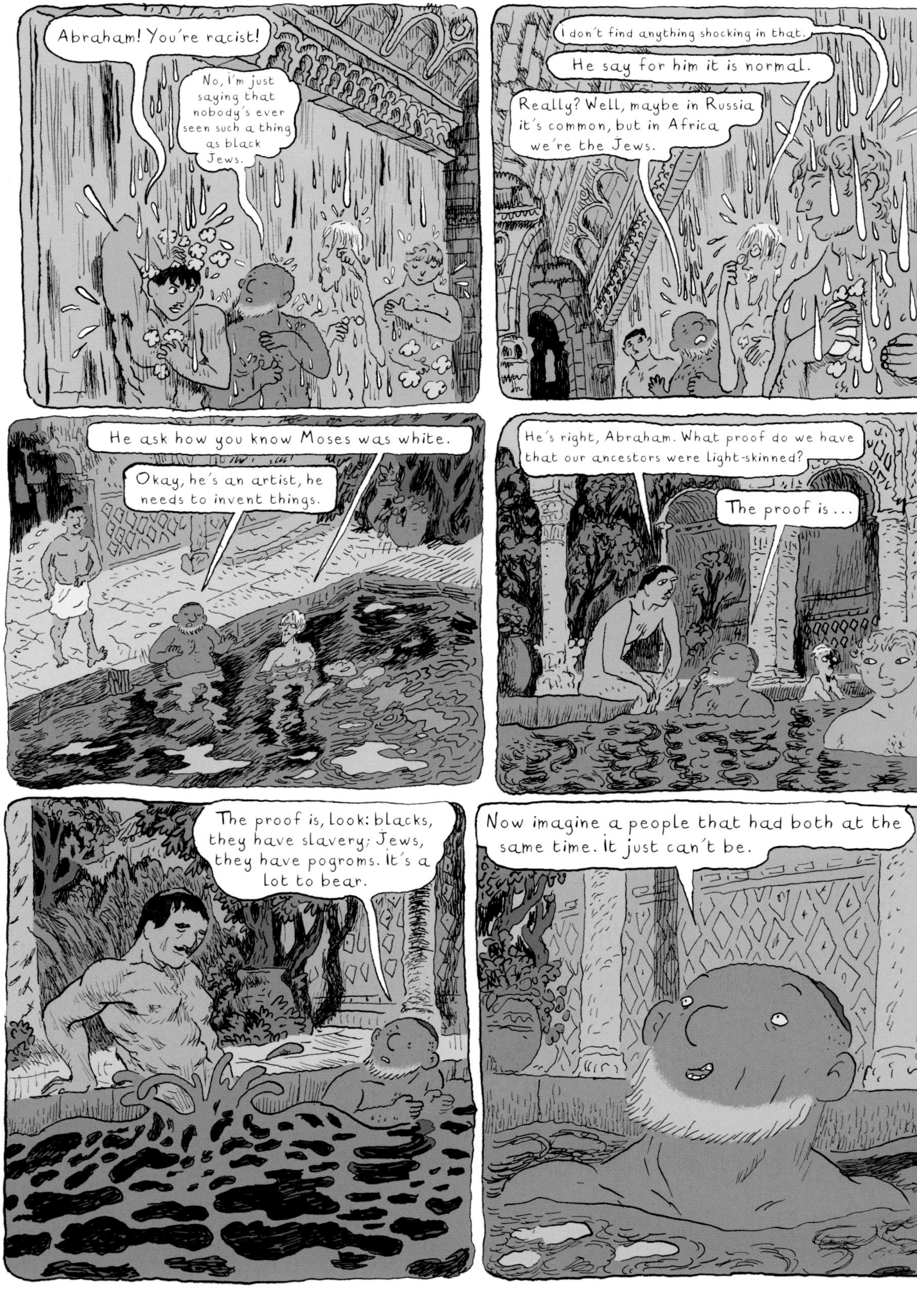
Abraham! You're racist!
No, I'm just saying that nobody's ever seen such a thing as black Jews.
I don't find anything shocking in that.
He say for him it is normal.
Really? Well, maybe in Russia it's common, but in Africa we're the Jews.
He ask how you know Moses was white.
Okay, he's an artist, he needs to invent things.
He's right, Abraham. What proof do we have that our ancestors were light-skinned?
The proof is...
The proof is, look: blacks, they have slavery; Jews, they have pogroms. It's a lot to bear.
Now imagine a people that had both at the same time. It just can't be.

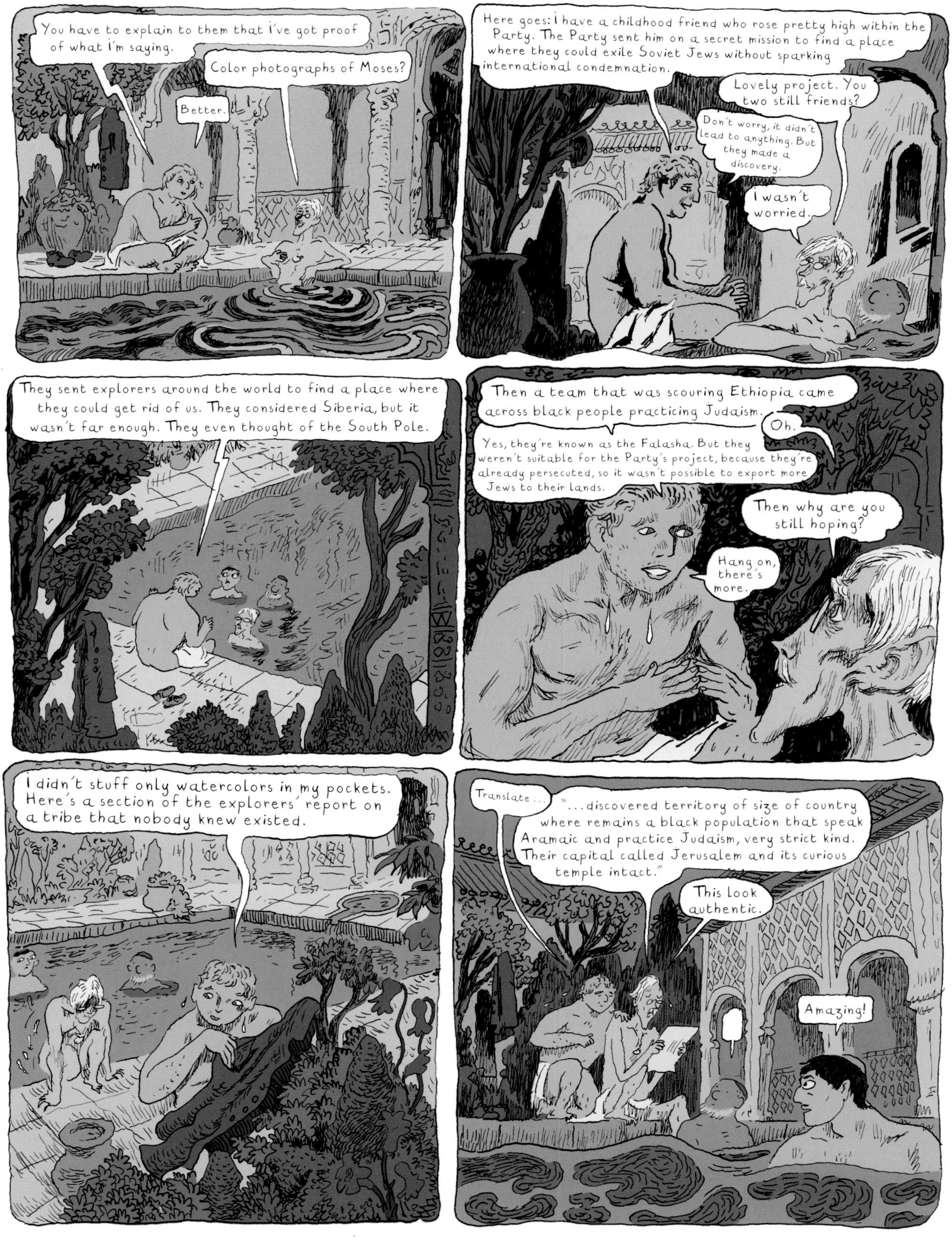

You have to explain to them that I've got proof of what I'm saying.
Color photographs of Moses?
Better.
Here goes: I have a childhood friend who rose pretty high within the Party. The Party sent him on a secret mission to find a place where they could exile Soviet Jews without sparking international condemnation.
Lovely project. You two still friends?
Don't worry, it didn't lead to anything. But they made a discovery.
I wasn't worried.
They sent explorers around the world to find a place where they could get rid of us. They considered Siberia, but it wasn't far enough. They even thought of the South Pole.
Then a team that was scouring Ethiopia came across black people practicing Judaism.
Oh.
Yes, they're known as the Falasha. But they weren't suitable for the Party's project, because they're already persecuted, so it wasn't possible to export more Jews to their lands.
Then why are you still hoping?
Hang on, there's more.
I didn't stuff only watercolors in my pockets. Here's a section of the explorers' report on a tribe that nobody knew existed.
Translate...
"...discovered territory of size of country where remains a black population that speak Aramaic and practice Judaism, very strict kind. Their capital called Jerusalem and its curious temple intact."
This look authentic.
Amazing!

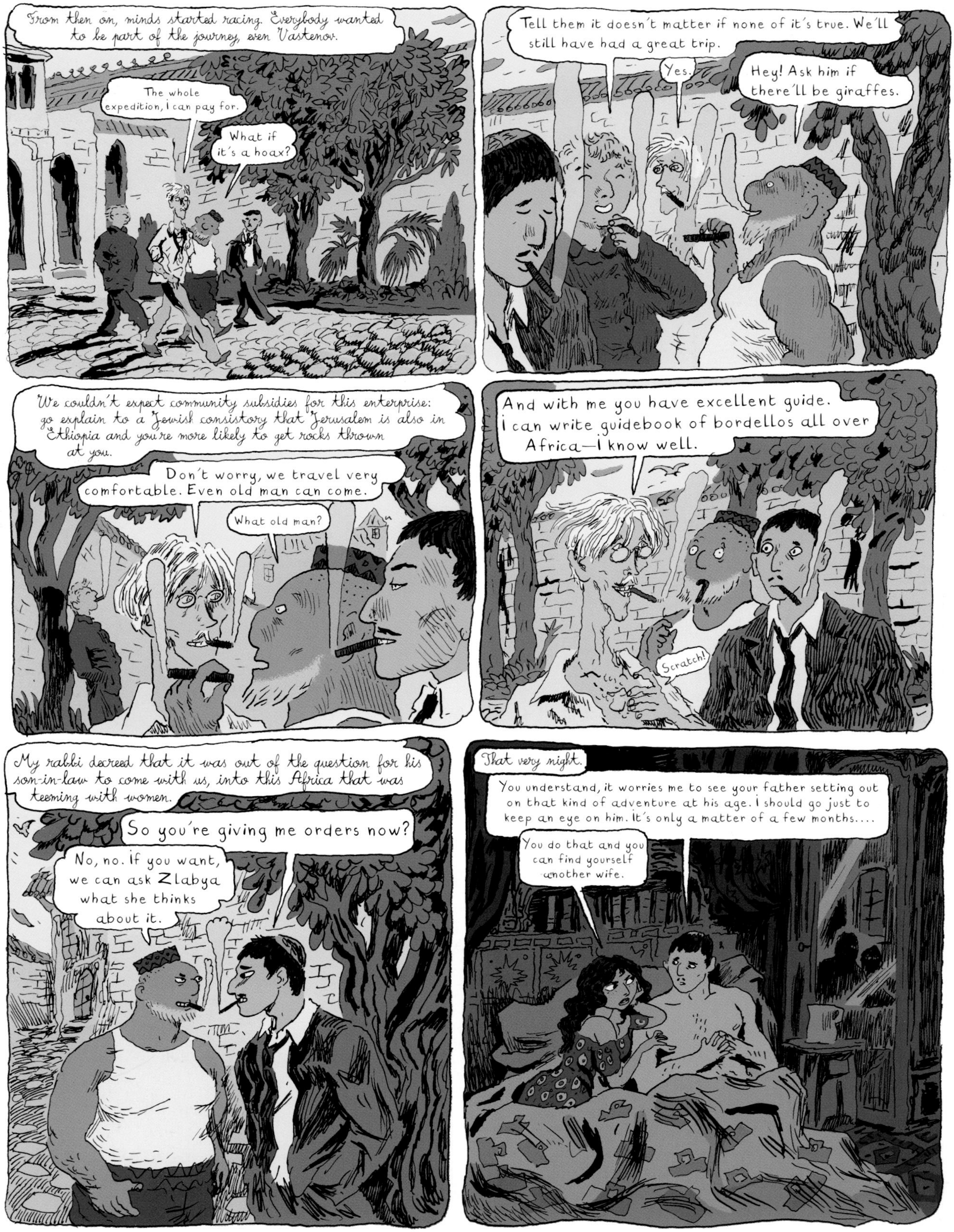
From then on, minds started racing. Everybody wanted to be part of the journey, even Vastenov.
The whole expedition, I can pay for.
What if it's a hoax?
Tell them it doesn't matter if none of it's true. We'll still have had a great trip.
Yes.
Hey! Ask him if there'll be giraffes.
We couldn't expect community subsidies for this enterprise: go explain to a Jewish consistory that Jerusalem is also in Ethiopia and you're more likely to get rocks thrown at you.
Don't worry, we travel very comfortable. Even old man can come.
What old man?
And with me you have excellent guide. I can write guidebook of bordellos all over Africa—I know well.
Scratch!
My rabbi decreed that it was out of the question for his son-in-law to come with us, into this Africa that was teeming with women.
So you're giving me orders now?
No, no. If you want, we can ask Zlabya what she thinks about it.
That very night.
You understand, it worries me to see your father setting out on that kind of adventure at his age. I should go just to keep an eye on him. It's only a matter of a few months....
You do that and you can find yourself another wife.

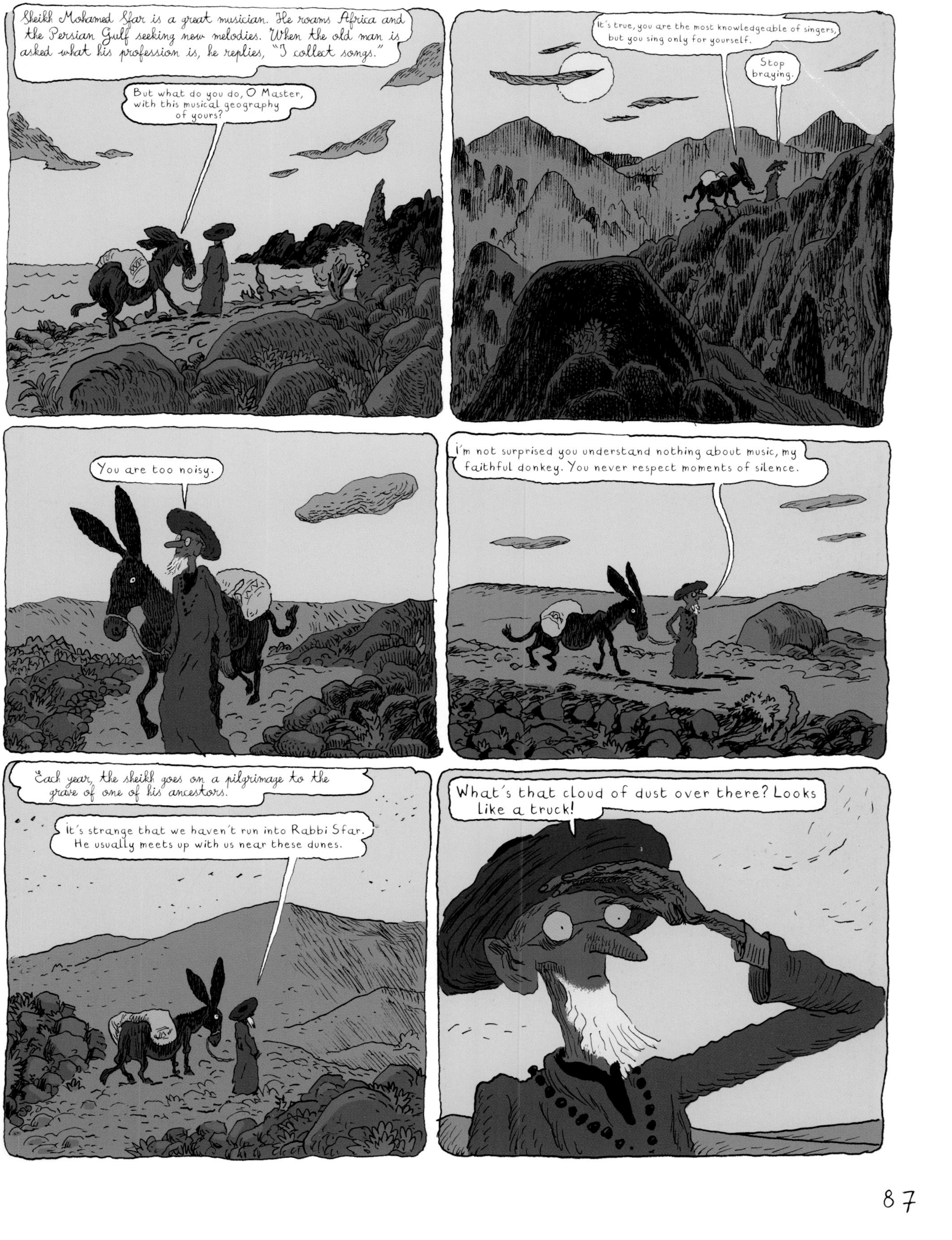
Sheikh Mohamed Sfar is a great musician. He roams Africa and the Persian Gulf seeking new melodies. When the old man is asked what his profession is, he replies, "I collect songs."
But what do you do, O Master, with this musical geography of yours?
It's true, you are the most knowledgeable of singers, but you sing only for yourself.
Stop braying.
You are too noisy.
I'm not surprised you understand nothing about music, my faithful donkey. You never respect moments of silence.
Each year, the sheikh goes on a pilgrimage to the grave of one of his ancestors.
It's strange that we haven't run into Rabbi Sfar. He usually meets up with us near these dunes.
What's that cloud of dust over there? Looks like a truck!

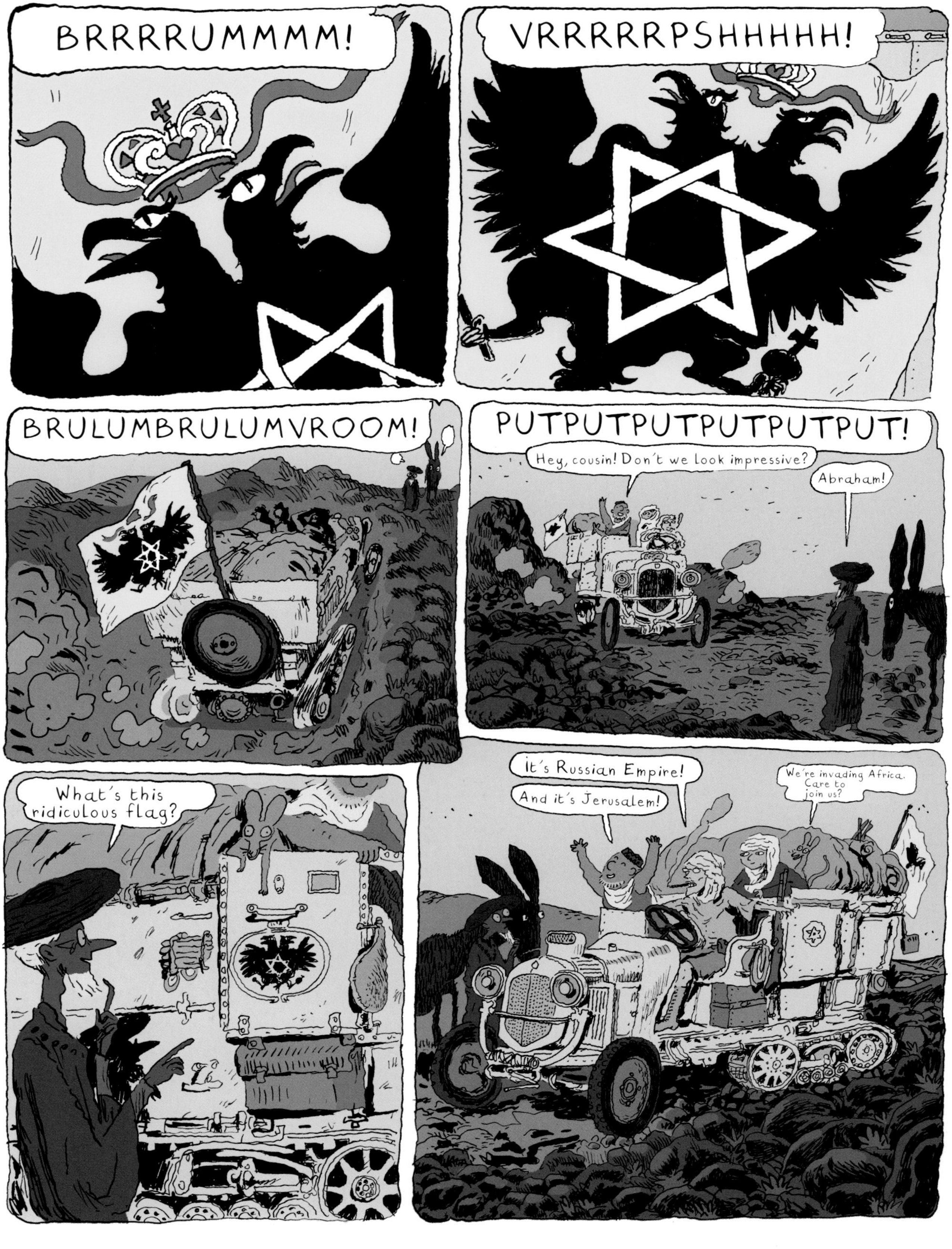
BRRRRUMMMM!
VRRRRRPSHHHHH!
BRULUMBRULUMVROOM!
PUTPUTPUTPUTPUTPUT!
Hey, cousin! Don't we look impressive?
Abraham!
What's this ridiculous flag?
It's Russian Empire!
And it's Jerusalem!
We're invading Africa. Care to join us?

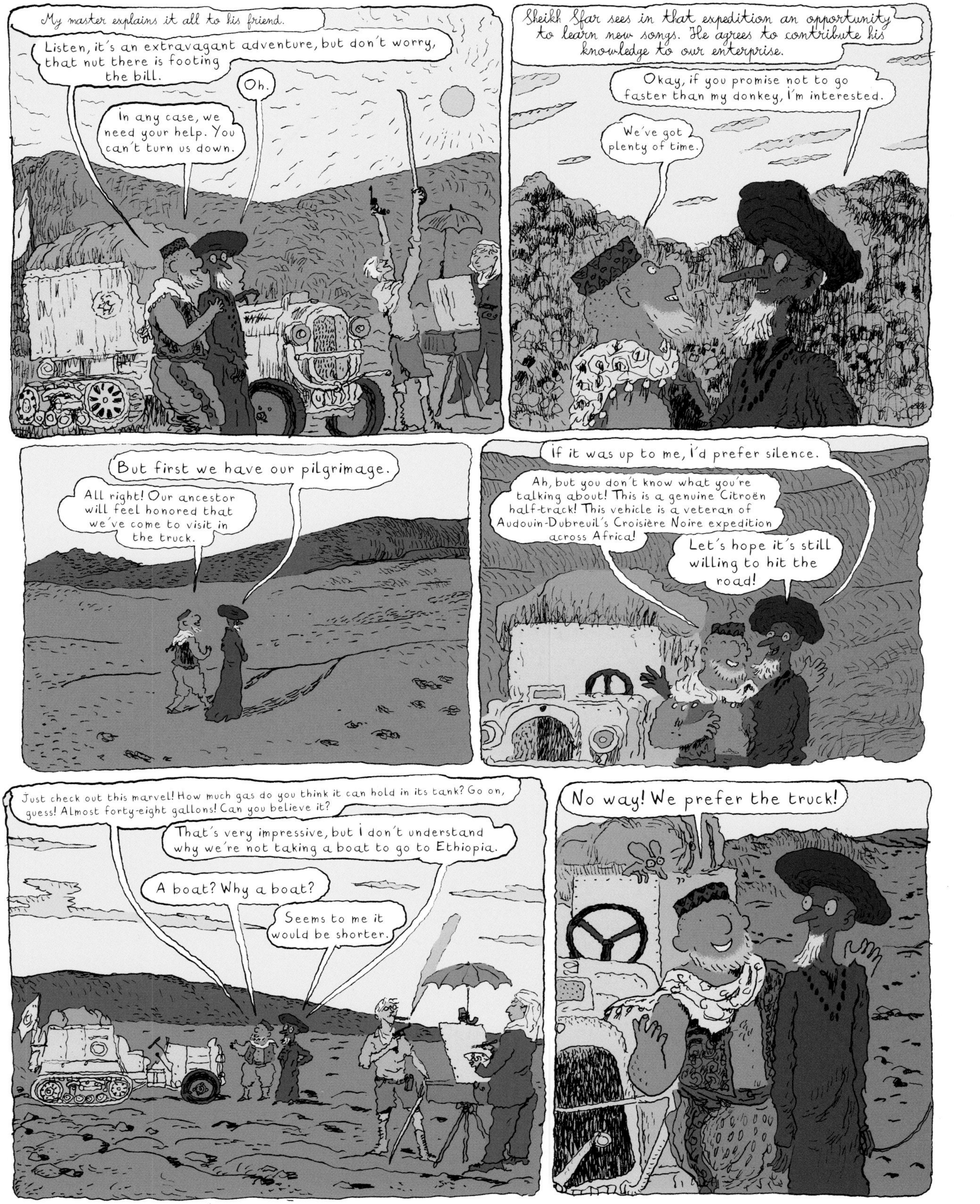
My master explains it all to his friend.
Listen, it's an extravagant adventure, but don't worry, that nut there is footing the bill.
Oh.
In any case, we need your help. You can't turn us down.
Sheikh Sfar sees in that expedition an opportunity to learn new songs. He agrees to contribute his knowledge to our enterprise.
Okay, if you promise not to go faster than my donkey, I'm interested.
We've got plenty of time.
But first we have our pilgrimage.
All right! Our ancestor will feel honored that we've come to visit in the truck.
If it was up to me, I'd prefer silence.
Ah, but you don't know what you're talking about! This is a genuine Citroën half-track! This vehicle is a veteran of Audouin-Dubreuil's Croisière Noire expedition across Africa!
Let's hope it's still willing to hit the road!
Just check out this marvel! How much gas do you think it can hold in its tank? Go on, guess! Almost forty-eight gallons! Can you believe it?
That's very impressive, but I don't understand why we're not taking a boat to go to Ethiopia.
A boat? Why a boat?
Seems to me it would be shorter.
No way! We prefer the truck!

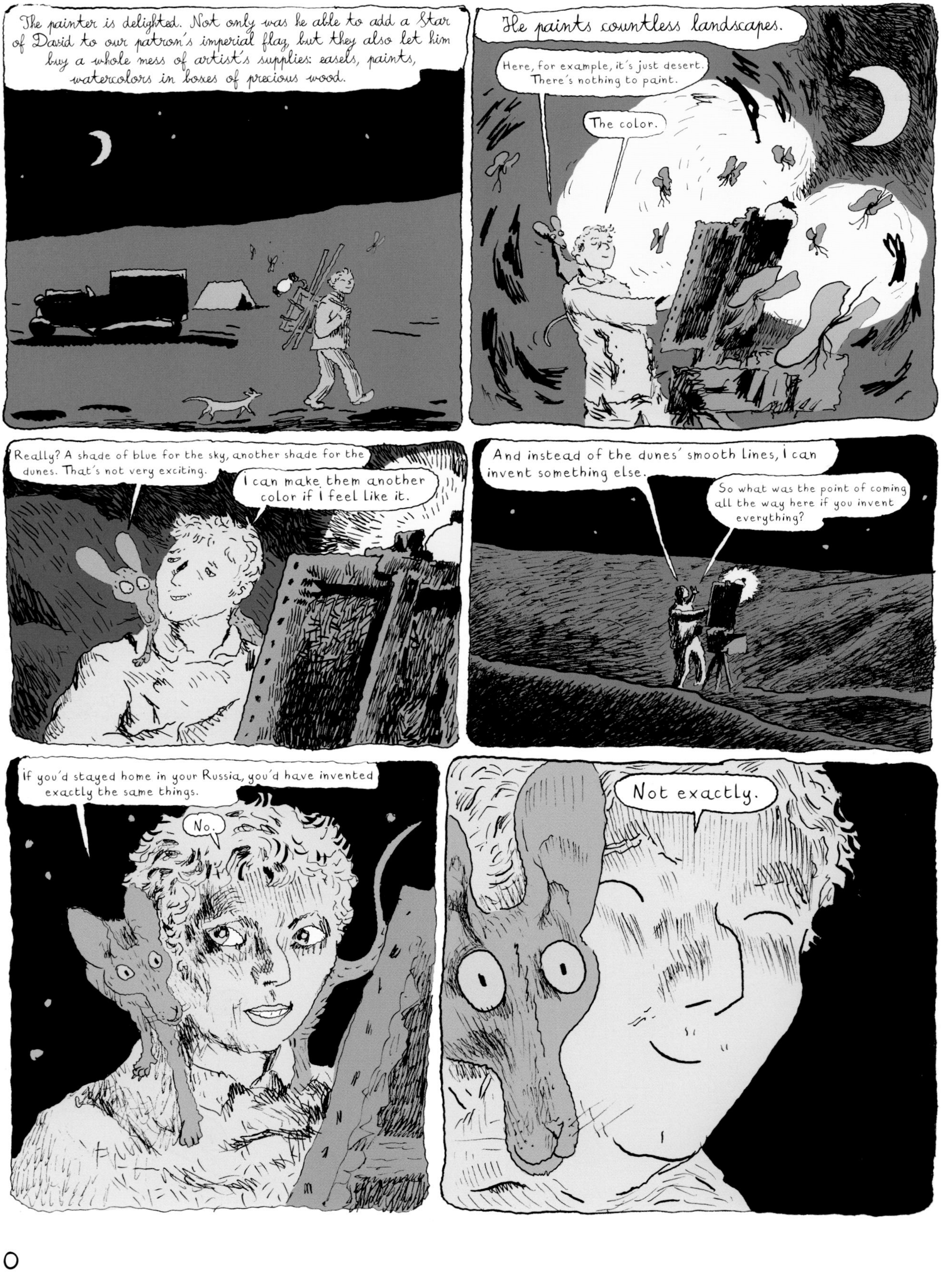
The painter is delighted. Not only was he able to add a Star of David to our patron's imperial flag, but they also let him buy a whole mess of artist's supplies: easels, paints, watercolors in boxes of precious wood.
He paints countless landscapes.
Here, for example, it's just desert. There's nothing to paint.
The color.
Really? A shade of blue for the sky, another shade for the dunes. That's not very exciting.
I can make them another color if I feel like it.
And instead of the dunes' smooth lines, I can invent something else.
So what was the point of coming all the way here if you invent everything?
If you'd stayed home in your Russia, you'd have invented exactly the same things.
No.
Not exactly.

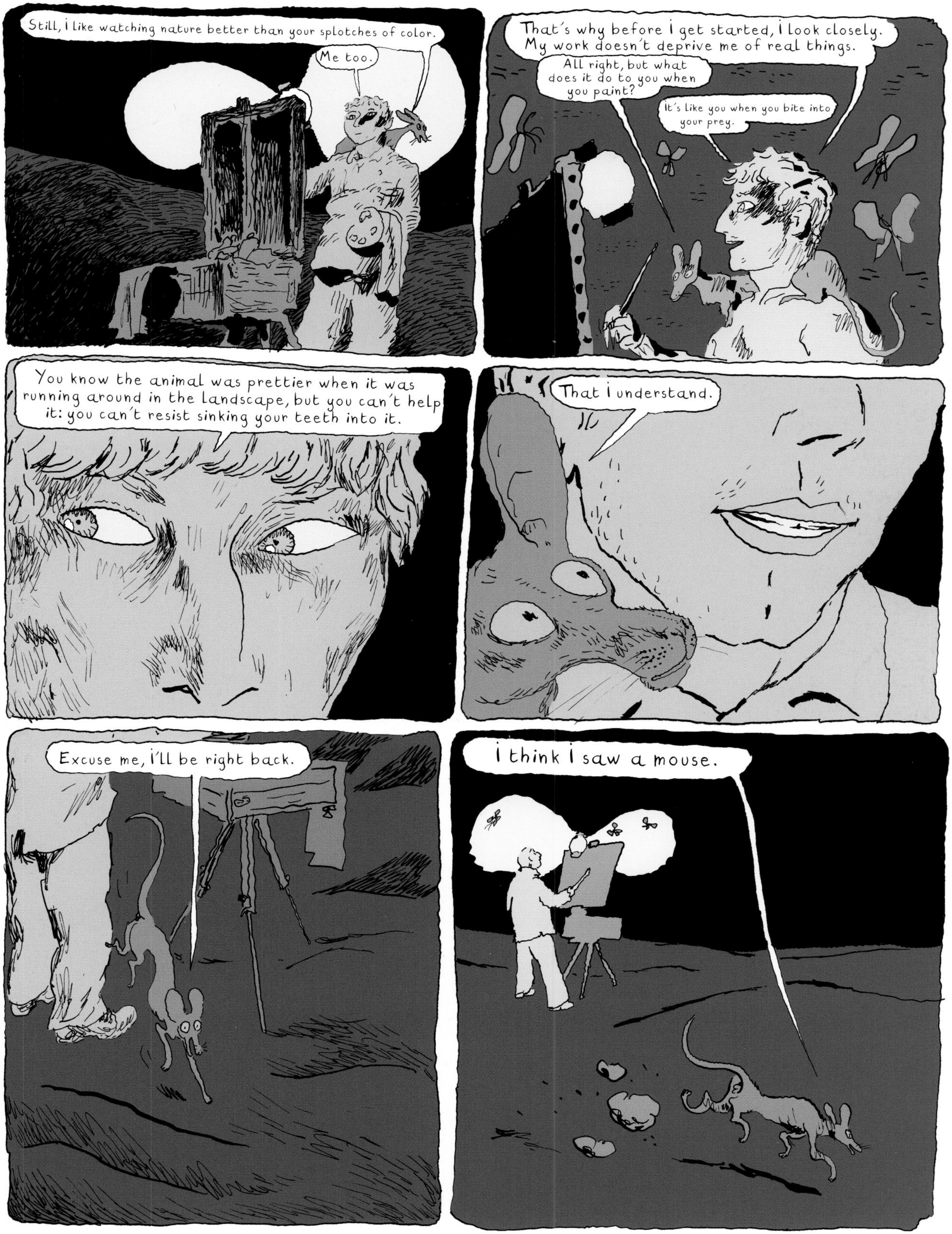

Still, I like watching nature better than your splotches of color.
Me too.
That's why before I get started, I look closely. My work doesn't deprive me of real things.
All right, but what does it do to you when you paint?
It's like you when you bite into your prey.
You know the animal was prettier when it was running around in the landscape, but you can't help it: you can't resist sinking your teeth into it.
That I understand.
Excuse me, I'll be right back.
I think I saw a mouse.

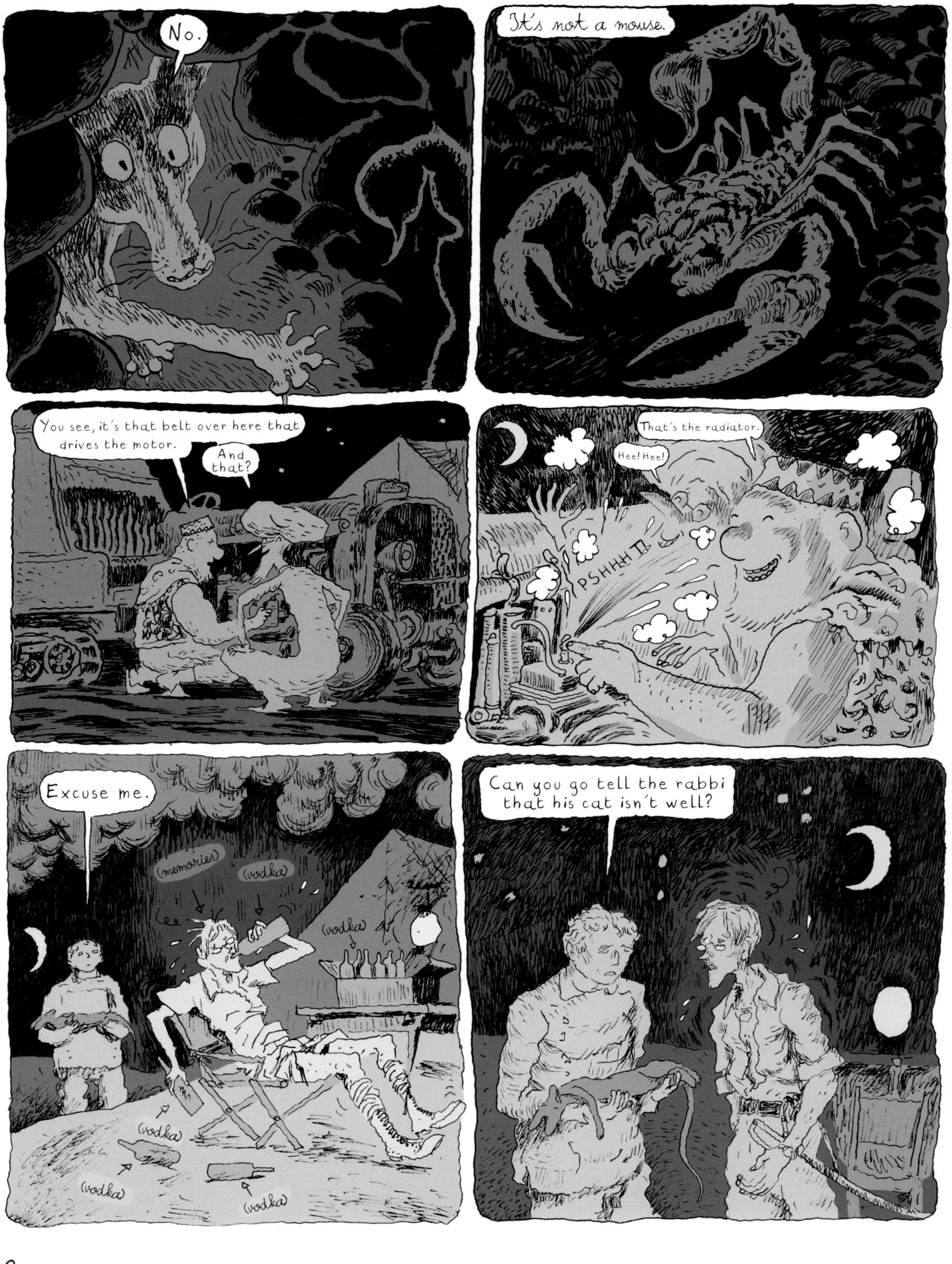
No.
It's not a mouse.
You see, it's that belt over here that drives the motor.
And that?
That's the radiator.
Hee! Hee!
PSHHHH
Excuse me.
(memories)
(vodka)
(vodka)
(vodka)
(vodka)
(vodka)
Can you go tell the rabbi that his cat isn't well?

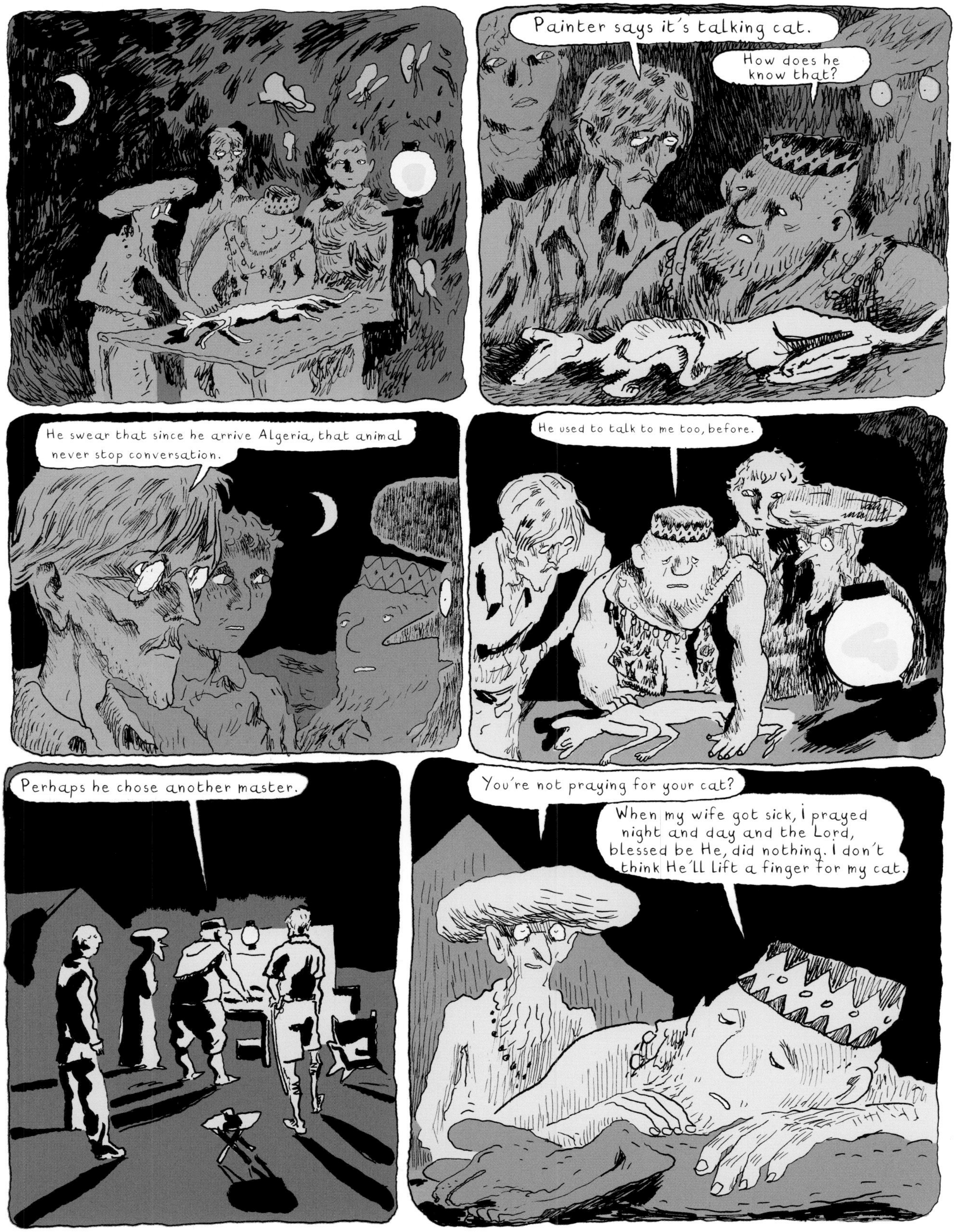
Painter says it's talking cat.
How does he know that?
He swear that since he arrive Algeria, that animal never stop conversation.
He used to talk to me too, before.
Perhaps he chose another master.
You're not praying for your cat?
When my wife got sick, I prayed night and day and the Lord, blessed be He, did nothing. I don't think He'll lift a finger for my cat.

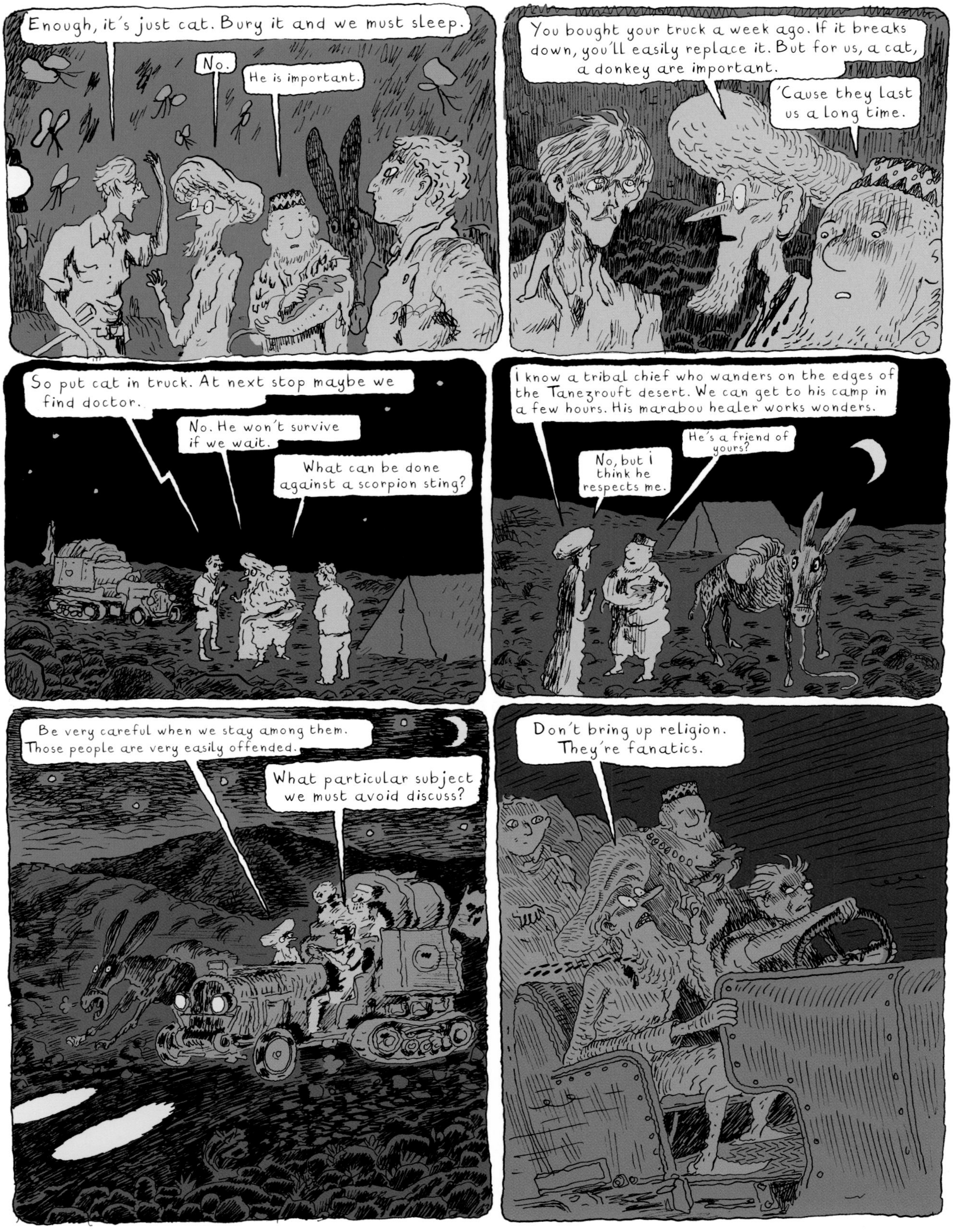

Enough, it's just cat. Bury it and we must sleep.
No.
He is important.
You bought your truck a week ago. If it breaks down, you'll easily replace it. But for us, a cat, a donkey are important.
'Cause they last us a long time.
So put cat in truck. At next stop maybe we find doctor.
No. He won't survive if we wait.
What can be done against a scorpion sting?
I know a tribal chief who wanders on the edges of the Tanezrouft desert. We can get to his camp in a few hours. His marabou healer works wonders.
He's a friend of yours?
No, but I think he respects me.
Be very careful when we stay among them. Those people are very easily offended.
What particular subject we must avoid discuss?
Don't bring up religion. They're fanatics.

My cat.

My cat who doesn't even have a name.

You're lucky my prince respects Sheikh Sfar. Otherwise I would never have dirtied my hands treating a cat. He'll live.

I thank you from the bottom of my heart, marabou. What is your name?

Professor Soliman.

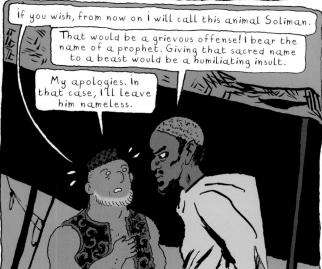

If you wish, from now on I will call this animal Soliman.

That would be a grievous offense! I bear the name of a prophet. Giving that sacred name to a beast would be a humiliating insult.

My apologies. In that case, I'll leave him nameless.

But I will pray for you often.

You are Jewish?

Yes.

Your prayers do not go far.

If you want to make me happy, embrace the faith of the Prophet Muhammad.

Listen, we pray to the same God.

That's what you say.

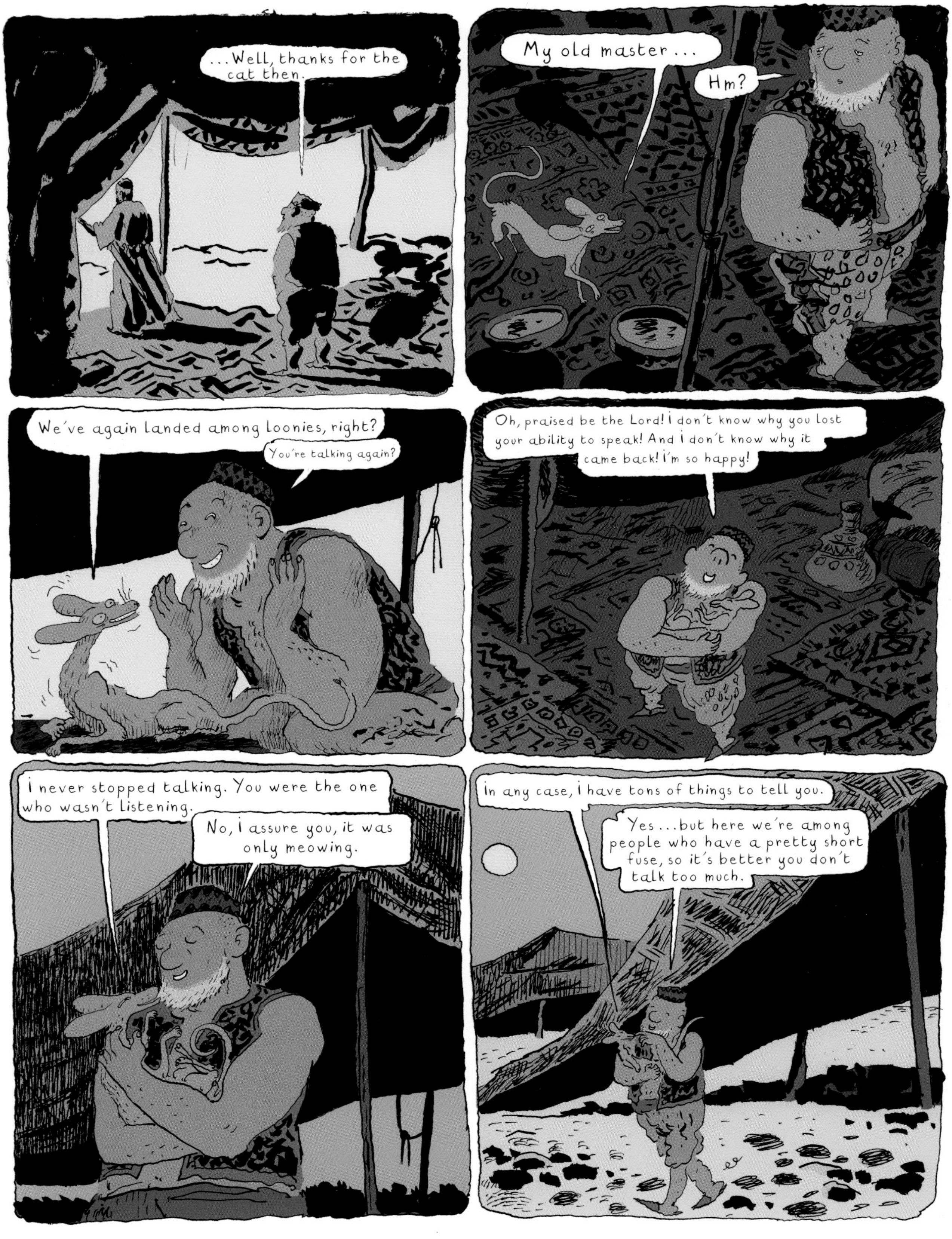
...Well, thanks for the cat then.
My old master...
Hm?
We've again landed among loonies, right?
You're talking again?
Oh, praised be the Lord! I don't know why you lost your ability to speak! And I don't know why it came back! I'm so happy!
I never stopped talking. You were the one who wasn't listening.
No, I assure you, it was only meowing.
In any case, I have tons of things to tell you.
Yes...but here we're among people who have a pretty short fuse, so it's better you don't talk too much.

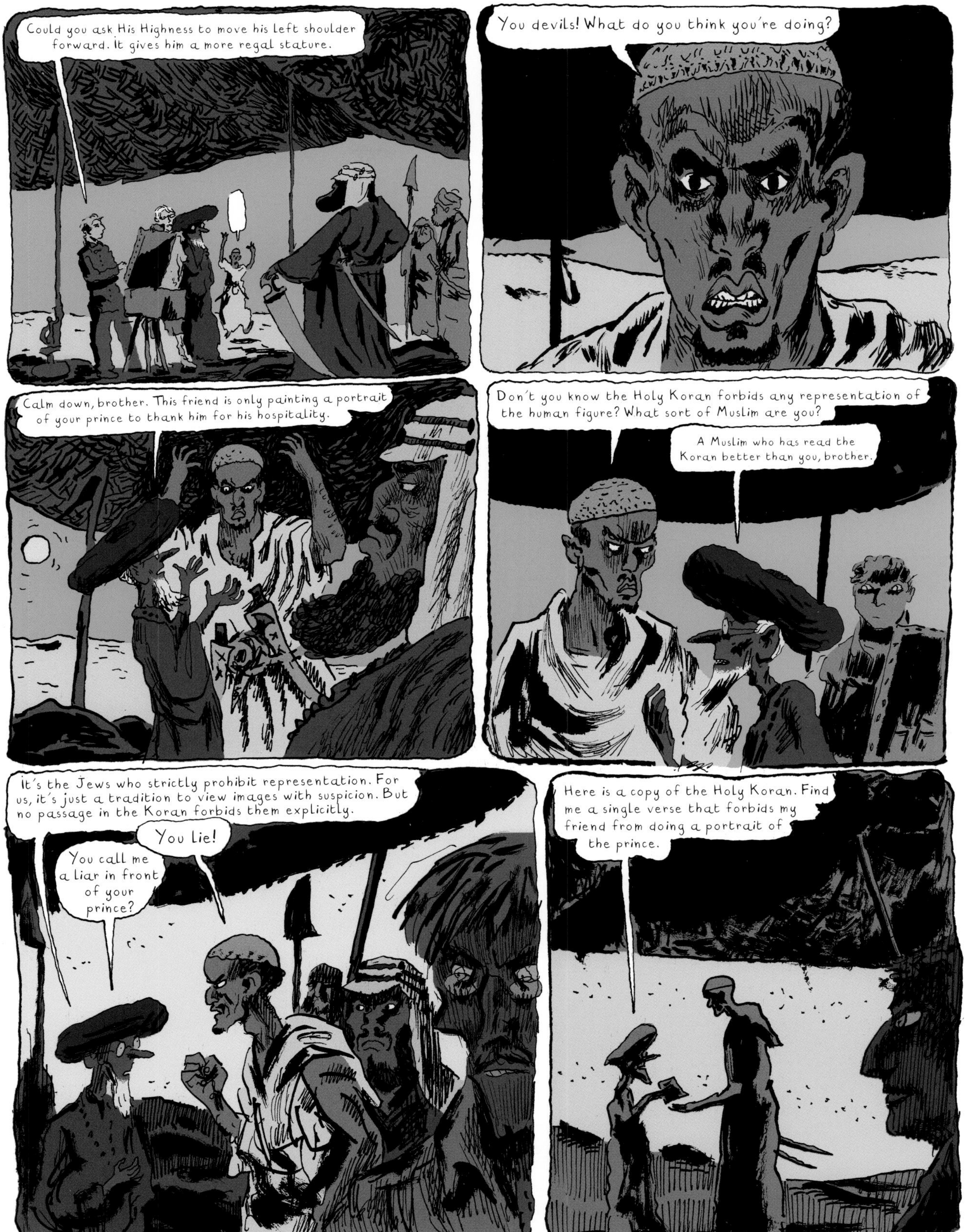

Could you ask His Highness to move his left shoulder forward. It gives him a more regal stature.
You devils! What do you think you're doing?
Calm down, brother. This friend is only painting a portrait of your prince to thank him for his hospitality.
Don't you know the Holy Koran forbids any representation of the human figure? What sort of Muslim are you?
A Muslim who has read the Koran better than you, brother.
It's the Jews who strictly prohibit representation. For us, it's just a tradition to view images with suspicion. But no passage in the Koran forbids them explicitly.
You lie!
You call me a liar in front of your prince?
Here is a copy of the Holy Koran. Find me a single verse that forbids my friend from doing a portrait of the prince.

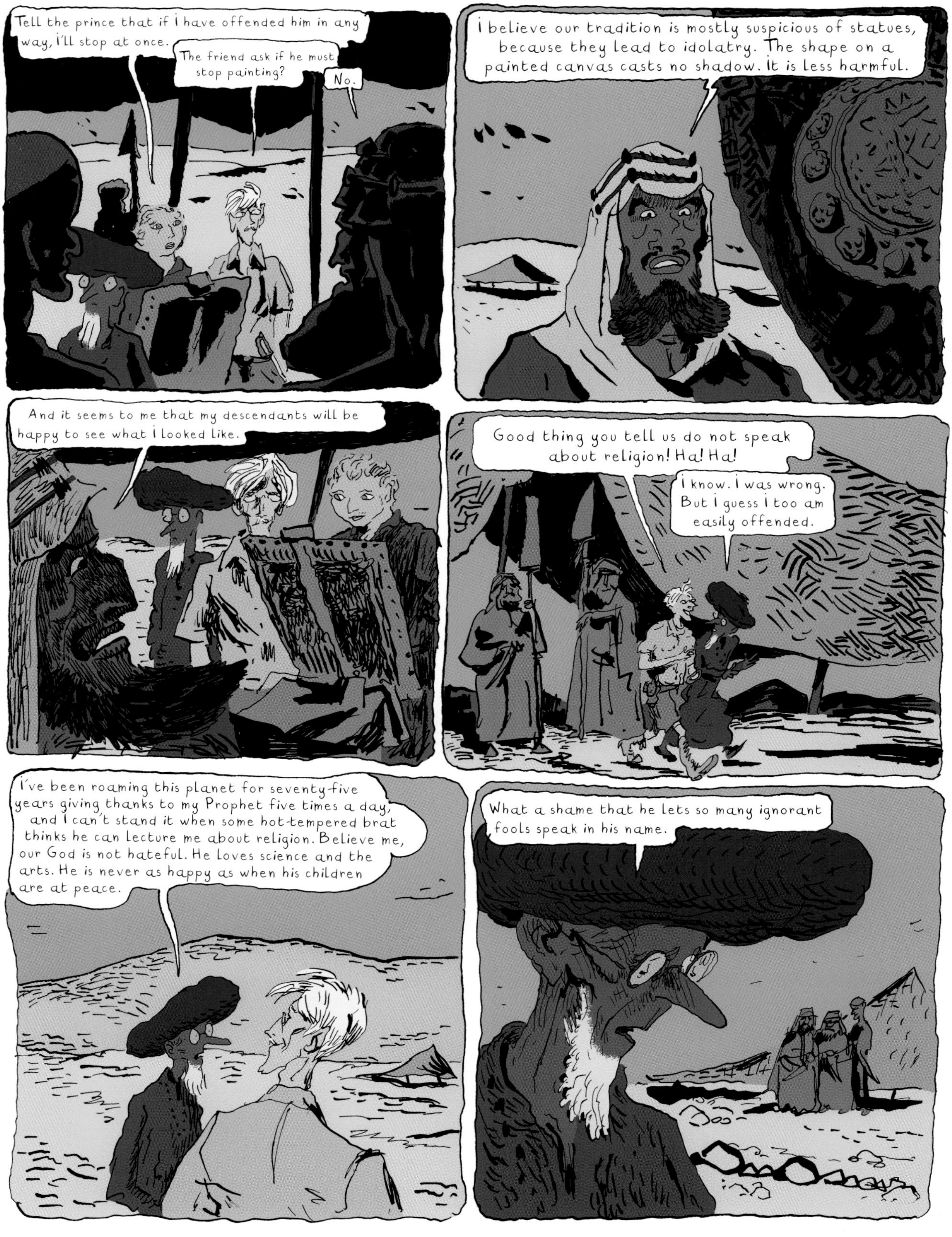
Tell the prince that if I have offended him in any way, I'll stop at once.
The friend ask if he must stop painting?
No.
I believe our tradition is mostly suspicious of statues, because they lead to idolatry. The shape on a painted canvas casts no shadow. It is less harmful.
And it seems to me that my descendants will be happy to see what I looked like.
Good thing you tell us do not speak about religion! Ha! Ha!
I know. I was wrong. But I guess I too am easily offended.
I've been roaming this planet for seventy-five years giving thanks to my Prophet five times a day, and I can't stand it when some hot-tempered brat thinks he can lecture me about religion. Believe me, our God is not hateful. He loves science and the arts. He is never as happy as when his children are at peace.
What a shame that he lets so many ignorant fools speak in his name.

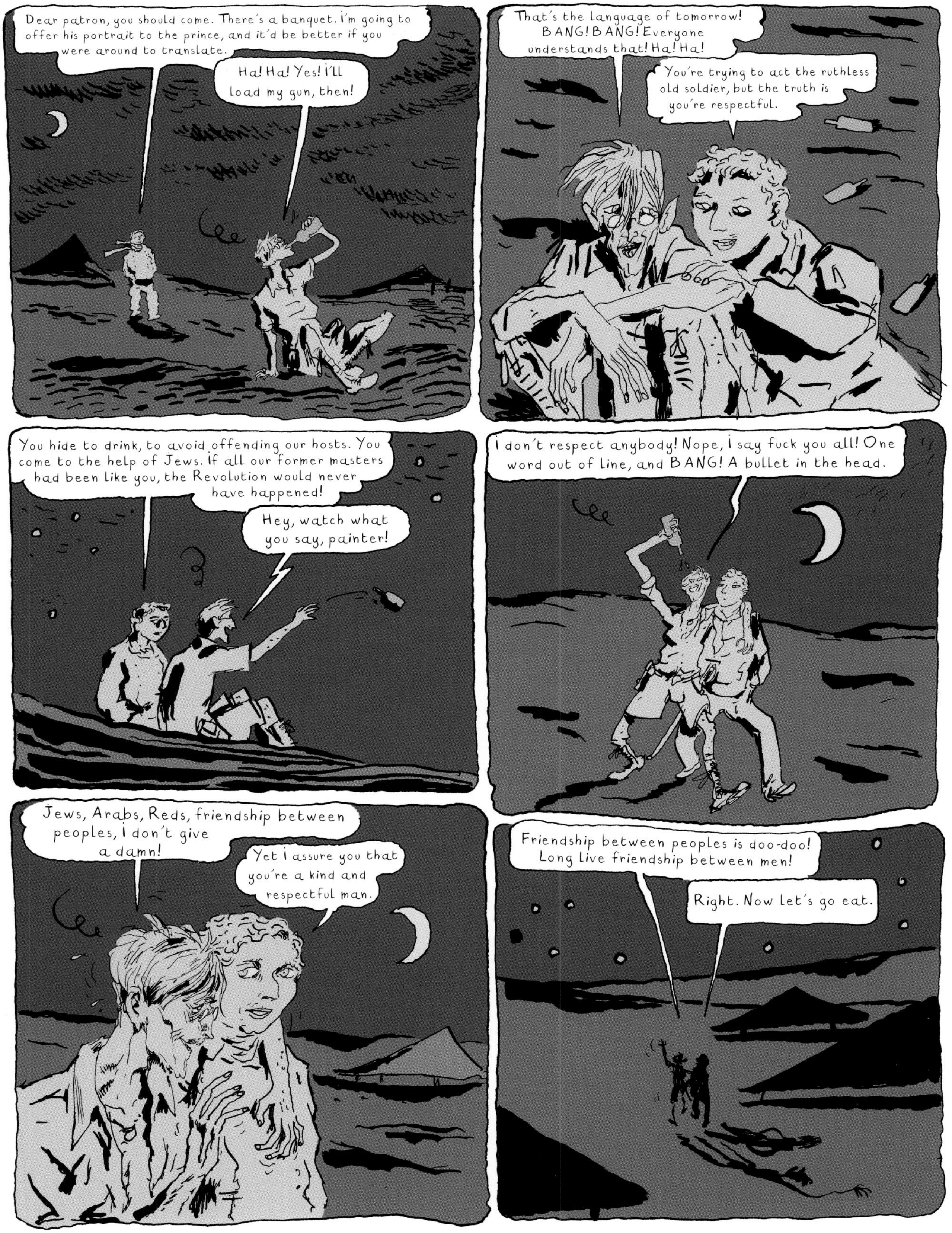

Dear patron, you should come. There's a banquet. I'm going to offer his portrait to the prince, and it'd be better if you were around to translate.
Ha! Ha! Yes! I'll load my gun, then!
That's the language of tomorrow! BANG! BANG! Everyone understands that! Ha! Ha!
You're trying to act the ruthless old soldier, but the truth is you're respectful.
You hide to drink, to avoid offending our hosts. You come to the help of Jews. If all our former masters had been like you, the Revolution would never have happened!
Hey, watch what you say, painter!
I don't respect anybody! Nope, I say fuck you all! One word out of line, and BANG! A bullet in the head.
Jews, Arabs, Reds, friendship between peoples, I don't give a damn!
Yet I assure you that you're a kind and respectful man.
Friendship between peoples is doo-doo! Long live friendship between men!
Right. Now let's go eat.

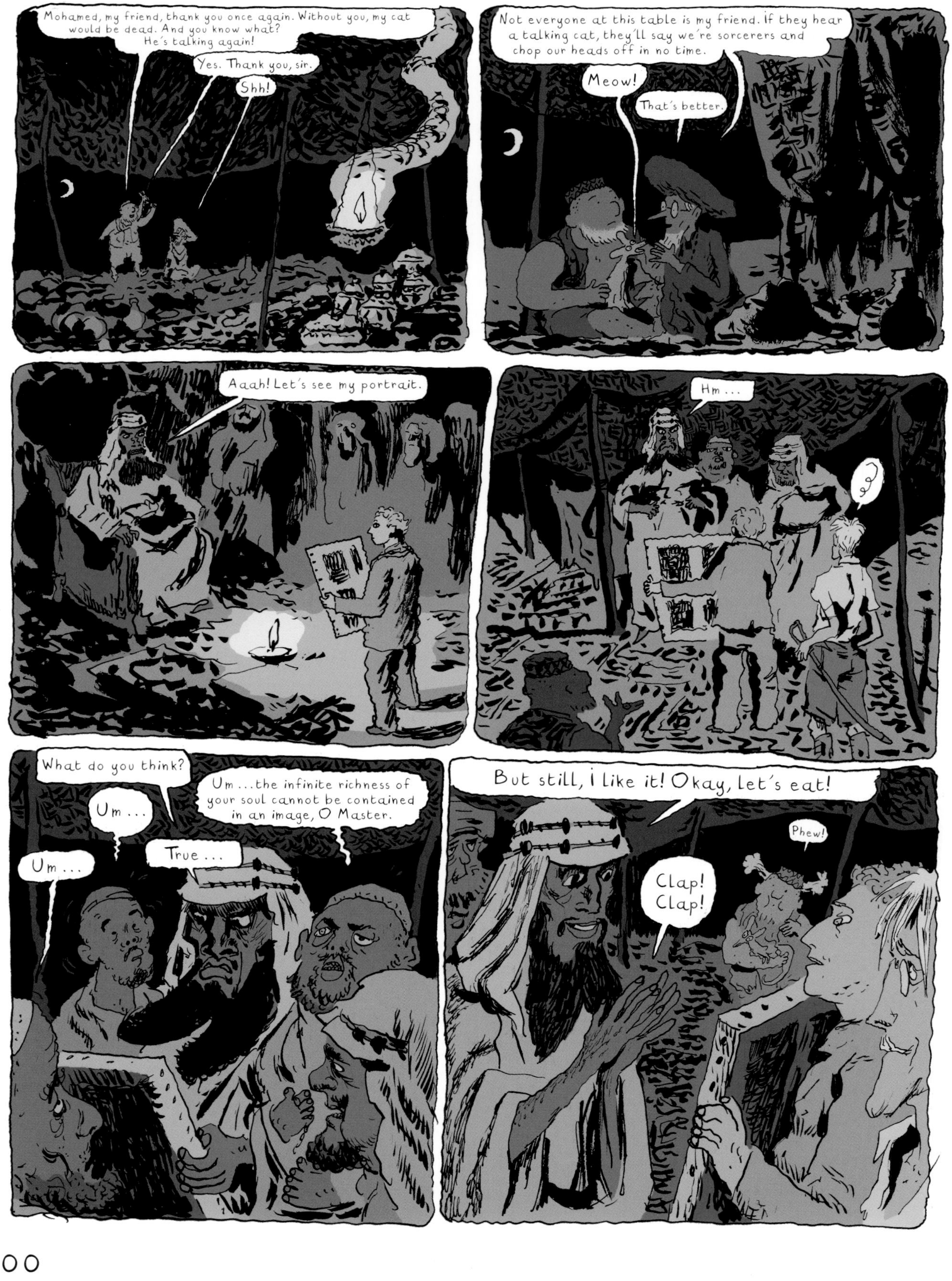
Mohamed, my friend, thank you once again. Without you, my cat would be dead. And you know what? He's talking again!
Yes. Thank you, sir.
Shh!
Not everyone at this table is my friend. If they hear a talking cat, they'll say we're sorcerers and chop our heads off in no time.
Meow!
That's better.
Aaah! Let's see my portrait.
Hm...
What do you think?
Um...
Um...
Um...the infinite richness of your soul cannot be contained in an image, O Master.
True...
But still, I like it! Okay, let's eat!
Clap! Clap!
Phew!

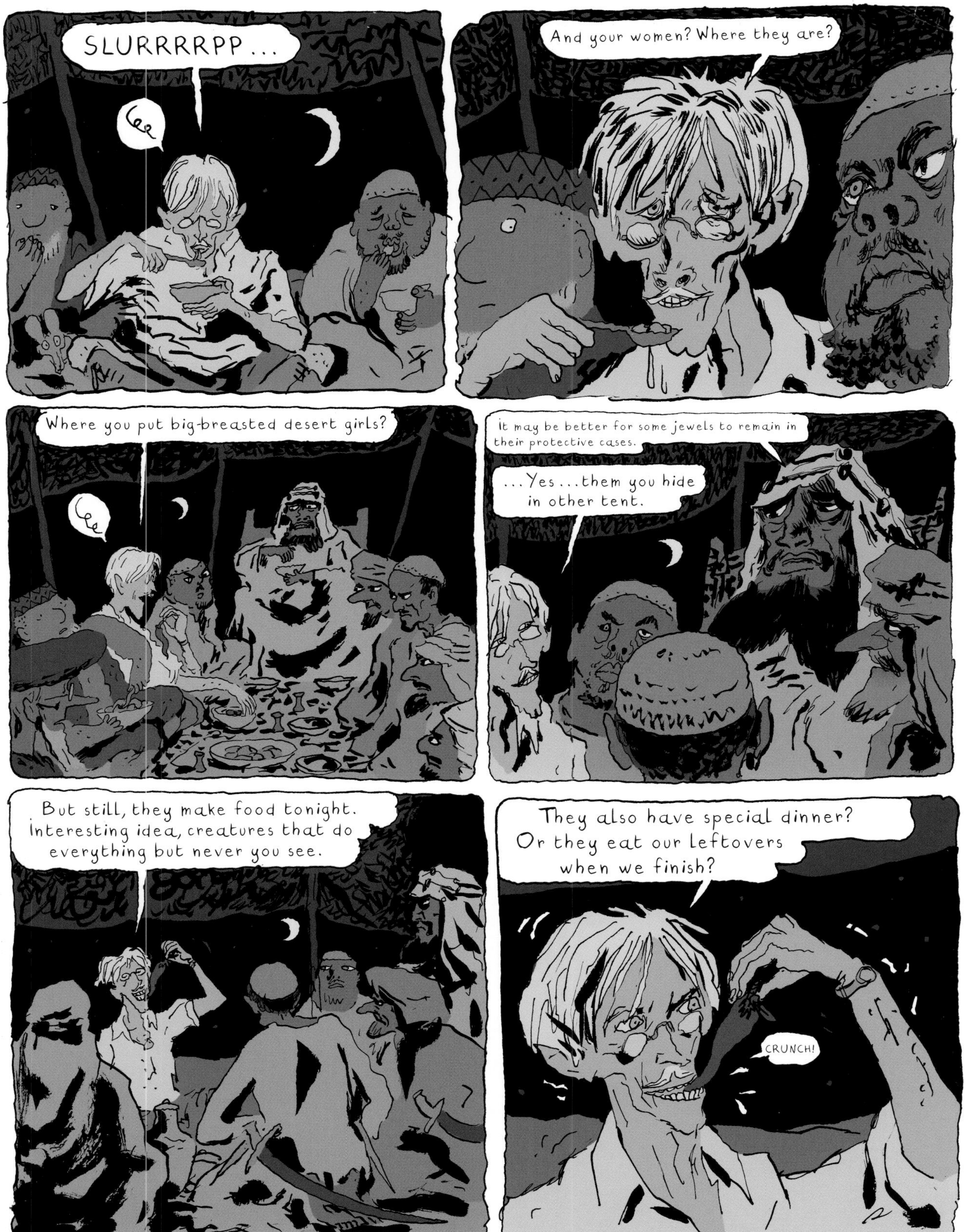

SLURRRRPP...
And your women? Where they are?
Where you put big-breasted desert girls?
It may be better for some jewels to remain in their protective cases.
...Yes...them you hide in other tent.
But still, they make food tonight. Interesting idea, creatures that do everything but never you see.
They also have special dinner? Or they eat our leftovers when we finish?
CRUNCH!

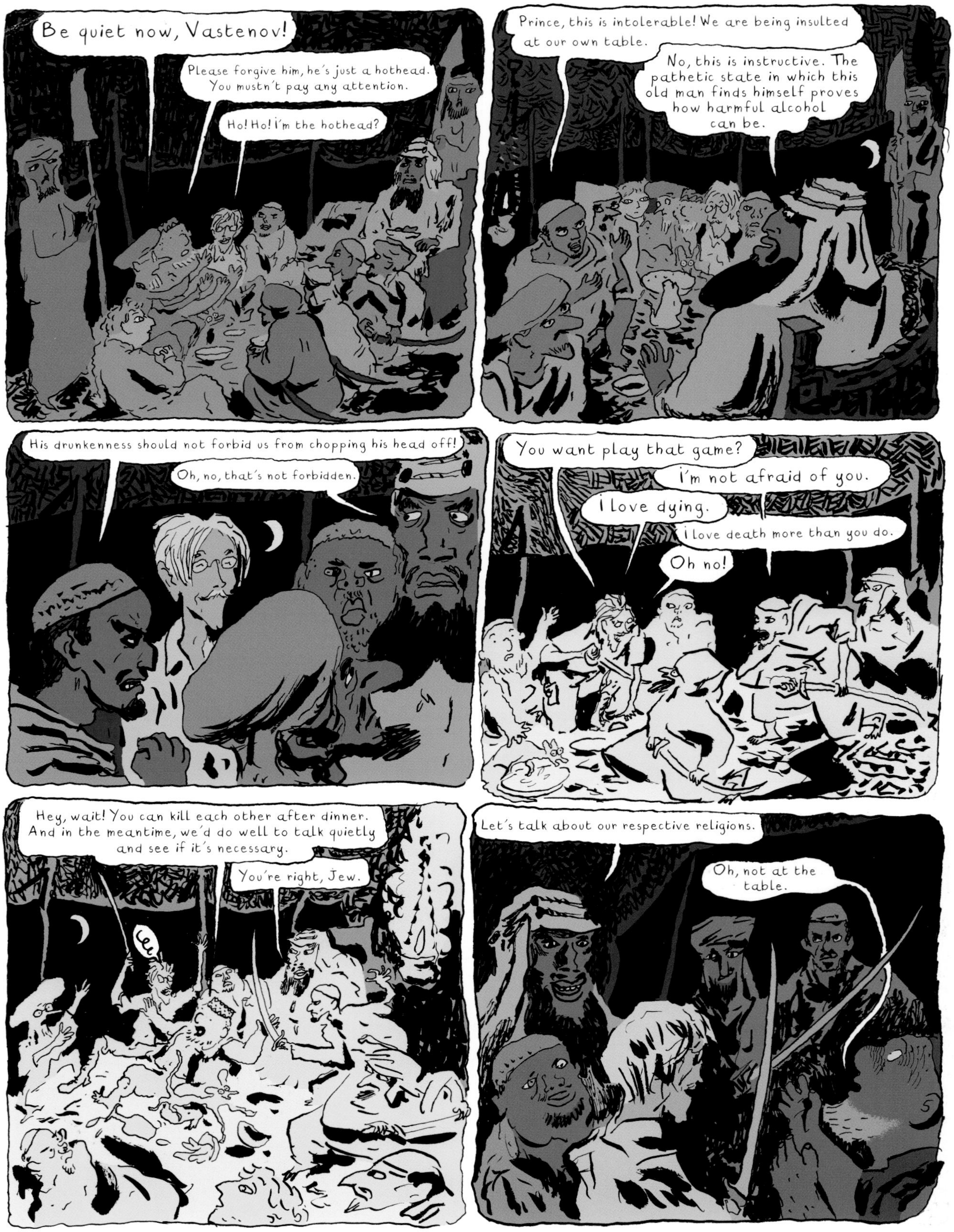

Be quiet now, Vastenov!
Please forgive him, he's just a hothead. You mustn't pay any attention.
Ho! Ho! I'm the hothead?
Prince, this is intolerable! We are being insulted at our own table.
No, this is instructive. The pathetic state in which this old man finds himself proves how harmful alcohol can be.
His drunkenness should not forbid us from chopping his head off!
Oh, no, that's not forbidden.
You want play that game?
I'm not afraid of you.
I love dying.
I love death more than you do.
Oh no!
Hey, wait! You can kill each other after dinner. And in the meantime, we'd do well to talk quietly and see if it's necessary.
You're right, Jew.
Let's talk about our respective religions.
Oh, not at the table.

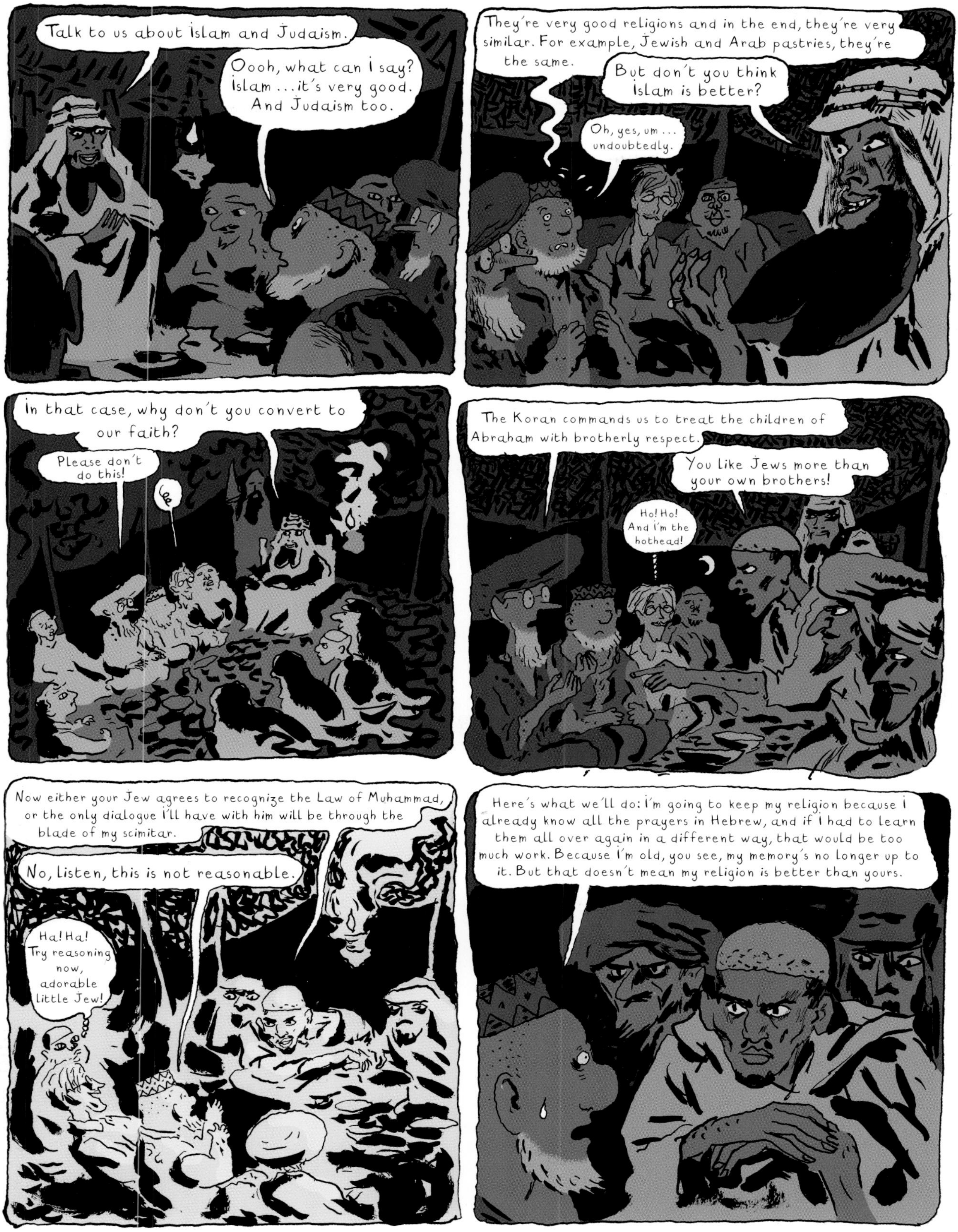

Talk to us about Islam and Judaism.
Oooh, what can I say? Islam ... it's very good. And Judaism too.
They're very good religions and in the end, they're very similar. For example, Jewish and Arab pastries, they're the same.
But don't you think Islam is better?
Oh, yes, um ... undoubtedly.
In that case, why don't you convert to our faith?
Please don't do this!
The Koran commands us to treat the children of Abraham with brotherly respect.
You like Jews more than your own brothers!
Ho! Ho! And I'm the hothead!
Now either your Jew agrees to recognize the Law of Muhammad, or the only dialogue I'll have with him will be through the blade of my scimitar.
No, listen, this is not reasonable.
Ha! Ha! Try reasoning now, adorable little Jew!
Here's what we'll do: I'm going to keep my religion because I already know all the prayers in Hebrew, and if I had to learn them all over again in a different way, that would be too much work. Because I'm old, you see, my memory's no longer up to it. But that doesn't mean my religion is better than yours.

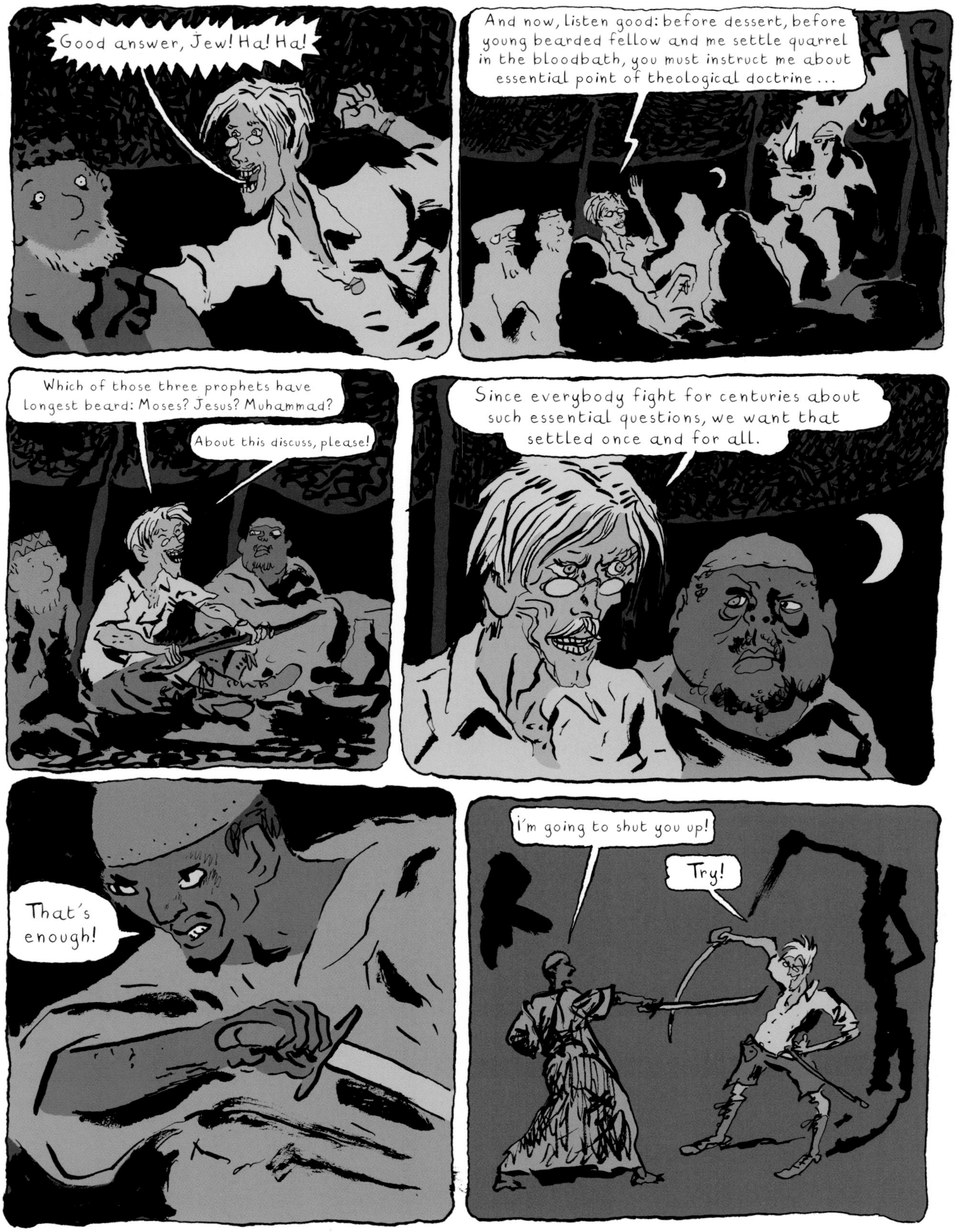
Good answer, Jew! Ha! Ha!
And now, listen good: before dessert, before young bearded fellow and me settle quarrel in the bloodbath, you must instruct me about essential point of theological doctrine . . .
Which of those three prophets have longest beard: Moses? Jesus? Muhammad?
About this discuss, please!
Since everybody fight for centuries about such essential questions, we want that settled once and for all.
That's enough!
I'm going to shut you up!
Try!

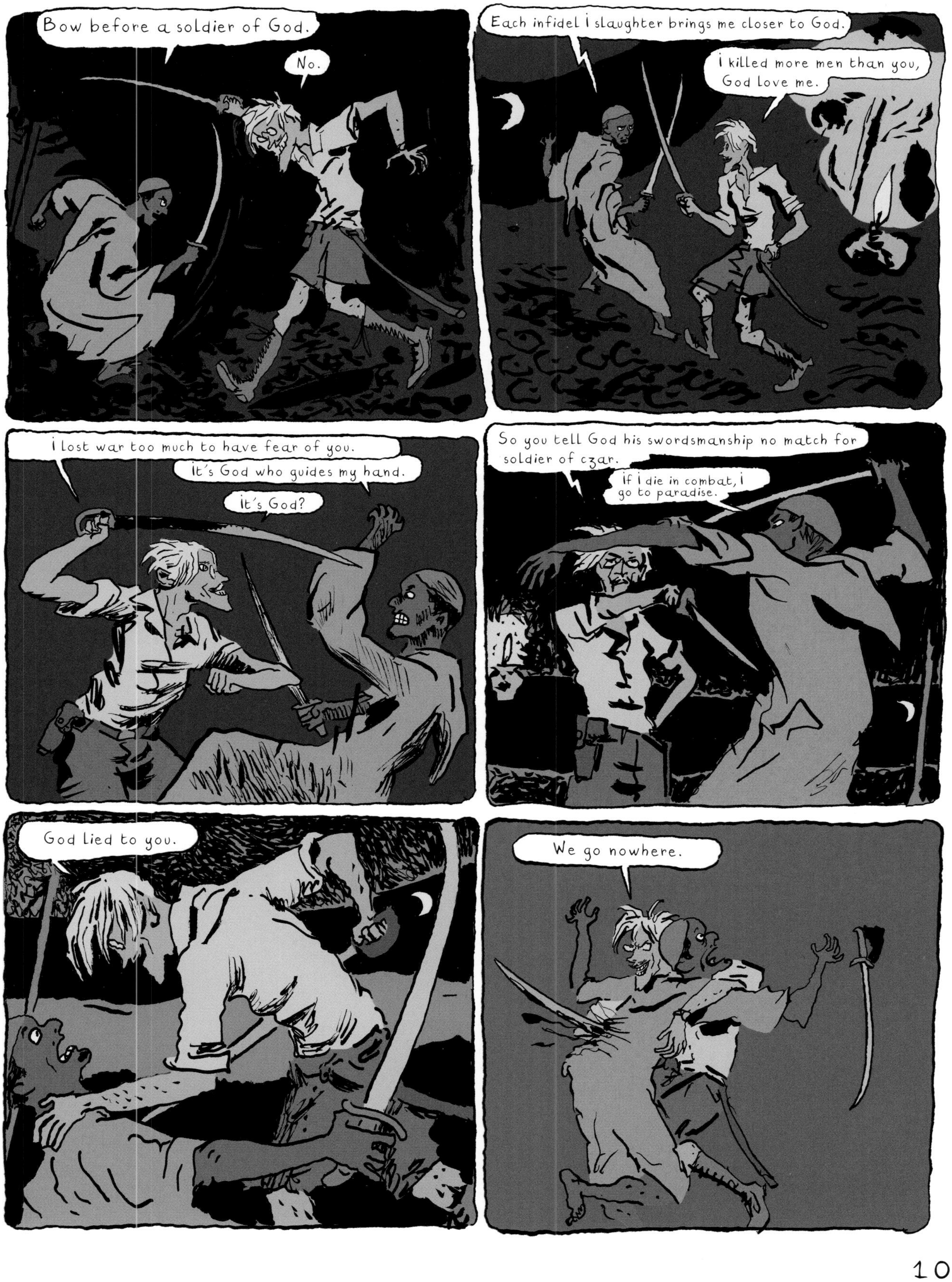
Bow before a soldier of God.
No.
Each infidel I slaughter brings me closer to God.
I killed more men than you, God love me.
I lost war too much to have fear of you.
It's God who guides my hand.
It's God?
So you tell God his swordsmanship no match for soldier of czar.
If I die in combat, I go to paradise.
God lied to you.
We go nowhere.

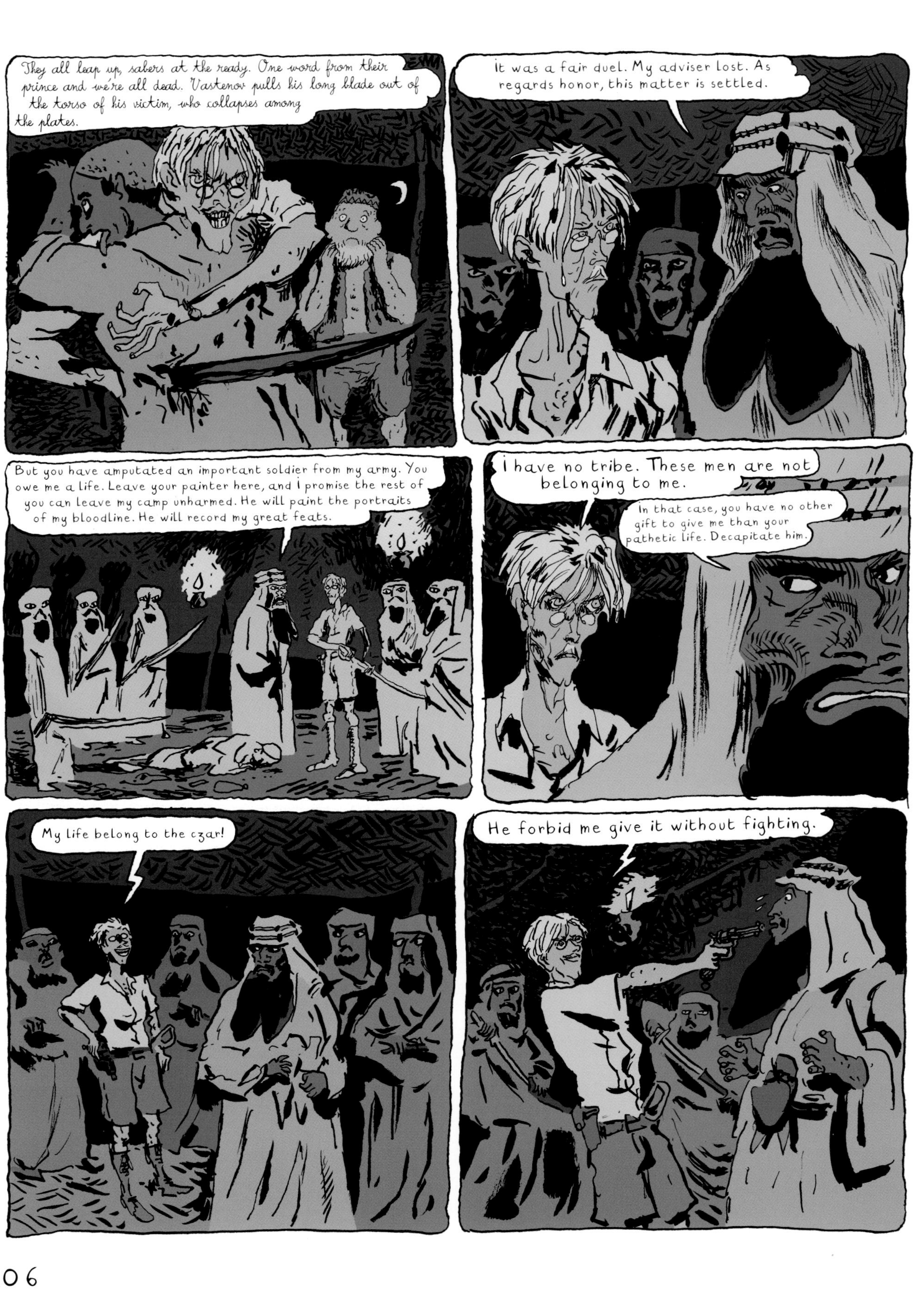
They all leap up, sabers at the ready. One word from their prince and we're all dead. Vastenov pulls his long blade out of the torso of his victim, who collapses among the plates.
It was a fair duel. My adviser lost. As regards honor, this matter is settled.
But you have amputated an important soldier from my army. You owe me a life. Leave your painter here, and I promise the rest of you can leave my camp unharmed. He will paint the portraits of my bloodline. He will record my great feats.
I have no tribe. These men are not belonging to me.
In that case, you have no other gift to give me than your pathetic life. Decapitate him.
My life belong to the czar!
He forbid me give it without fighting.

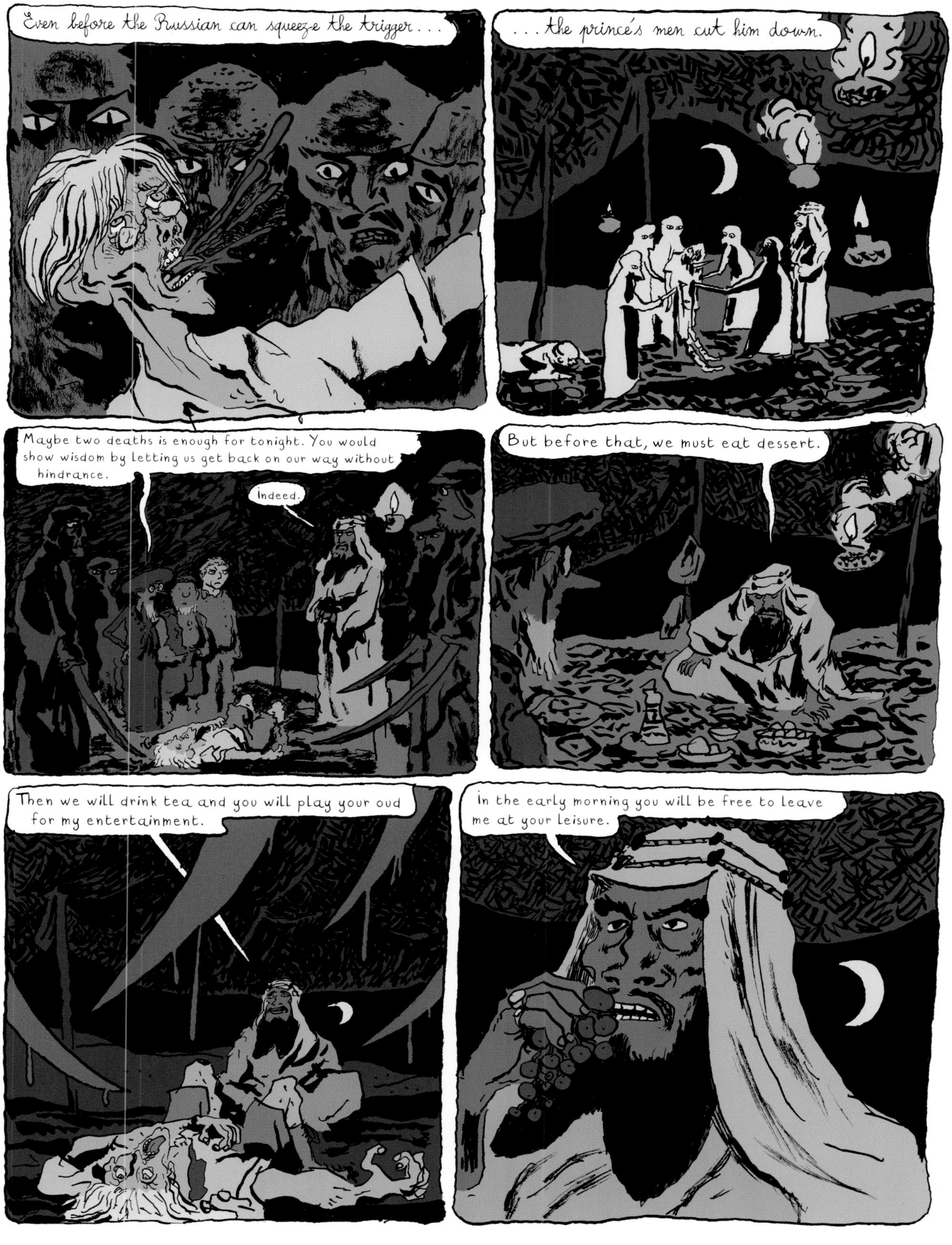

Even before the Russian can squeeze the trigger . . .
. . . the prince's men cut him down.
Maybe two deaths is enough for tonight. You would show wisdom by letting us get back on our way without hindrance.
Indeed.
But before that, we must eat dessert.
Then we will drink tea and you will play your oud for my entertainment.
In the early morning you will be free to leave me at your leisure.

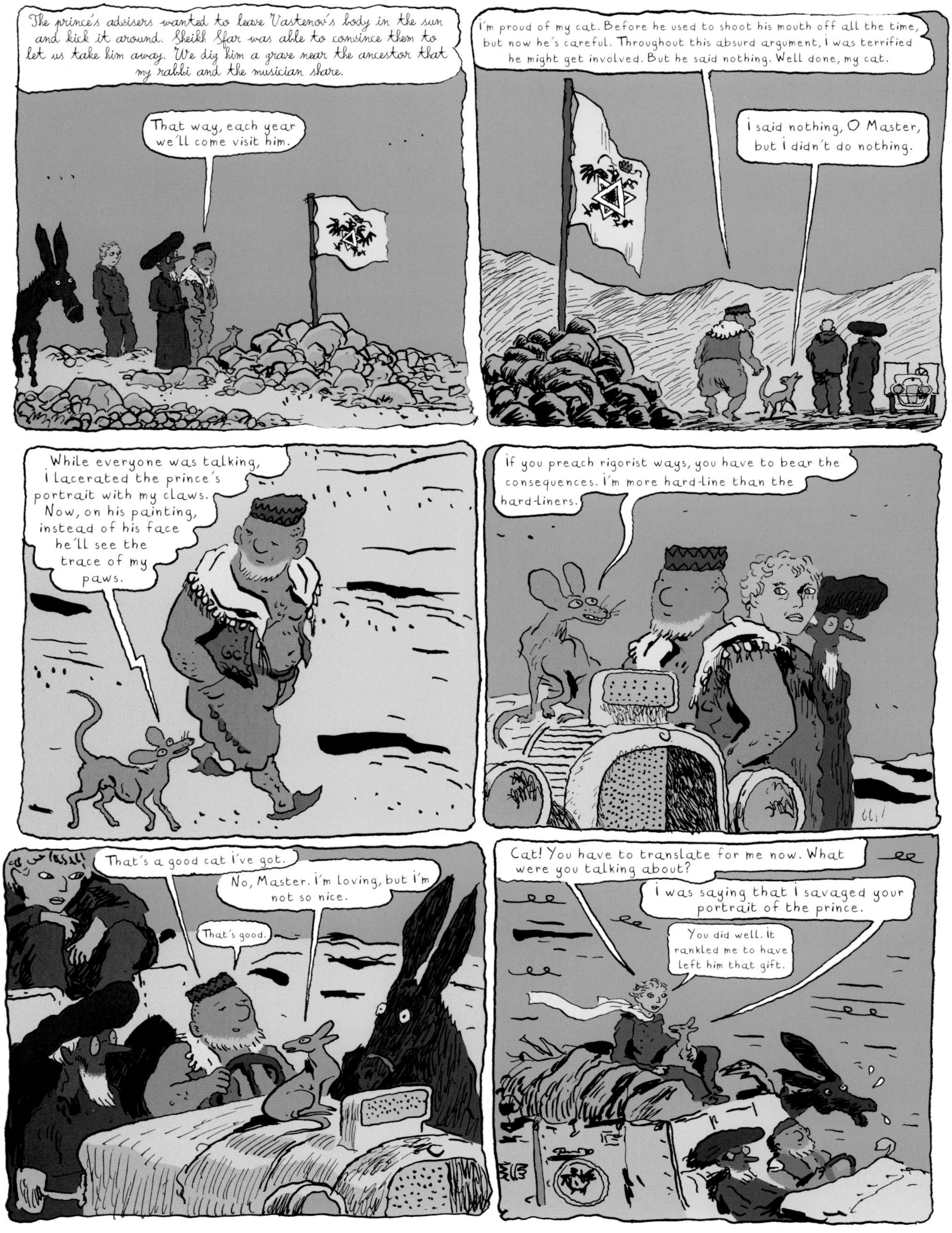
The prince's advisers wanted to leave Vastenov's body in the sun and kick it around. Sheikh Sfar was able to convince them to let us take him away. We dig him a grave near the ancestor that my rabbi and the musician share.
That way, each year we'll come visit him.
...
I'm proud of my cat. Before he used to shoot his mouth off all the time, but now he's careful. Throughout this absurd argument, I was terrified he might get involved. But he said nothing. Well done, my cat.
I said nothing, O Master, but I didn't do nothing.
While everyone was talking, I lacerated the prince's portrait with my claws. Now, on his painting, instead of his face he'll see the trace of my paws.
If you preach rigorist ways, you have to bear the consequences. I'm more hard-line than the hard-liners.
That's a good cat I've got.
No, Master. I'm loving, but I'm not so nice.
That's good.
Cat! You have to translate for me now. What were you talking about?
I was saying that I savaged your portrait of the prince.
You did well. It rankled me to have left him that gift.

Now we just need to cross the entire continent to find the painter's Jerusalem.

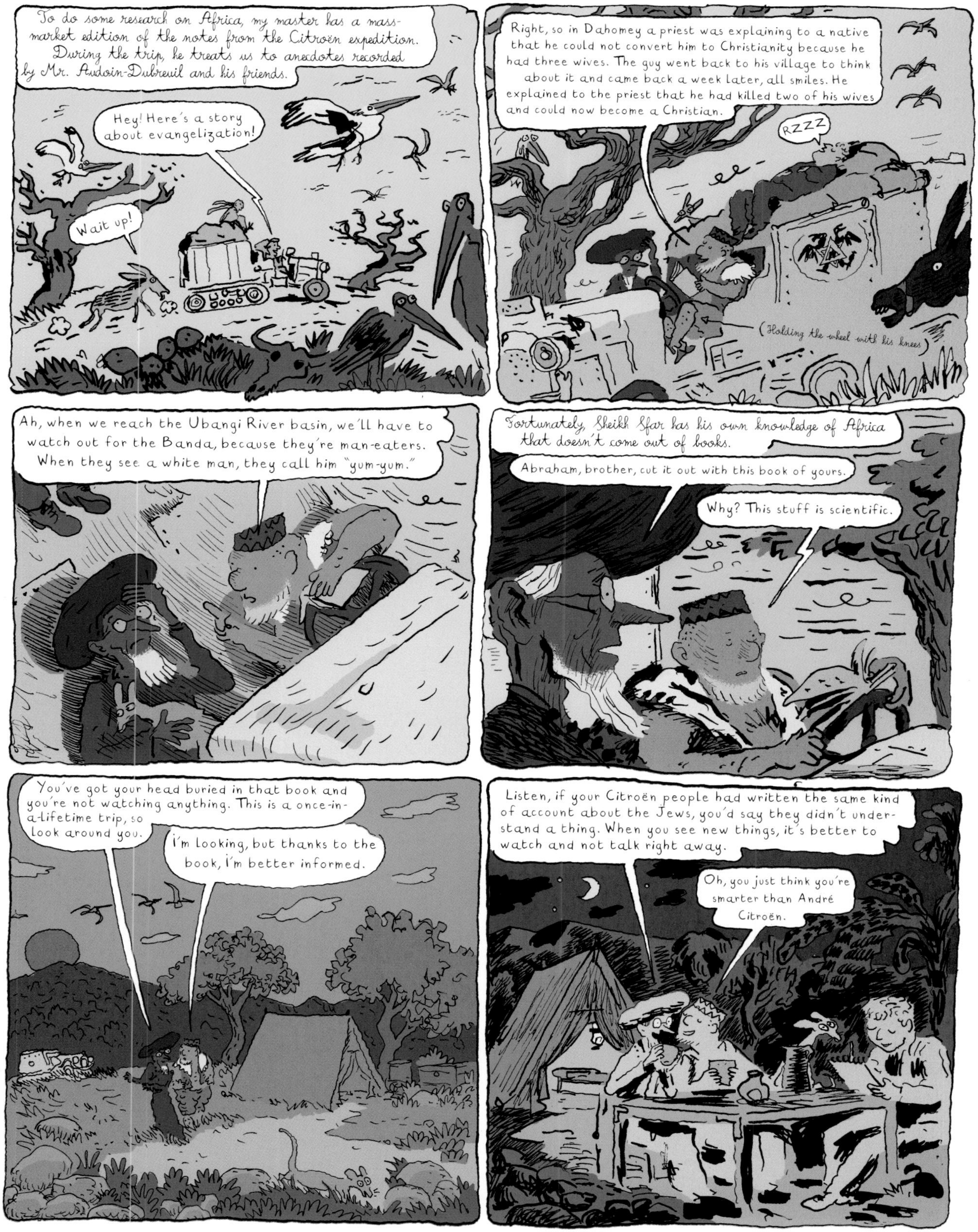
To do some research on Africa, my master has a mass-market edition of the notes from the Citroën expedition. During the trip, he treats us to anecdotes recorded by Mr. Audoin-Dubreuil and his friends.
Hey! Here's a story about evangelization!
Wait up!
Right, so in Dahomey a priest was explaining to a native that he could not convert him to Christianity because he had three wives. The guy went back to his village to think about it and came back a week later, all smiles. He explained to the priest that he had killed two of his wives and could now become a Christian.
RZZZ
(Holding the wheel with his knees)
Ah, when we reach the Ubangi River basin, we'll have to watch out for the Banda, because they're man-eaters. When they see a white man, they call him "yum-yum."
Fortunately, Sheikh Sfar has his own knowledge of Africa that doesn't come out of books.
Abraham, brother, cut it out with this book of yours.
Why? This stuff is scientific.
You've got your head buried in that book and you're not watching anything. This is a once-in-a-lifetime trip, so look around you.
I'm looking, but thanks to the book, I'm better informed.
Listen, if your Citroën people had written the same kind of account about the Jews, you'd say they didn't understand a thing. When you see new things, it's better to watch and not talk right away.
Oh, you just think you're smarter than André Citroën.

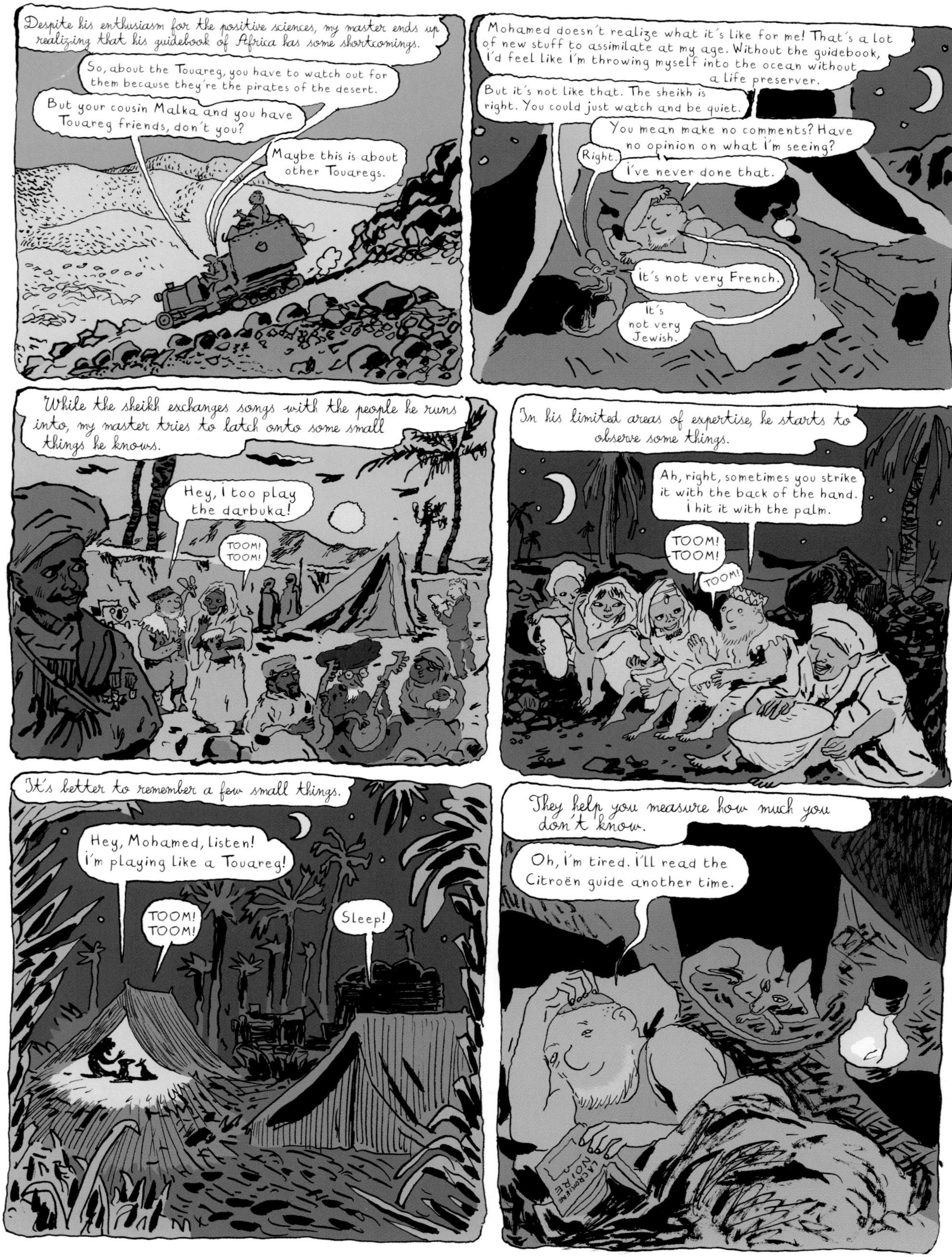

Despite his enthusiasm for the positive sciences, my master ends up realizing that his guidebook of Africa has some shortcomings.
So, about the Touareg, you have to watch out for them because they're the pirates of the desert.
But your cousin Malka and you have Touareg friends, don't you?
Maybe this is about other Touaregs.
Mohamed doesn't realize what it's like for me! That's a lot of new stuff to assimilate at my age. Without the guidebook, I'd feel like I'm throwing myself into the ocean without a life preserver.
But it's not like that. The sheikh is right. You could just watch and be quiet.
You mean make no comments? Have no opinion on what I'm seeing?
Right.
I've never done that.
It's not very French.
It's not very Jewish.
While the sheikh exchanges songs with the people he runs into, my master tries to latch onto some small things he knows.
Hey, I too play the darbuka!
TOOM! TOOM!
In his limited areas of expertise, he starts to observe some things.
Ah, right, sometimes you strike it with the back of the hand. I hit it with the palm.
TOOM! TOOM!
TOOM!
It's better to remember a few small things.
Hey, Mohamed, listen! I'm playing like a Touareg!
TOOM! TOOM!
Sleep!
They help you measure how much you don't know.
Oh, I'm tired. I'll read the Citroën guide another time.
LA CROISIÈRE NOIRE

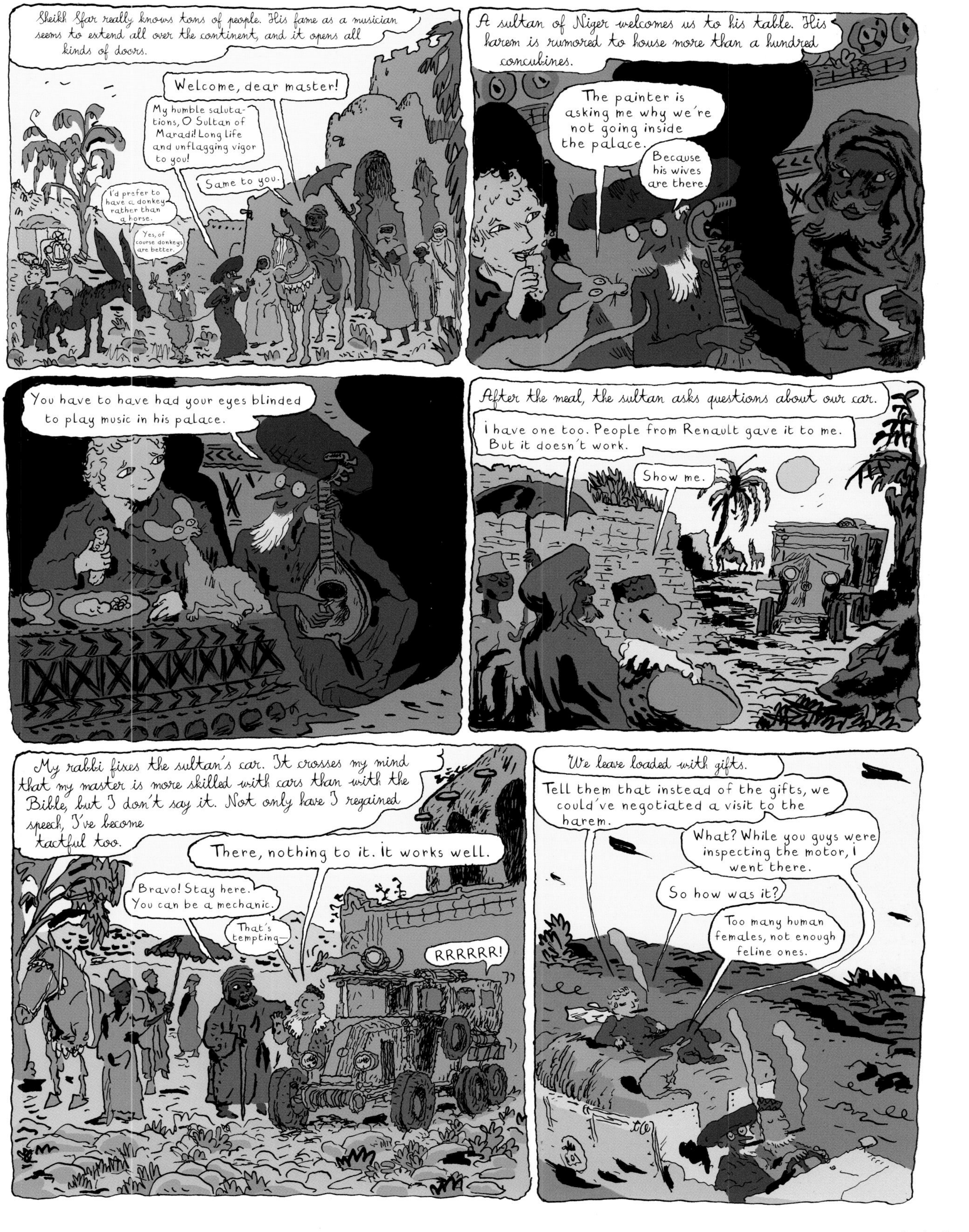
Sheikh Sfar really knows tons of people. His fame as a musician seems to extend all over the continent, and it opens all kinds of doors.
Welcome, dear master!
My humble salutations, O Sultan of Maradi! Long life and unflagging vigor to you!
Same to you.
I'd prefer to have a donkey rather than a horse.
Yes, of course donkeys are better.
A sultan of Niger welcomes us to his table. His harem is rumored to house more than a hundred concubines.
The painter is asking me why we're not going inside the palace.
Because his wives are there.
You have to have had your eyes blinded to play music in his palace.
After the meal, the sultan asks questions about our car.
I have one too. People from Renault gave it to me. But it doesn't work.
Show me.
My rabbi fixes the sultan's car. It crosses my mind that my master is more skilled with cars than with the Bible, but I don't say it. Not only have I regained speech, I've become tactful too.
There, nothing to it. It works well.
Bravo! Stay here. You can be a mechanic.
That's tempting—
RRRRRR!
We leave loaded with gifts.
Tell them that instead of the gifts, we could've negotiated a visit to the harem.
What? While you guys were inspecting the motor, I went there.
So how was it?
Too many human females, not enough feline ones.

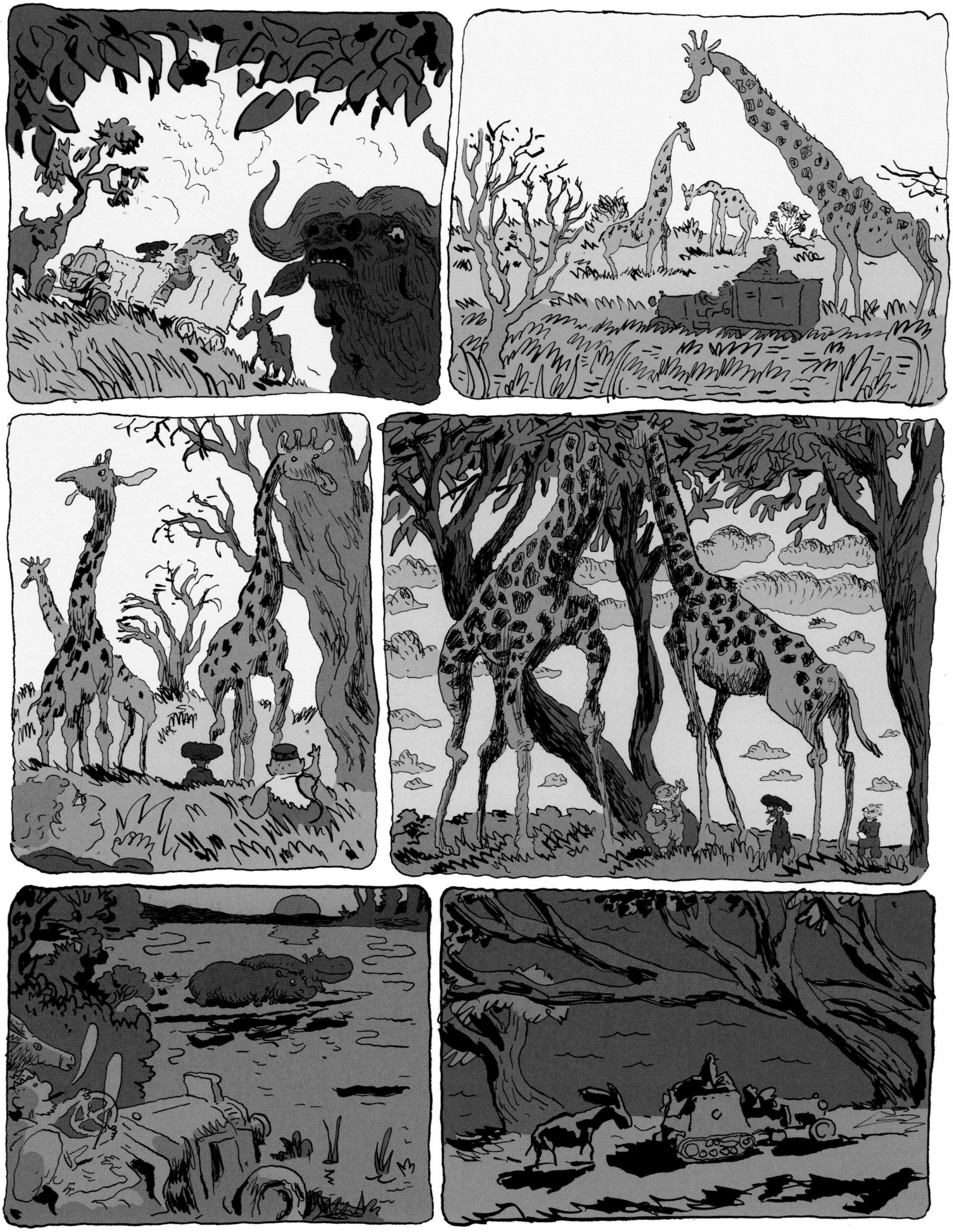

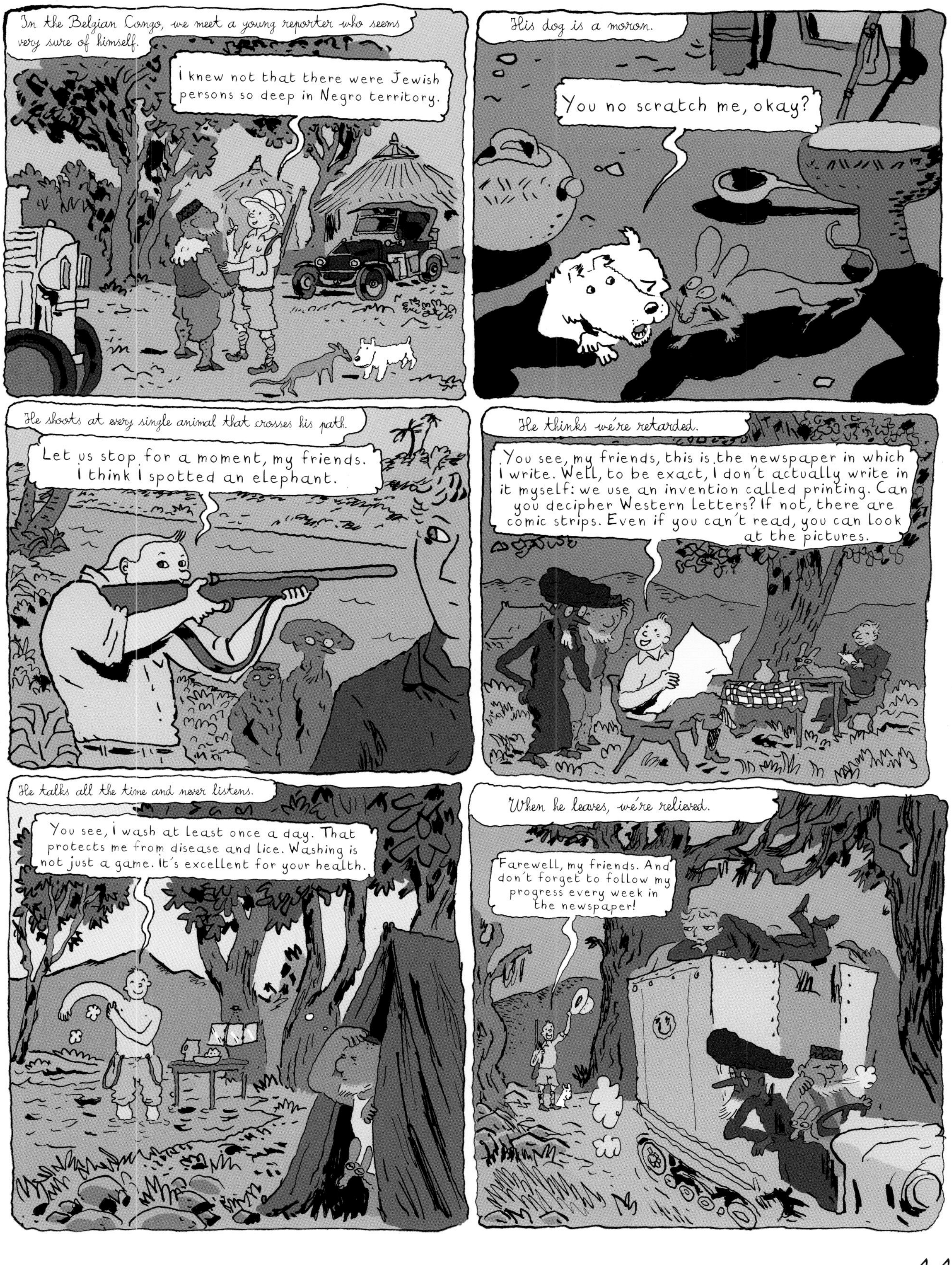
In the Belgian Congo, we meet a young reporter who seems very sure of himself.
I knew not that there were Jewish persons so deep in Negro territory.
His dog is a moron.
You no scratch me, okay?
He shoots at every single animal that crosses his path.
Let us stop for a moment, my friends. I think I spotted an elephant.
He thinks we're retarded.
You see, my friends, this is the newspaper in which I write. Well, to be exact, I don't actually write in it myself: we use an invention called printing. Can you decipher Western letters? If not, there are comic strips. Even if you can't read, you can look at the pictures.
He talks all the time and never listens.
You see, I wash at least once a day. That protects me from disease and lice. Washing is not just a game. It's excellent for your health.
When he leaves, we're relieved.
Farewell, my friends. And don't forget to follow my progress every week in the newspaper!

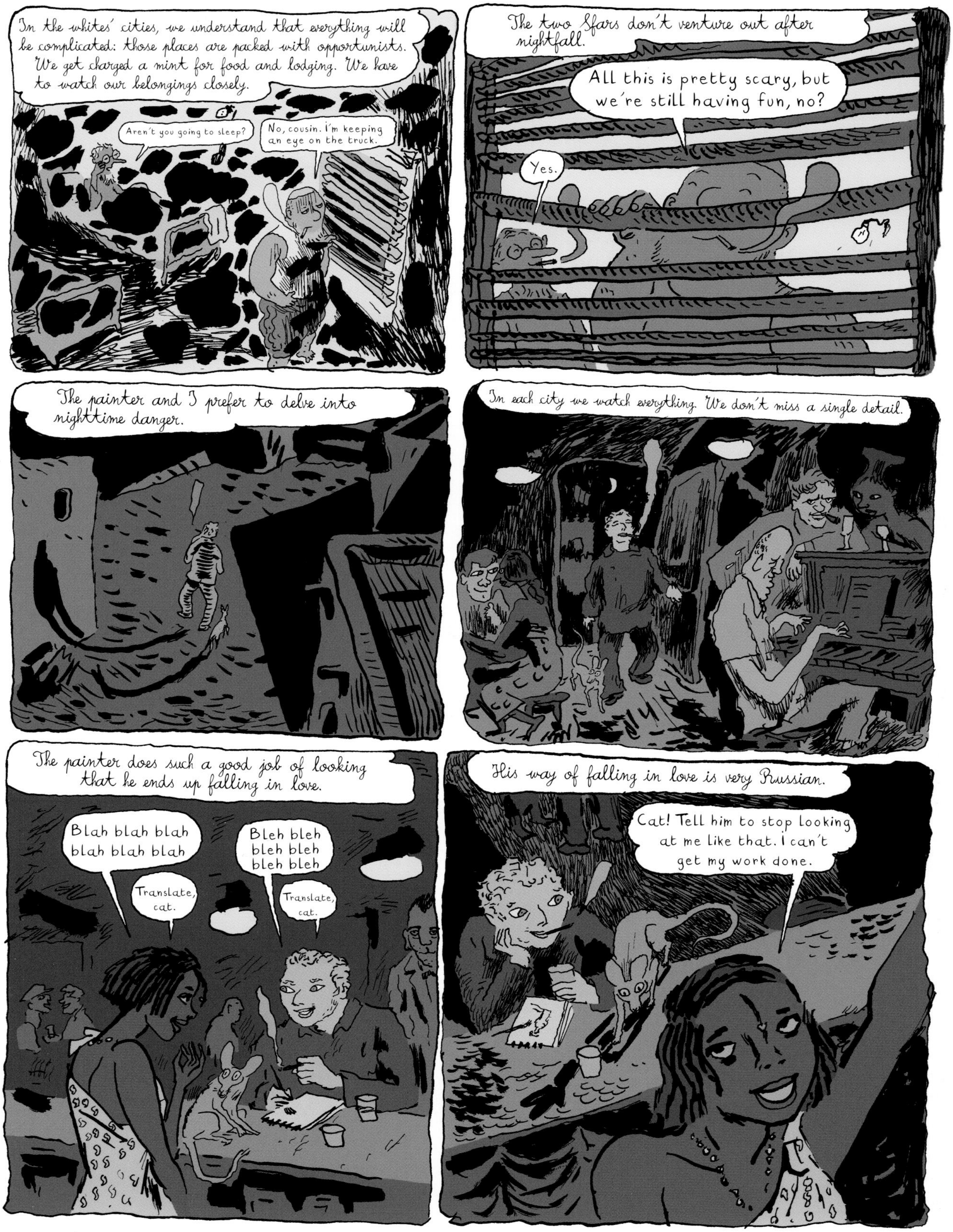
In the whites' cities, we understand that everything will be complicated: those places are packed with opportunists. We get charged a mint for food and lodging. We have to watch our belongings closely.
Aren't you going to sleep?
No, cousin. I'm keeping an eye on the truck.
The two Sfars don't venture out after nightfall.
All this is pretty scary, but we're still having fun, no?
Yes.
The painter and I prefer to delve into nighttime danger.
In each city we watch everything. We don't miss a single detail.
The painter does such a good job of looking that he ends up falling in love.
Blah blah blah blah blah blah
Translate, cat.
Bleh bleh bleh bleh bleh bleh
Translate, cat.
His way of falling in love is very Russian.
Cat! Tell him to stop looking at me like that. I can't get my work done.

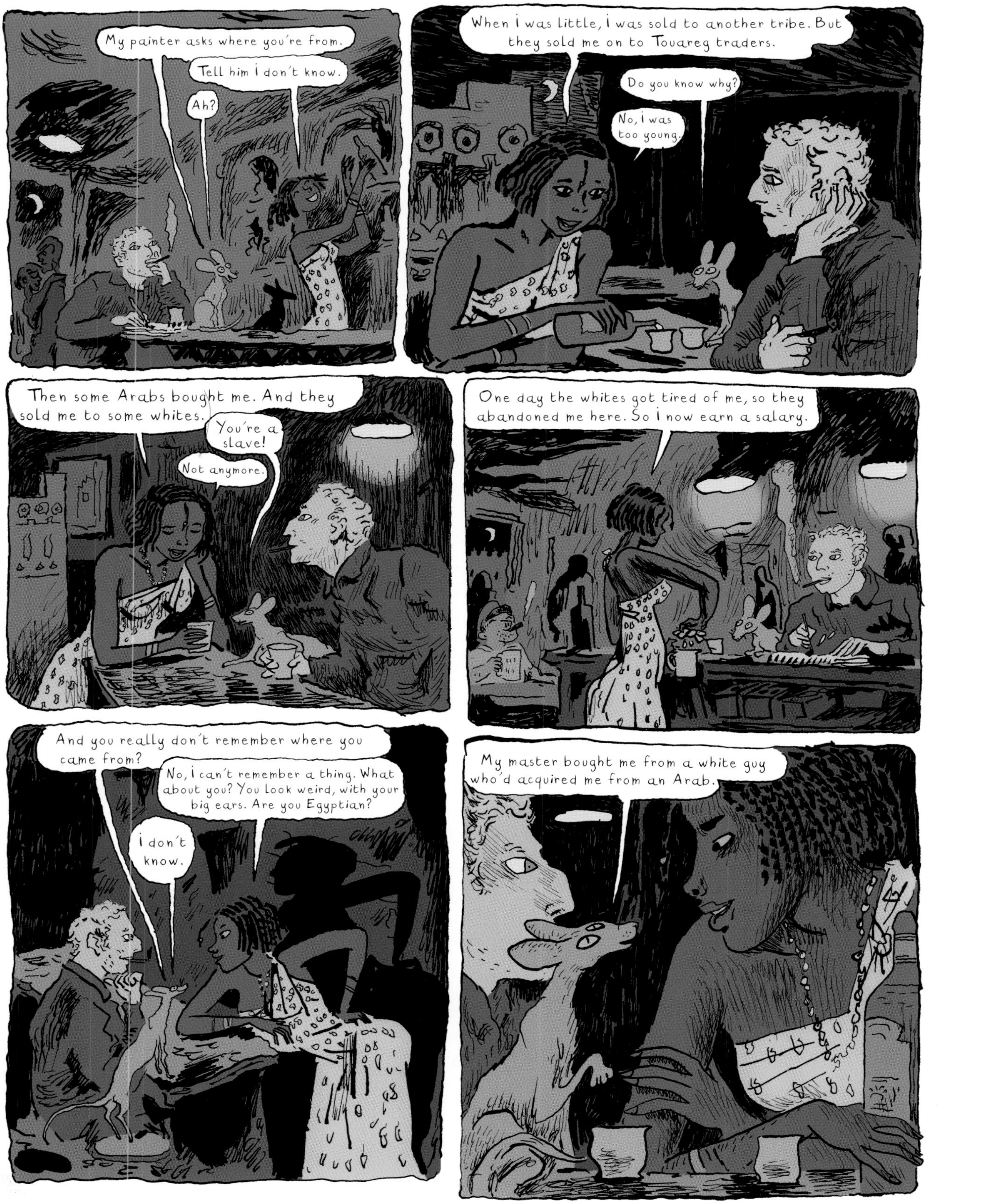
My painter asks where you're from.
Tell him I don't know.
Ah?
When I was little, I was sold to another tribe. But they sold me on to Touareg traders.
Do you know why?
No, I was too young.
Then some Arabs bought me. And they sold me to some whites.
You're a slave!
Not anymore.
One day the whites got tired of me, so they abandoned me here. So I now earn a salary.
And you really don't remember where you came from?
No, I can't remember a thing. What about you? You look weird, with your big ears. Are you Egyptian?
I don't know.
My master bought me from a white guy who'd acquired me from an Arab.

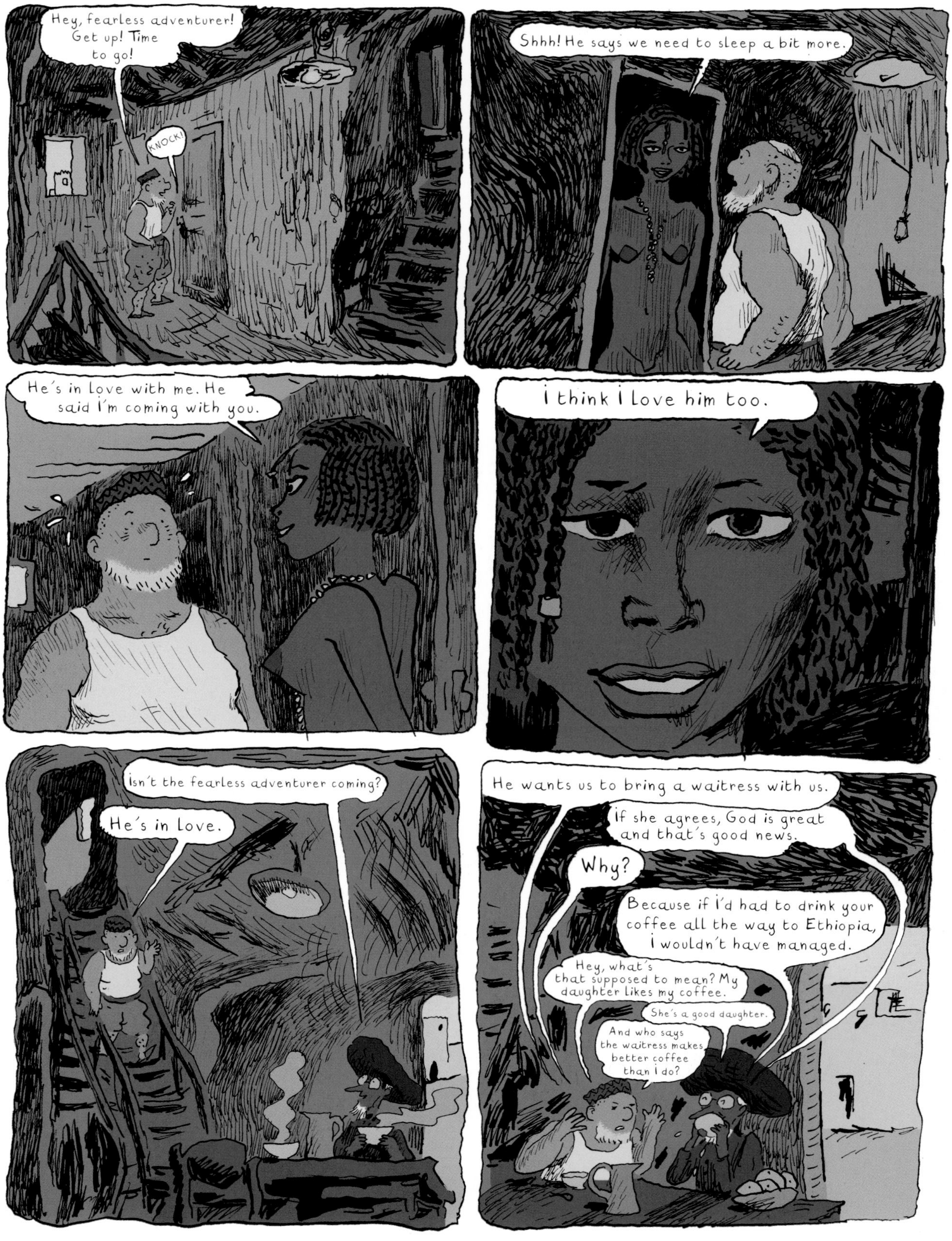
Hey, fearless adventurer! Get up! Time to go!
KNOCK!
Shhh! He says we need to sleep a bit more.
He's in love with me. He said I'm coming with you.
I think I love him too.
Isn't the fearless adventurer coming?
He's in love.
He wants us to bring a waitress with us.
If she agrees, God is great and that's good news.
Why?
Because if I'd had to drink your coffee all the way to Ethiopia, I wouldn't have managed.
Hey, what's that supposed to mean? My daughter likes my coffee.
She's a good daughter.
And who says the waitress makes better coffee than I do?

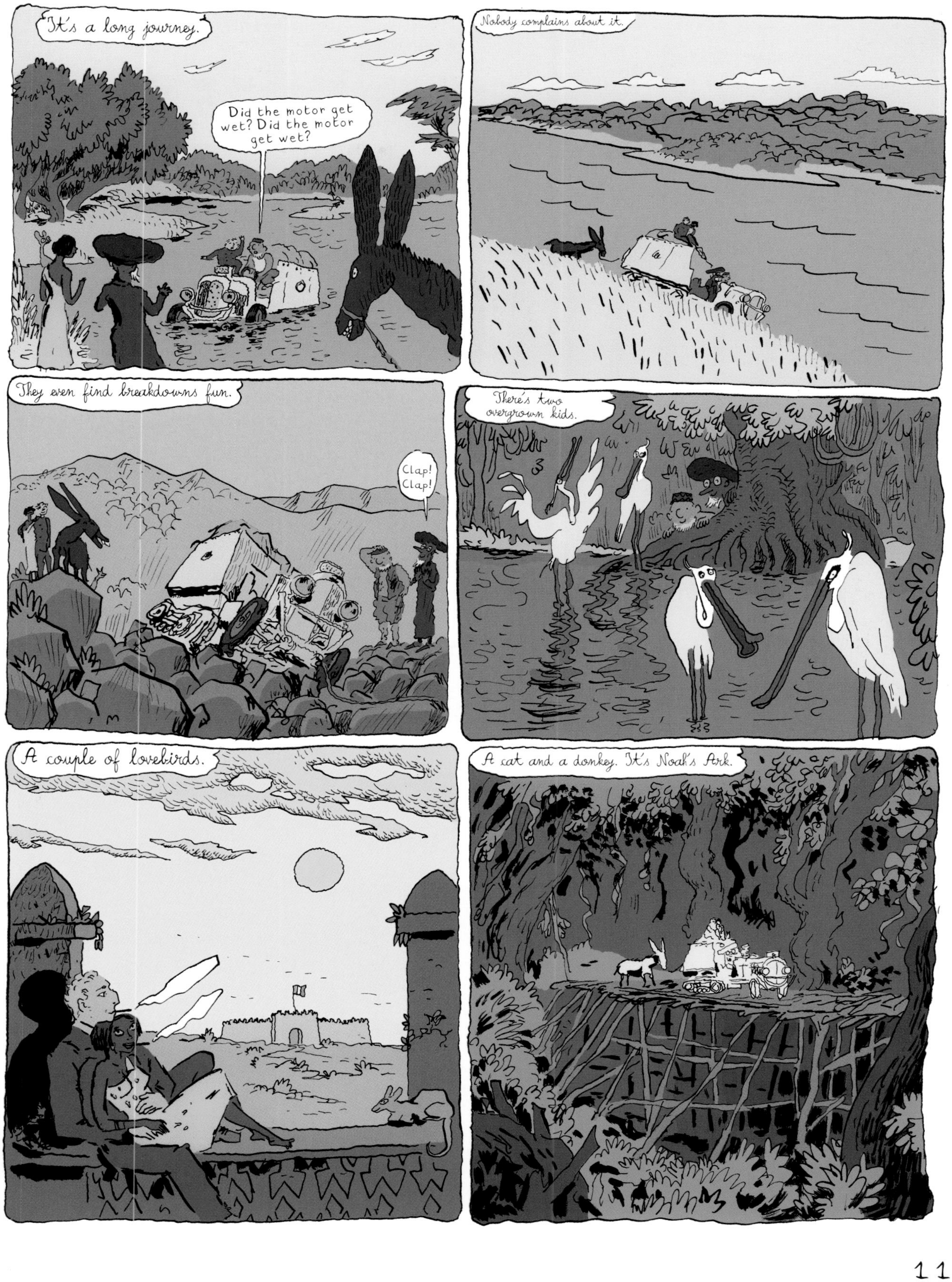
It's a long journey.
Did the motor get wet? Did the motor get wet?
Nobody complains about it.
They even find breakdowns fun.
Clap! Clap!
There's two overgrown kids.
A couple of lovebirds.
A cat and a donkey. It's Noah's Ark.

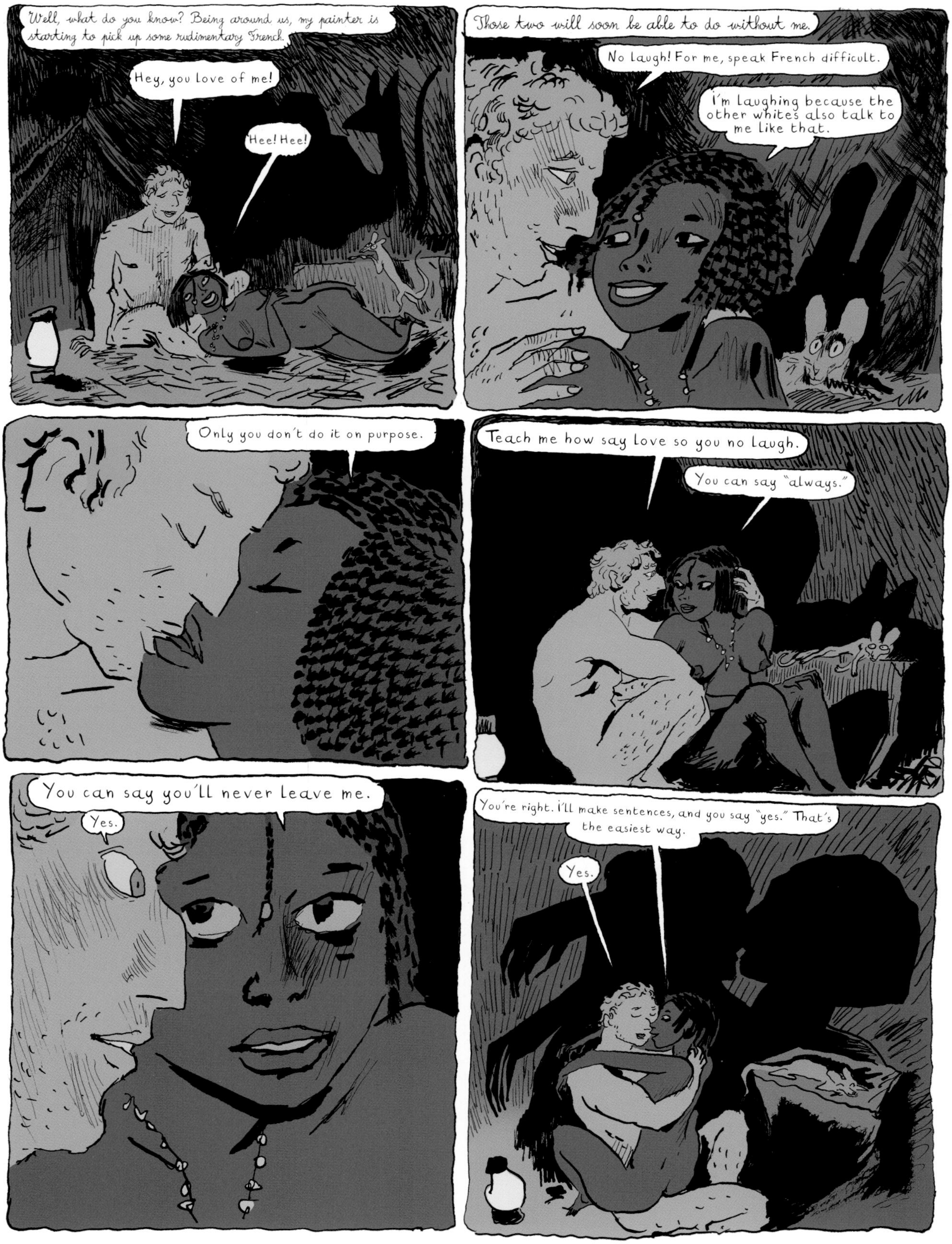
Well, what do you know? Being around us, my painter is starting to pick up some rudimentary French.
Hey, you love of me!
Hee! Hee!
Those two will soon be able to do without me.
No laugh! For me, speak French difficult.
I'm laughing because the other whites also talk to me like that.
Only you don't do it on purpose.
Teach me how say love so you no laugh.
You can say "always."
You can say you'll never leave me.
Yes.
You're right. I'll make sentences, and you say "yes." That's the easiest way.
Yes.

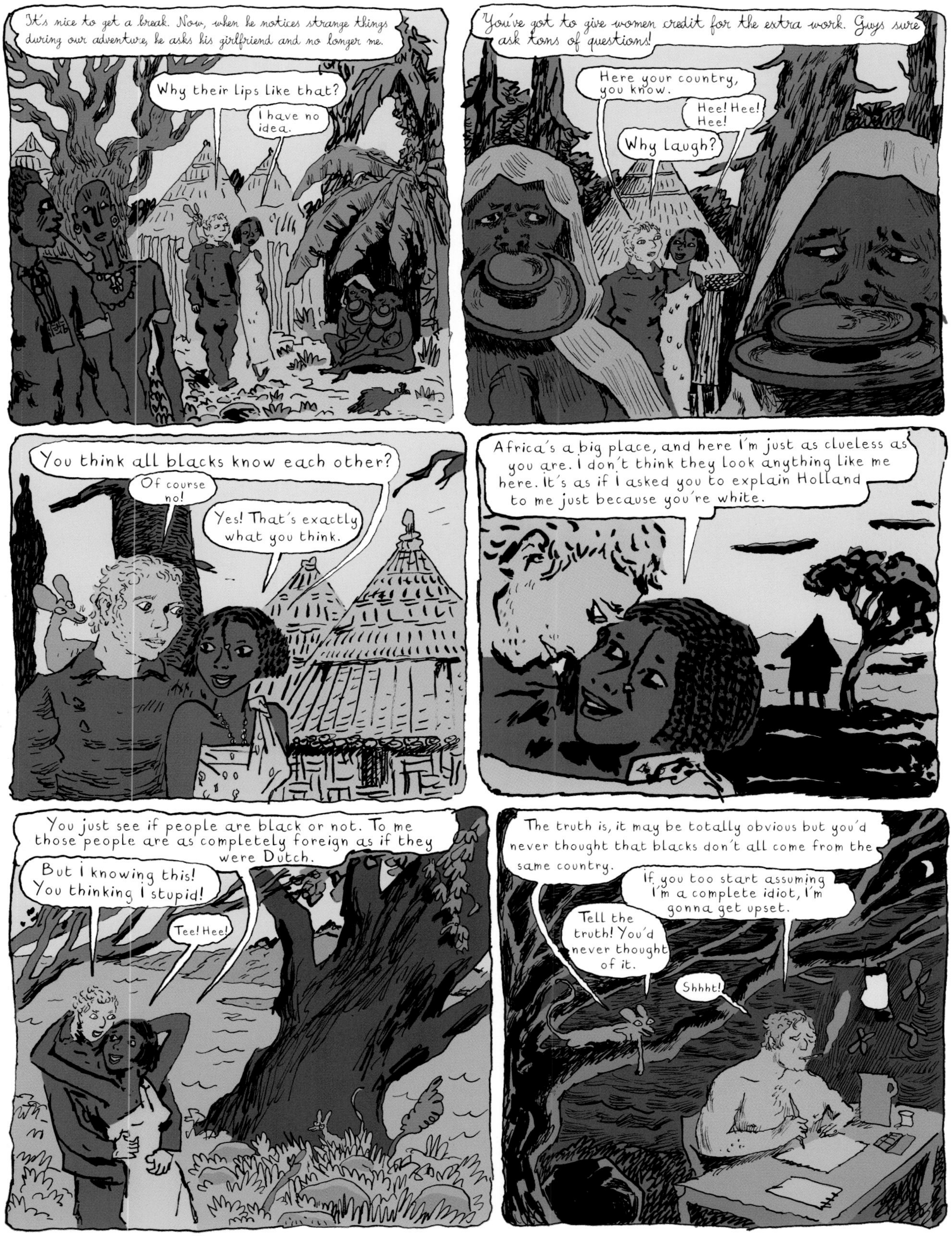

It's nice to get a break. Now, when he notices strange things during our adventure, he asks his girlfriend and no longer me.
Why their lips like that?
I have no idea.
You've got to give women credit for the extra work. Guys sure ask tons of questions!
Here your country, you know.
Hee! Hee! Hee!
Why laugh?
You think all blacks know each other?
Of course no!
Yes! That's exactly what you think.
Africa's a big place, and here I'm just as clueless as you are. I don't think they look anything like me here. It's as if I asked you to explain Holland to me just because you're white.
You just see if people are black or not. To me those people are as completely foreign as if they were Dutch.
But I knowing this! You thinking I stupid!
Tee! Hee!
The truth is, it may be totally obvious but you'd never thought that blacks don't all come from the same country.
If you too start assuming I'm a complete idiot, I'm gonna get upset.
Tell the truth! You'd never thought of it.
Shhht!

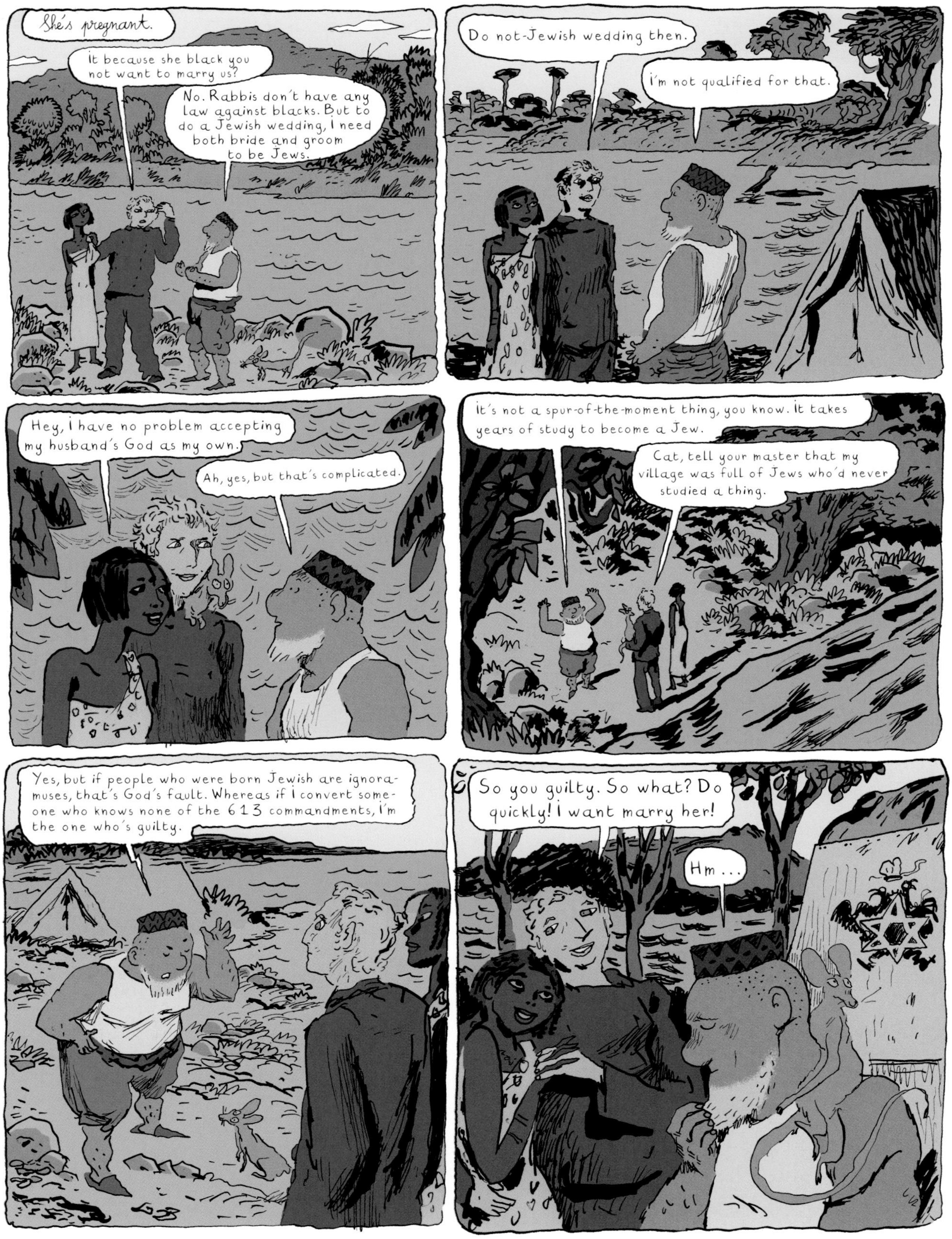
She's pregnant.
It because she black you not want to marry us?
No. Rabbis don't have any law against blacks. But to do a Jewish wedding, I need both bride and groom to be Jews.
Do not-Jewish wedding then.
I'm not qualified for that.
Hey, I have no problem accepting my husband's God as my own.
Ah, yes, but that's complicated.
It's not a spur-of-the-moment thing, you know. It takes years of study to become a Jew.
Cat, tell your master that my village was full of Jews who'd never studied a thing.
Yes, but if people who were born Jewish are ignoramuses, that's God's fault. Whereas if I convert someone who knows none of the 613 commandments, I'm the one who's guilty.
So you guilty. So what? Do quickly! I want marry her!
Hm...

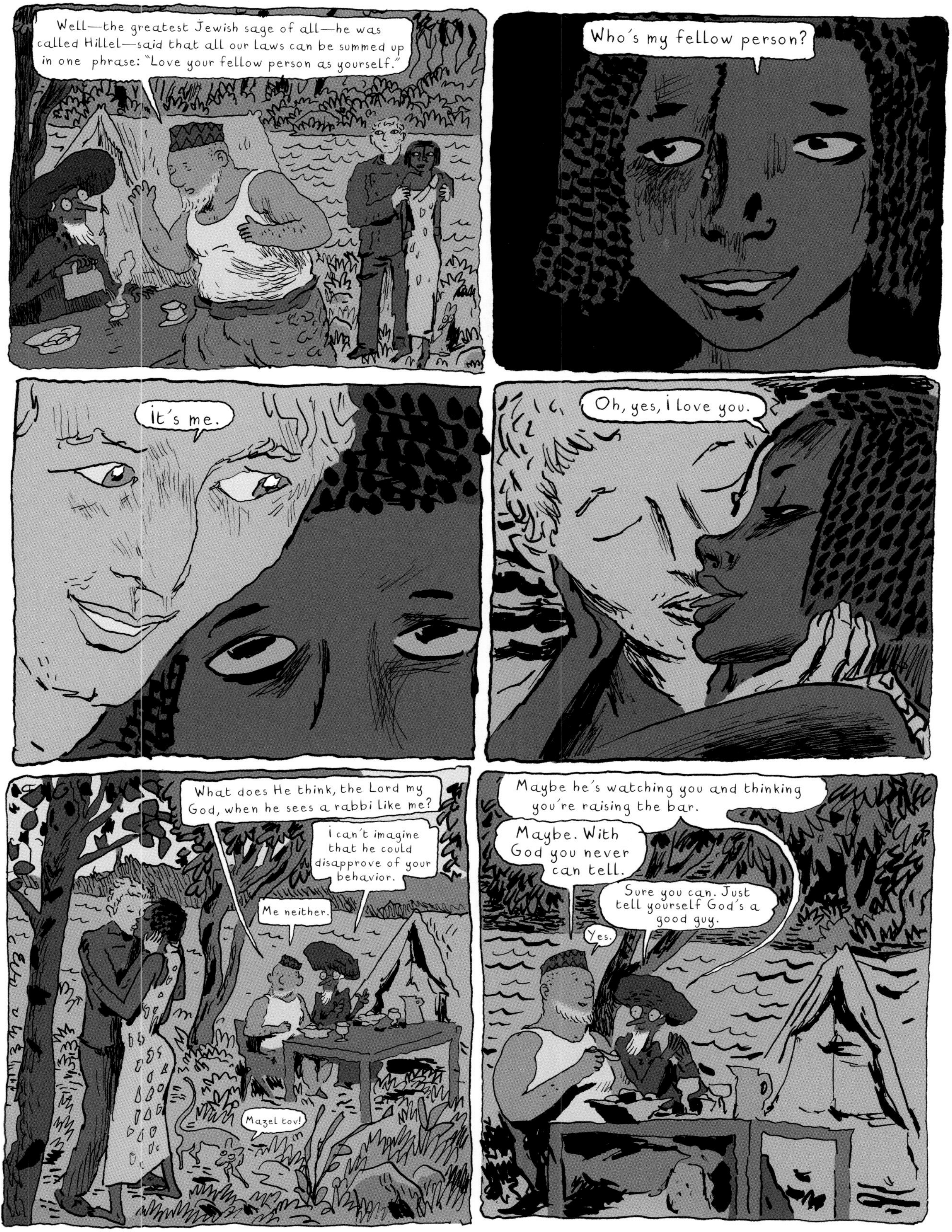

Well—the greatest Jewish sage of all—he was called Hillel—said that all our laws can be summed up in one phrase: "Love your fellow person as yourself."
Who's my fellow person?
It's me.
Oh, yes, I love you.
What does He think, the Lord my God, when he sees a rabbi like me?
I can't imagine that he could disapprove of your behavior.
Me neither.
Mazel tov!
Maybe he's watching you and thinking you're raising the bar.
Maybe. With God you never can tell.
Sure you can. Just tell yourself God's a good guy.
Yes.

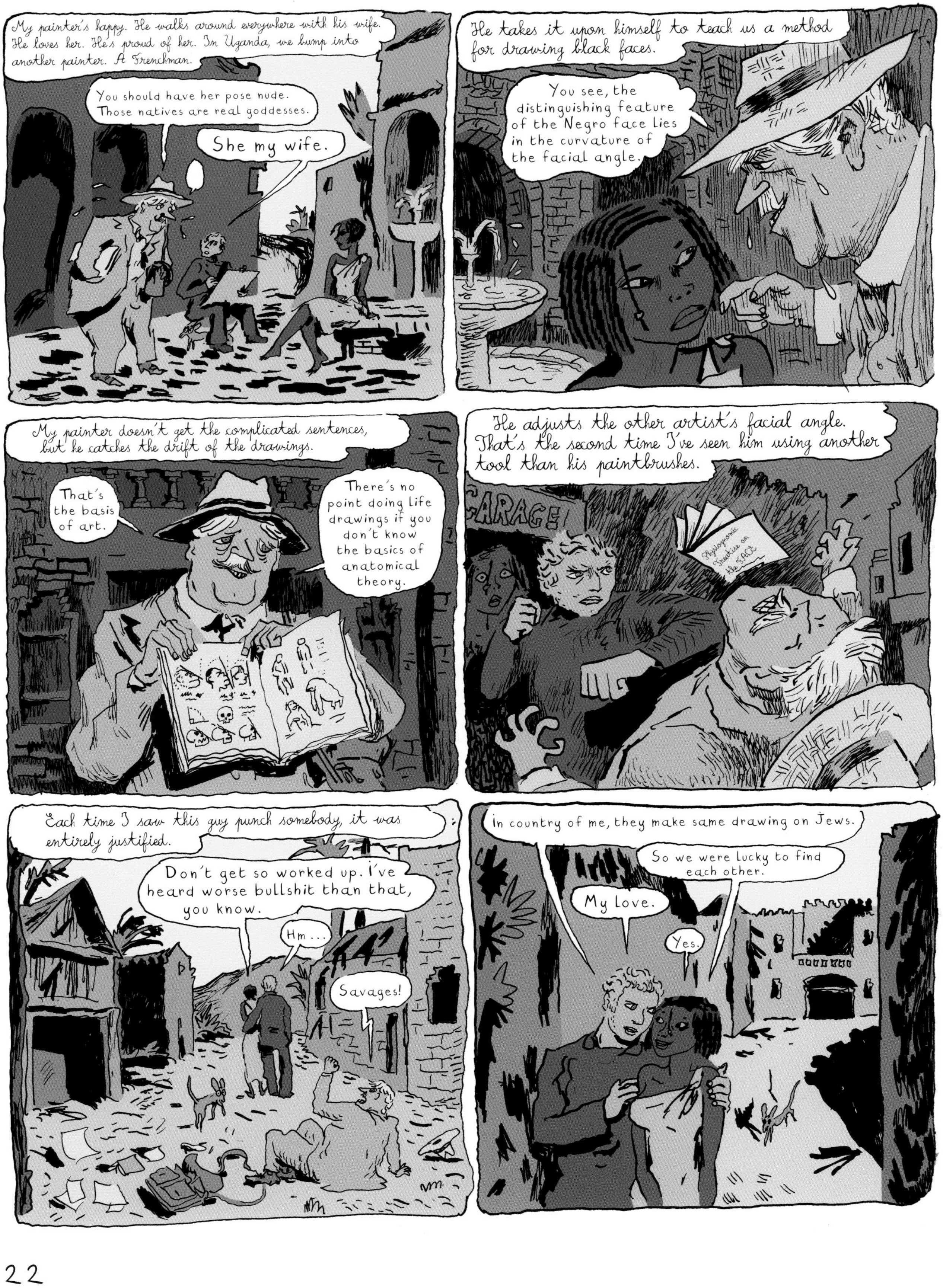

My painter's happy. He walks around everywhere with his wife. He loves her. He's proud of her. In Uganda, we bump into another painter. A Frenchman.
You should have her pose nude. Those natives are real goddesses.
She my wife.
He takes it upon himself to teach us a method for drawing black faces.
You see, the distinguishing feature of the Negro face lies in the curvature of the facial angle.
My painter doesn't get the complicated sentences, but he catches the drift of the drawings.
That's the basis of art.
There's no point doing life drawings if you don't know the basics of anatomical theory.
He adjusts the other artist's facial angle. That's the second time I've seen him using another tool than his paintbrushes.
ARAGE
Physiognomic Treatise on the FACE
Each time I saw this guy punch somebody, it was entirely justified.
Don't get so worked up. I've heard worse bullshit than that, you know.
Hm...
Savages!
In country of me, they make same drawing on Jews.
So we were lucky to find each other.
My Love.
Yes.

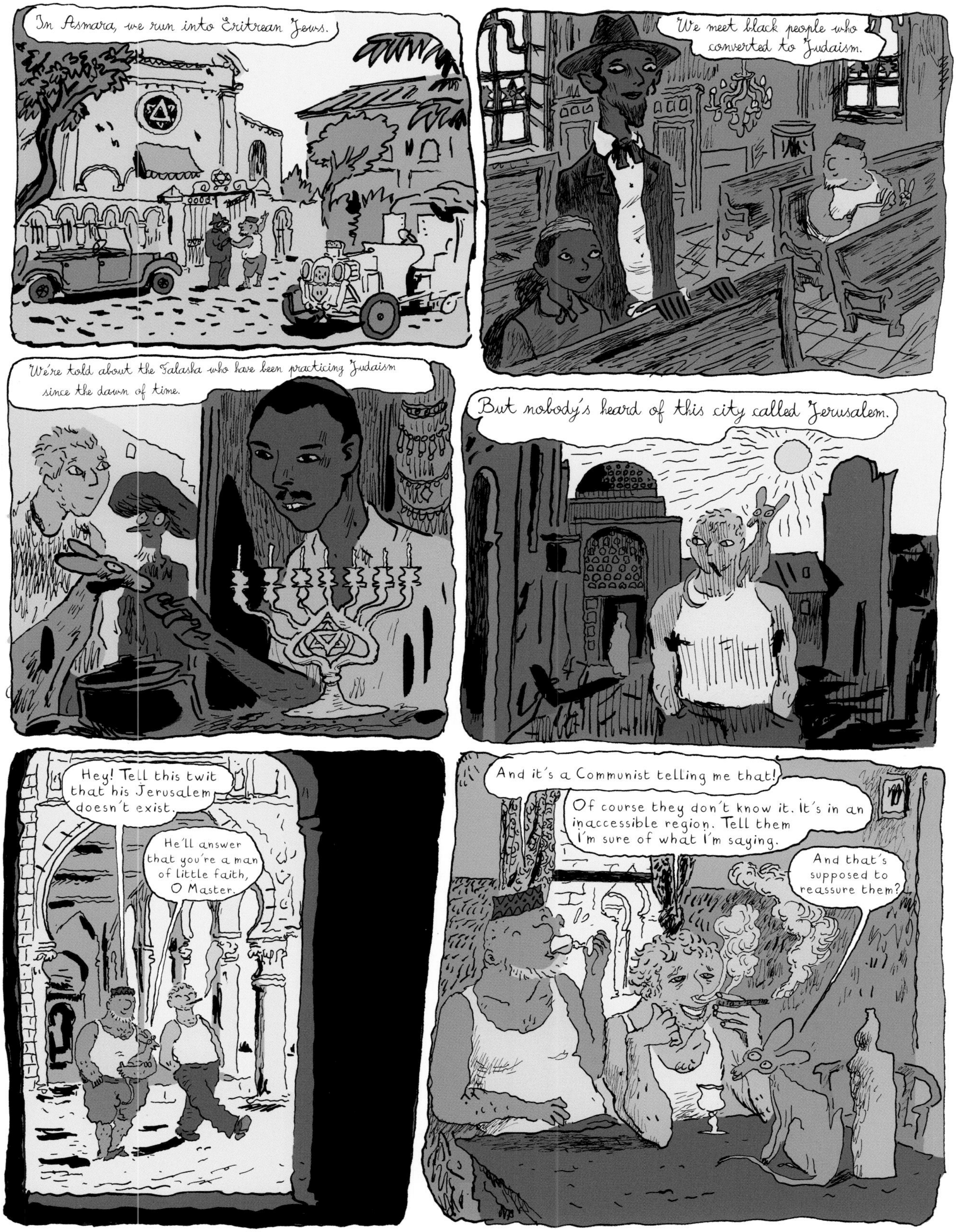
In Asmara, we run into Eritrean Jews.
We meet black people who converted to Judaism.
We're told about the Falasha who have been practicing Judaism since the dawn of time.
But nobody's heard of this city called Jerusalem.
Hey! Tell this twit that his Jerusalem doesn't exist.
He'll answer that you're a man of little faith, O Master.
And it's a Communist telling me that!
Of course they don't know it. It's in an inaccessible region. Tell them I'm sure of what I'm saying.
And that's supposed to reassure them?

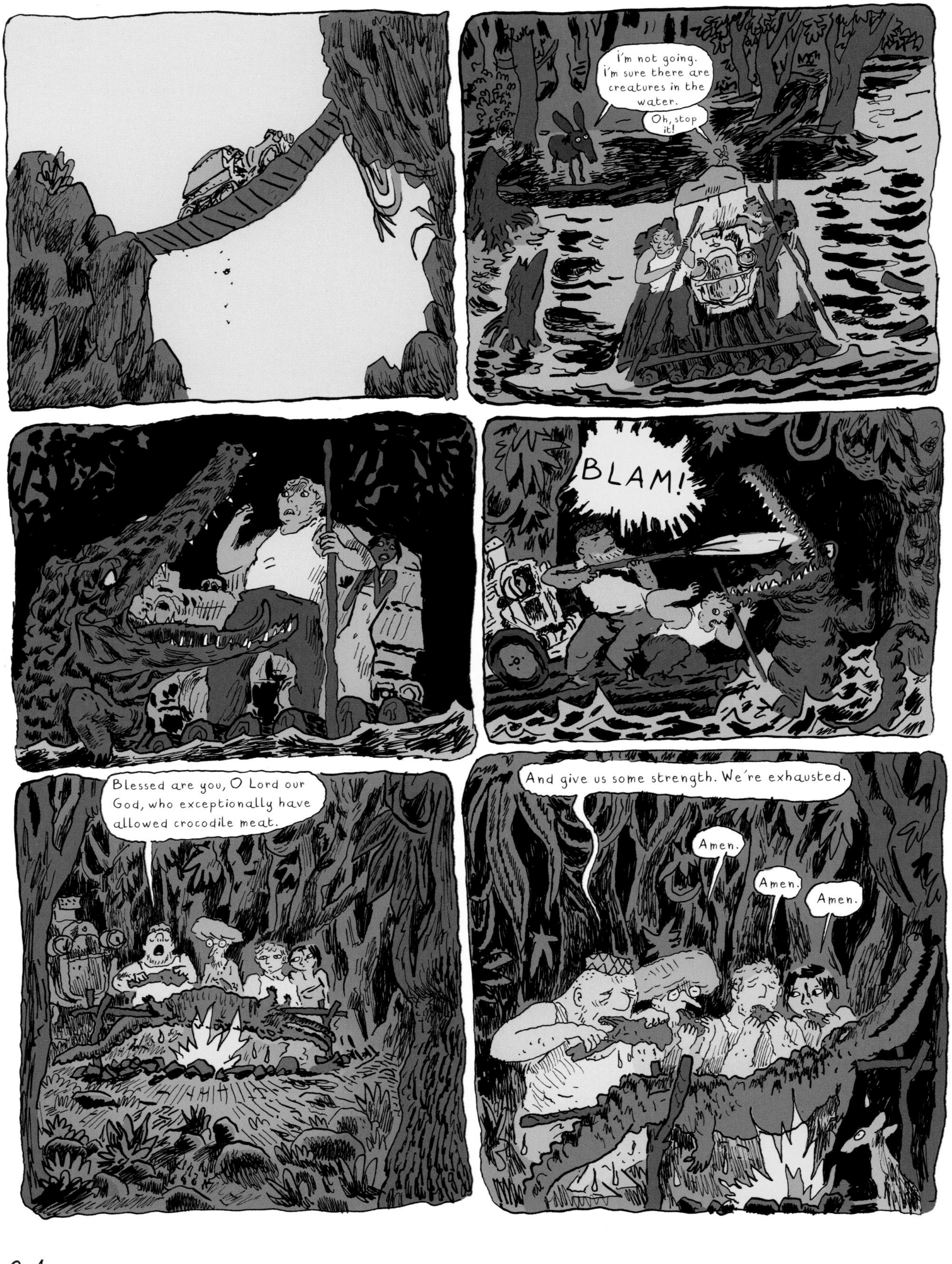
I'm not going. I'm sure there are creatures in the water.
Oh, stop it!
BLAM!
Blessed are you, O Lord our God, who exceptionally have allowed crocodile meat.
And give us some strength. We're exhausted.
Amen.
Amen.
Amen.

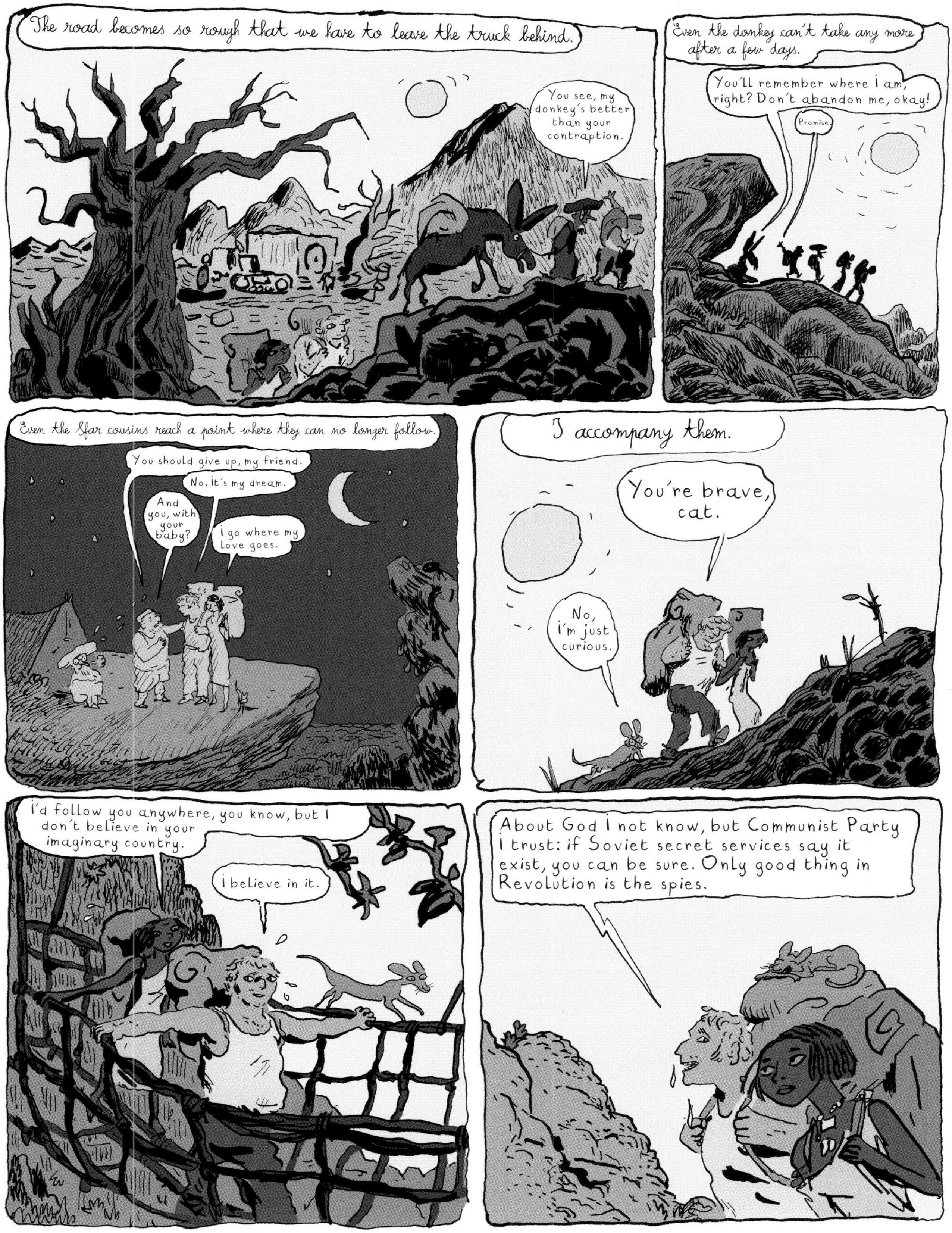

The road becomes so rough that we have to leave the truck behind.
You see, my donkey's better than your contraption.
Even the donkey can't take any more after a few days.
You'll remember where I am, right? Don't abandon me, okay!
Promise
Even the Sfar cousins reach a point where they can no longer follow.
You should give up, my friend.
No. It's my dream.
And you, with your baby?
I go where my love goes.
I accompany them.
You're brave, cat.
No, I'm just curious.
I'd follow you anywhere, you know, but I don't believe in your imaginary country.
I believe in it.
About God I not know, but Communist Party I trust: if Soviet secret services say it exist, you can be sure. Only good thing in Revolution is the spies.

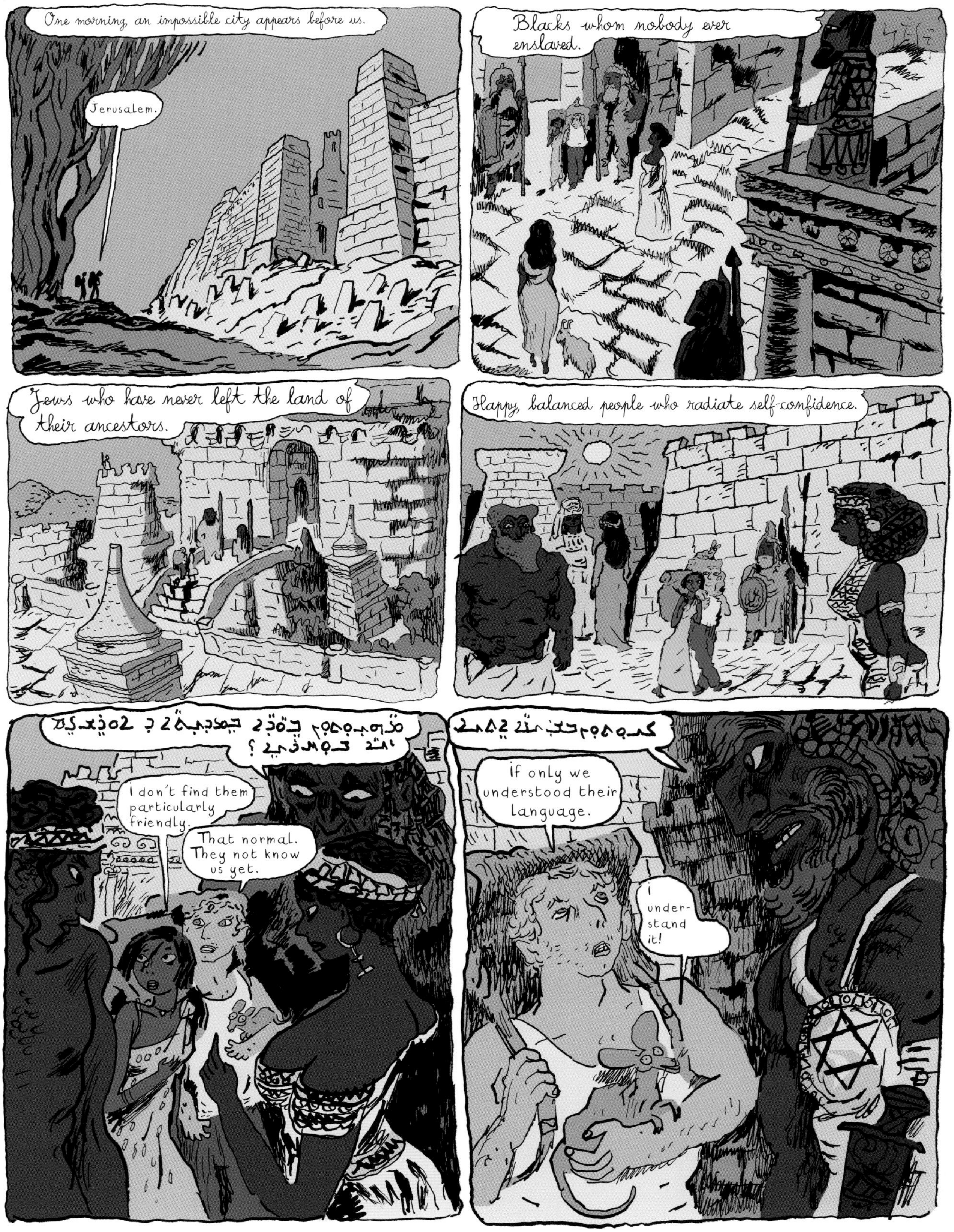
One morning, an impossible city appears before us.
Jerusalem.
Blacks whom nobody ever enslaved.
Jews who have never left the land of their ancestors.
Happy, balanced people who radiate self-confidence.
I don't find them particularly friendly.
That normal. They not know us yet.
If only we understood their language.
I under-stand it!

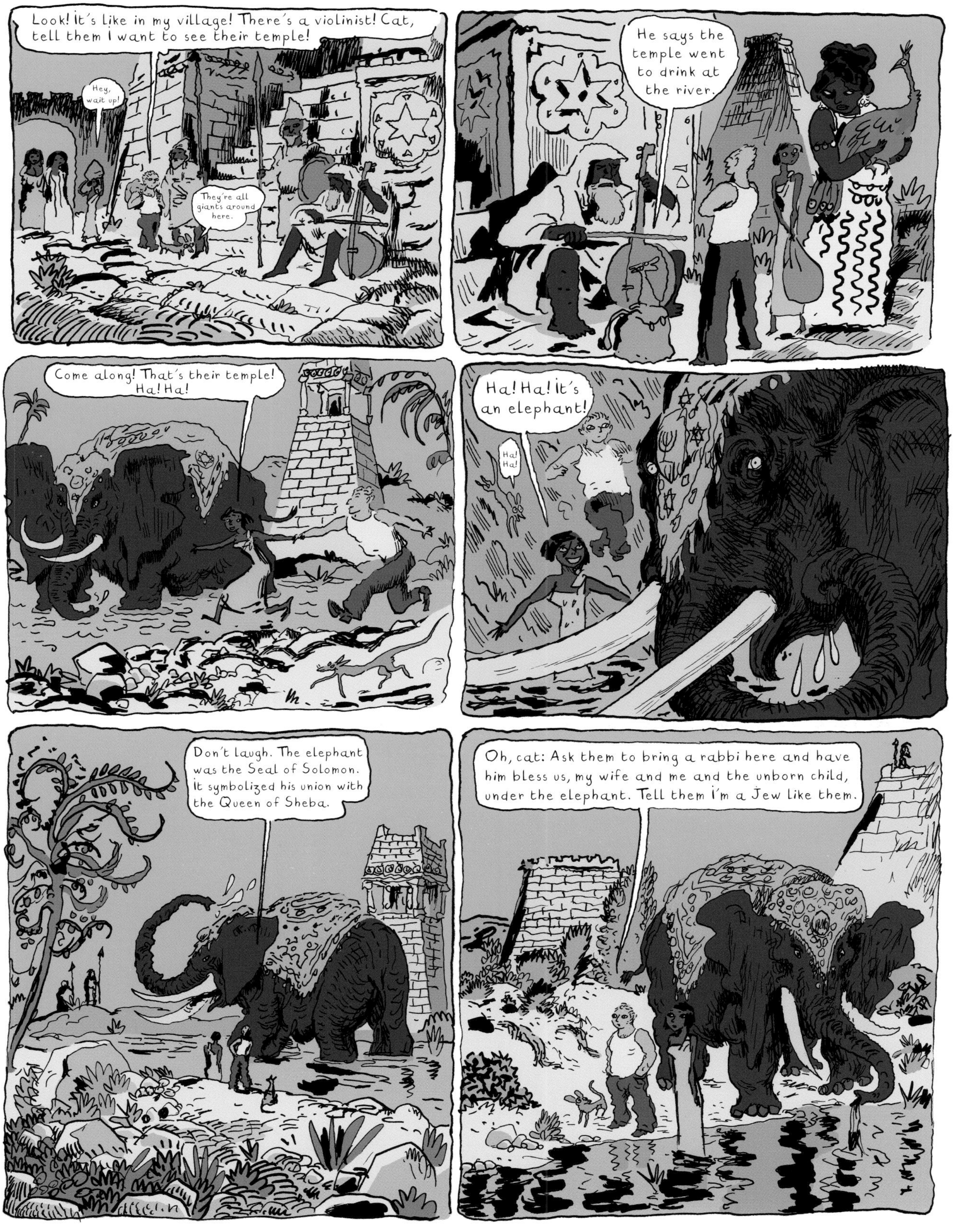
Look! It's like in my village! There's a violinist! Cat, tell them I want to see their temple!
Hey, wait up!
They're all giants around here.
He says the temple went to drink at the river.
Come along! That's their temple! Ha! Ha!
Ha! Ha! It's an elephant!
Ha! Ha!
Don't laugh. The elephant was the Seal of Solomon. It symbolized his union with the Queen of Sheba.
Oh, cat: Ask them to bring a rabbi here and have him bless us, my wife and me and the unborn child, under the elephant. Tell them I'm a Jew like them.

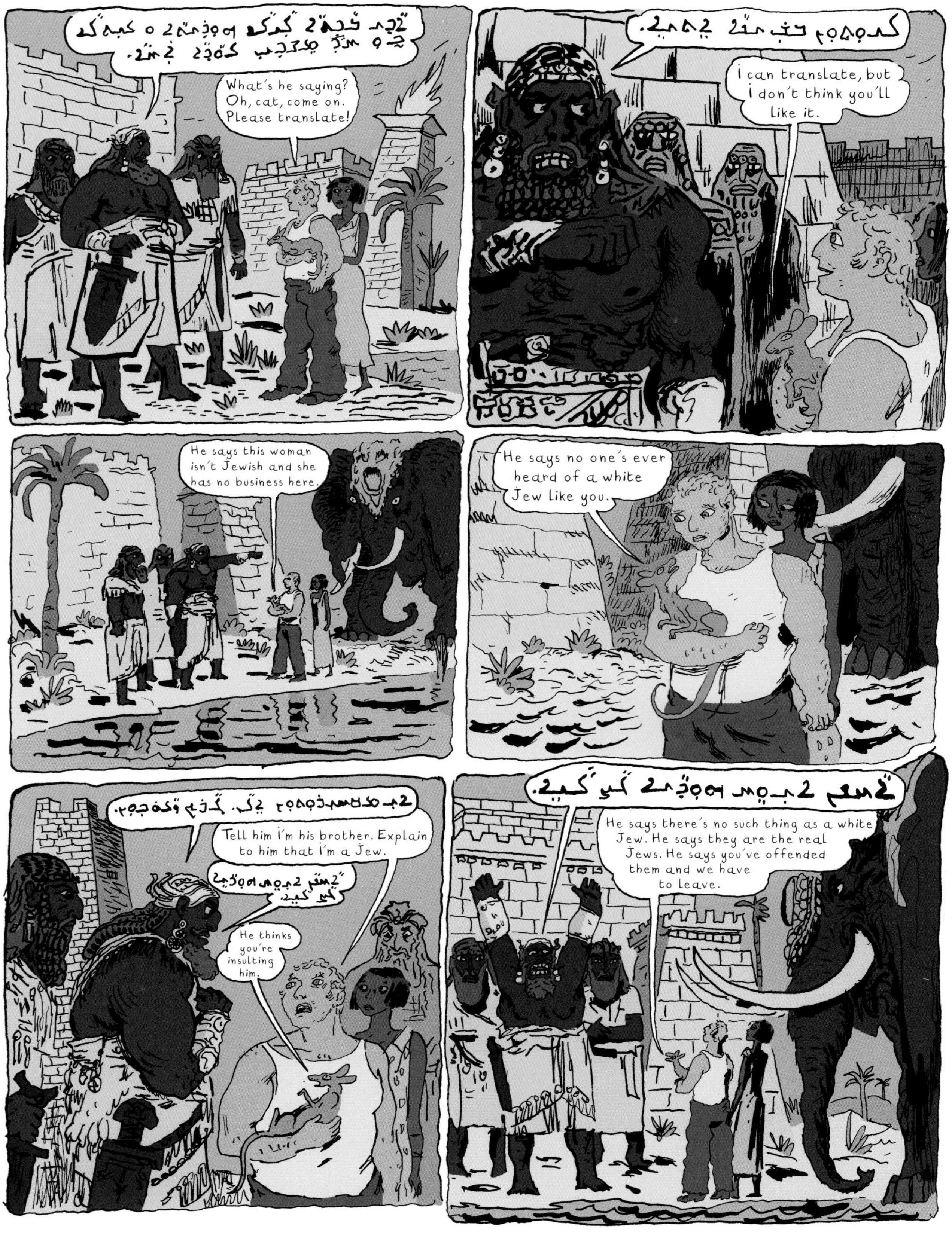
What's he saying? Oh, cat, come on. Please translate!
I can translate, but I don't think you'll like it.
He says this woman isn't Jewish and she has no business here.
He says no one's ever heard of a white Jew like you.
Tell him I'm his brother. Explain to him that I'm a Jew.
He thinks you're insulting him.
He says there's no such thing as a white Jew. He says they are the real Jews. He says you've offended them and we have to leave.

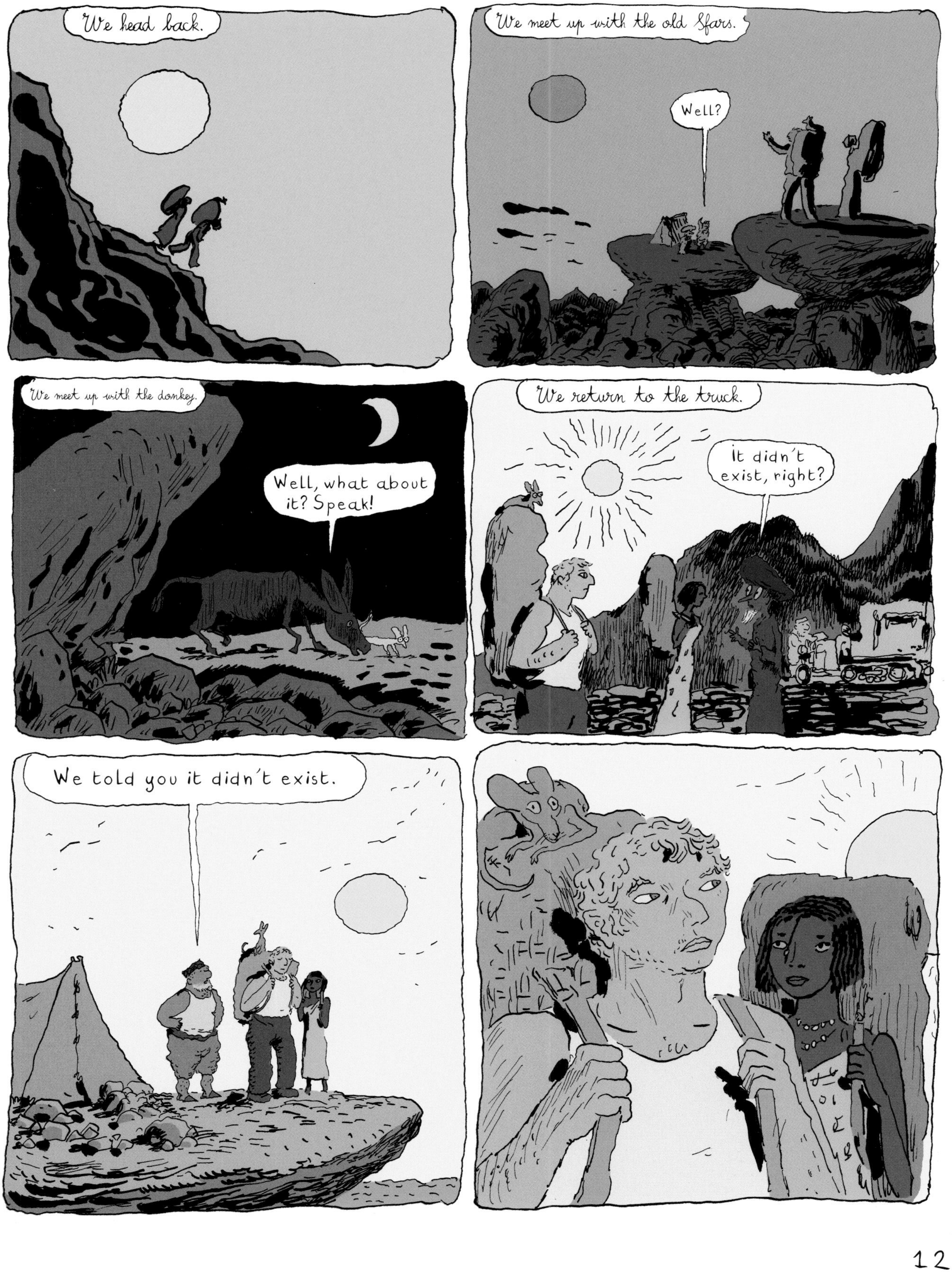
We head back.
We meet up with the old Sfars.
Well?
We meet up with the donkey.
Well, what about it? Speak!
We return to the truck.
It didn't exist, right?
We told you it didn't exist.

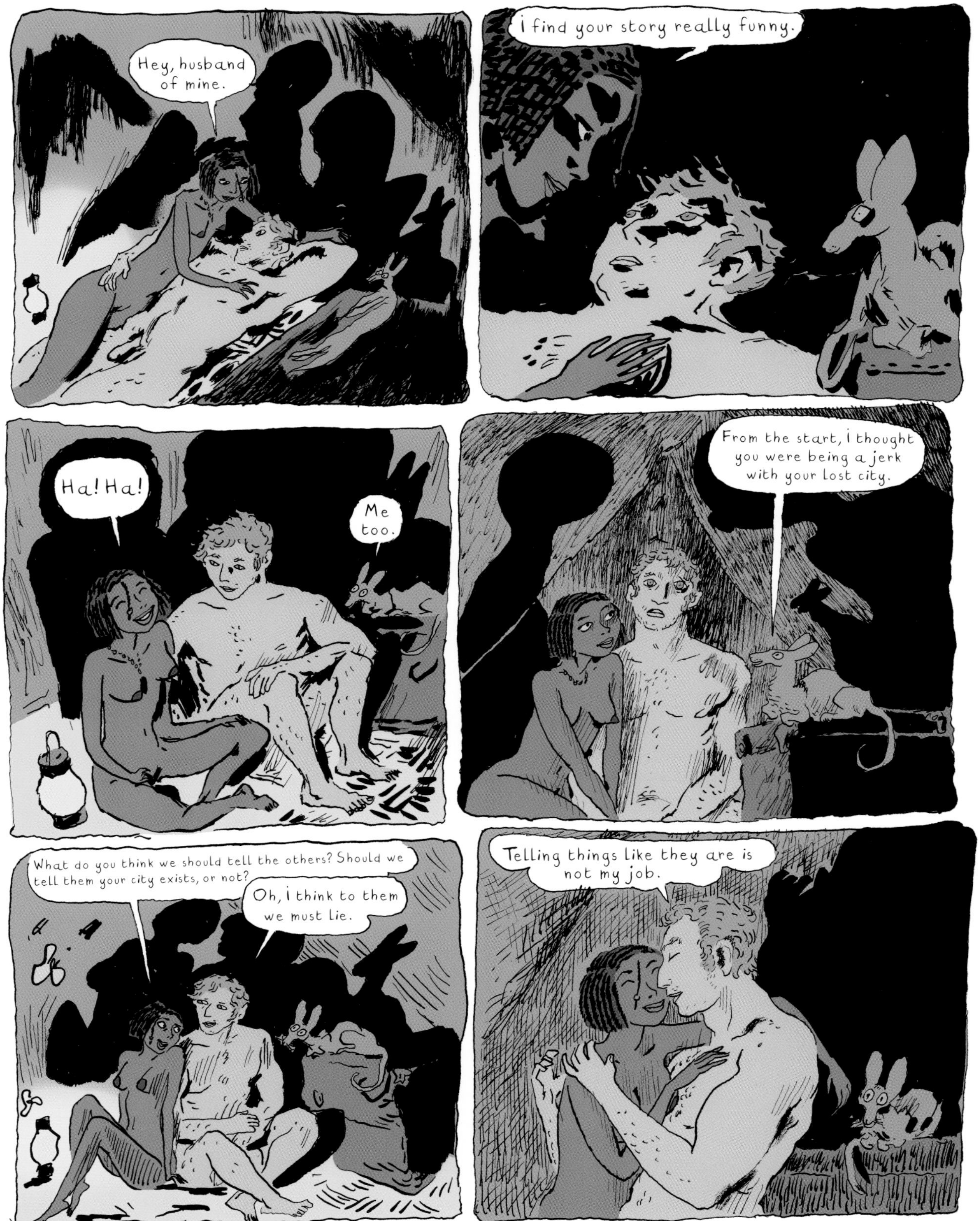
Hey, husband of mine.
I find your story really funny.
Ha! Ha!
Me too.
From the start, I thought you were being a jerk with your lost city.
What do you think we should tell the others? Should we tell them your city exists, or not?
Oh, I think to them we must lie.
Telling things like they are is not my job.

About the Author

Joann Sfar was awarded the prestigious Jury Prize at Angoulême
for the first volume of *The Rabbi's Cat*. He has drawn more than
a hundred comic books for children and adults, including *Little Vampire
Goes to School* (a *New York Times* best seller) and *Little Vampire Does
Kung Fu!* (nominated for an Eisner Award). He lives in Paris
with his wife, two children, and the model for the rabbi's cat.

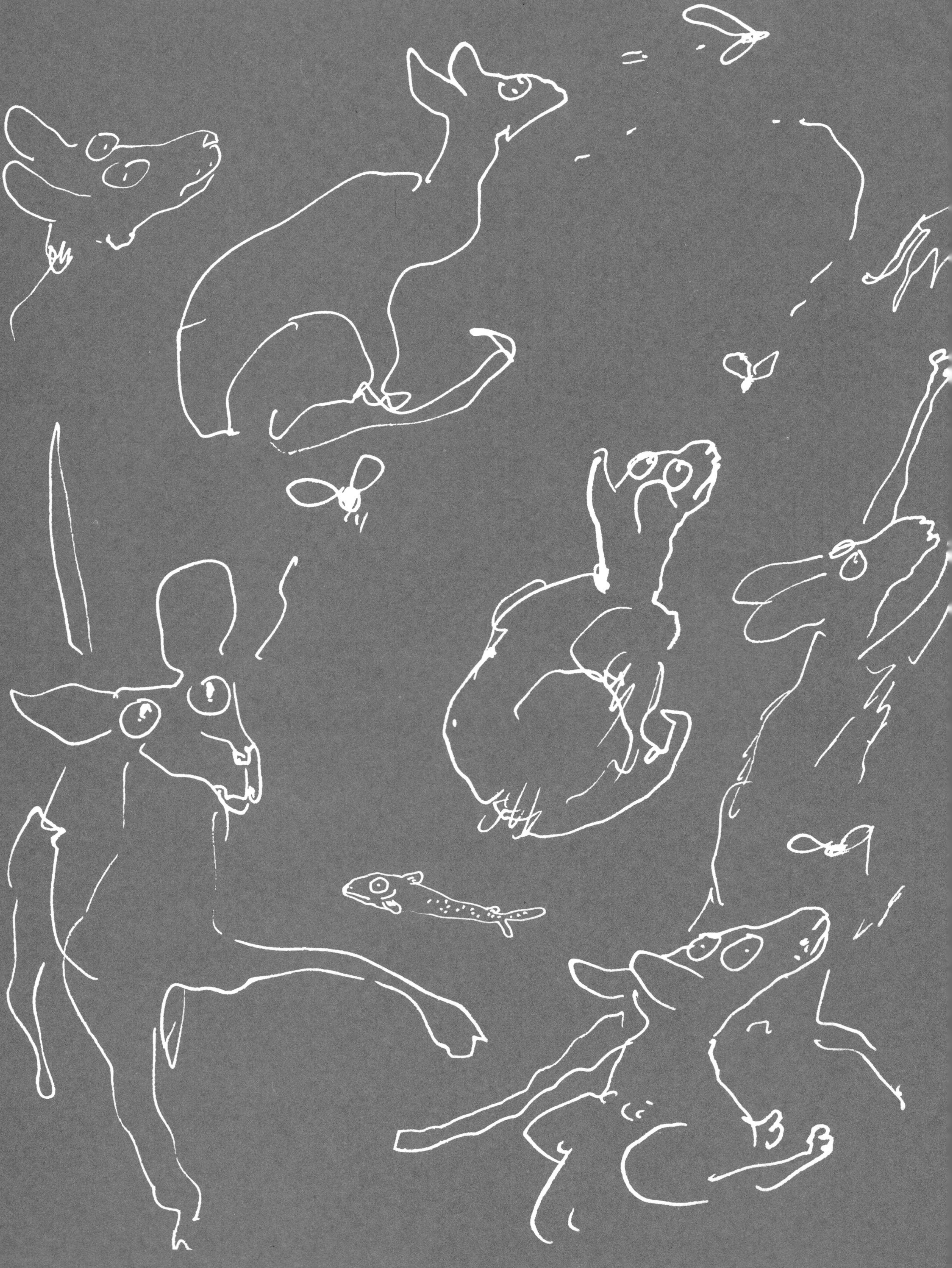